# Great
# Walks
## of
# Vancouver

## Charles Clapham

**THE LOWER MAINLAND AT YOUR FEET**

Edited by Neall Calvert
Designed by Andrew Johnstone
Printed in Hong Kong

∏

**Granville Island**
P u b l i s h i n g

Granville Island Publishing
Suite 212 – 1656 Duranleau
Vancouver B.C.  V6H 3S4
Tel: (604) 688-0320
Email: info@granvilleislandpublishing.com
www.granvilleislandpublishing.com

**National Library of Canada Cataloguing in Publication**

Clapham, Charles, 1925-
    Great walks of Vancouver : the Lower Mainland at your
feet / by Charles Clapham.

ISBN 1-894694-30-9

    1. Walking--British Columbia—Vancouver metropolitan
area—Guidebooks. 2. Walking—British Columbia—Lower
Mainland—Guidebooks. 3. Hiking—British Columbia—
Vancouver Metropolitan Area—Guidebooks. 4. Hiking—British
Columbia—Lower Mainland—Guidebooks. 5. Vancouver
Metropolitan Area (B.C.)—Guidebooks. 6. Lower Mainland
(B.C.)—Guidebooks. I. Title.

GV199.44.C22V34 2004        917.11'33045        C2004-901460-9

To Doris,
who accompanied me on all the trips.
When her hips wore out,
she had them replaced and carried on.

# Contents

# Introduction

Vancouver is a profoundly rural city, although you wouldn't think
so from your automobile. You see traffic jams, urban sprawl and
shopping malls. But often you can walk just a short distance from a
busy urban centre and be in near-wilderness. The busy shopping centre of Park Royal is situated on the banks of the Capilano River.
Capilano Mall sits beside MacKay Creek. Coquitlam Centre, with its
bustling commercial activity, is on the edge of Hoy Creek. And
Lougheed Mall is a stone's throw from Stoney Creek. You only find
this out by walking the city. If you think you know Vancouver by
travelling through it by automobile, you will not recognize the city
that you learn by exploring on foot.

Greater Vancouver is fortunate in being blessed with an abundance of walking routes. You can link parks, dikes, ravines, trails and
quiet roads to walk from almost any point in Vancouver to any other
(there are a few difficult places to reach but not many). *Great Walks
of Vancouver* describes a 500-km (300-mile) network of trails that let
you explore the whole area on foot.

Simon Fraser reached Vancouver down the river which bears his
name. The book's first section (Walk the Fraser, its Tributaries and

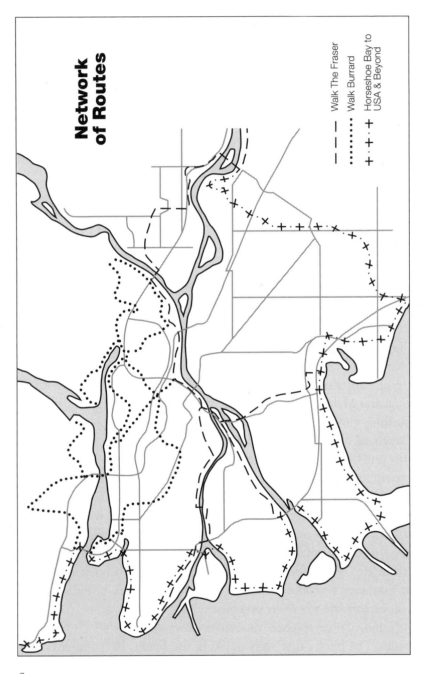

Network of Routes

— — — Walk The Fraser
·········· Walk Burrard
+ · + · + Horseshoe Bay to USA & Beyond

Arms) retraces Simon Fraser's route, following the Fraser River from the mouth of its north arm to the city of Mission. Eleven river walks explore farms, fishing, industry and historical communities which originated because of the river. They pass through places with such resonant names as New Westminster, Mary Hill, Port Haney, Fort Langley, Lehman's Landing and Mission. A further four walks discover the charms of the tributaries and other arms of the Fraser River.

The Canadian Pacific Railway brought immigrants to Port Moody at the end of Burrard Inlet, causing people to settle around its shores. The book's second section (Walk Burrard: Around the Inlet and Burnaby Mountain) shows Vancouver's green and ravined face. Eleven walks take you around Burrard Inlet, starting and finishing at Canada Place. These introduce you to the surprising abundance of rural scenery that exists in Vancouver's urban area. This set of walks updates my earlier *Walk the Burrard Loop* book. A further three walks lead over and around Burnaby Mountain in the centre of the loop.

A third group of settlers came from the sea or settled by the sea. Names such as Caulfeild, Vancouver, Spanish Banks, Marpole, Steveston, Ladner, Tsawwassen and Semiahmoo recall individuals and groups who visited or decided to settle by the sea, either recently or long ago. The book's third section (Walk Horseshoe Bay to the USA and Beyond) explores these places and the marine waterfront of Vancouver's western edges, ending at the Peace Arch. It is an update of my earlier *Walk Horseshoe Bay to the U.S.A.* book. A further three walks take you east from the Peace Arch to Fort Langley, passing through fertile lands developed by a fourth group of settlers—the farmers who fought the mosquitoes, the mud and the marshes to open up the delta lands to grow crops.

The Fraser walks, the Burrard walks and the Horseshoe-Bay-to-the-USA walks meet each other in various places, making a network of walks. Using them, you can plan your own outings from almost anywhere in Vancouver to almost anywhere else in the region.

# Getting There and Back

Many people drive to the start of a trail, take their walk, turn around and come back to their vehicle. Most books about walking in Vancouver describe walks taken in this way. However, this doesn't work if you want to keep walking in one direction until you reach your destination. Instead you can try one of these ways:

**Transit:** Take a bus from home to the day's starting point and get a bus home at the end.

**Bus-shuttle:** Drive to the end of the day's walk and get a bus back to the start. You can park at the end of the walk, arriving there just before the bus so that you have only a short wait.

**Car-shuttle:** Arrange to walk with a friend who also has a vehicle, and meet at the planned end-point of the walk. Park one vehicle there and drive together in the other to the starting point. Park and take the day's walk. When you finish, get in the vehicle there and drive back to reclaim the one at the start.

If you do not know how far you will be going on a given day, you can often leave your vehicle at the start and begin walking. The book notes the bus stops en route so that you can use transit to get back to your vehicle.

Maps accompany the written descriptions. The accompanying legend explains the symbols used in the maps.

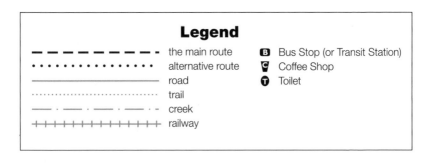

### Legend

| | | | |
|---|---|---|---|
| — — — — — — — · | the main route | **B** | Bus Stop (or Transit Station) |
| · · · · · · · · · · · · · · · · | alternative route | **C** | Coffee Shop |
| ———————————— | road | **T** | Toilet |
| ···················· | trail | | |
| — · — · — · — · — · | creek | | |
| +++++++++++++++ | railway | | |

# Transit Services

**TransLink** (604-953-3333) provides public bus service within the Greater Vancouver Regional District.

**Central Fraser Valley Transit** (604-854-3232) provides public bus service within Abbotsford, Mission and Chilliwack.

**City Link** (604-878-1290 in the Fraser Valley or 604-482-8747 via Greyhound in Vancouver) provides bus service connecting Vancouver and intermediate points with the downtown Abbotsford Bus Exchange.

**Greyhound Canada** (604-482-8747) provides bus service connecting Vancouver and intermediate points with its Abbotsford depot near the Trans-Canada Highway. It offers a daily 6:15 a.m. bus from Vancouver via Maple Ridge to Mission, with return buses at 2:10 p.m. (daily) and 8:05 p.m. (daily, except Saturday).

Bus times quoted in this book are based on September 2003 timetables. However, schedules change and it is worth obtaining the current timetable or calling the appropriate agency before departing, especially for infrequent buses or where transfers are required.

The website **www.translink.bc.ca** is also useful, because it gives the times that buses reach individual stops. Checking the schedules on the Internet ensures that the bus serves the stop in question and that you are not misreading the timetable.

# Planning How Far to Walk Each Day

I like to plan my walks so that I will have time to get home afterwards, clean up, and have the evening free for other activities. For this reason, I like to start each day's walk between 9 and 10 o'clock, depending on how long it takes to reach the starting point. I walk for up to an hour, then find a coffee shop (if possible) and take a half-hour break. I resume walking for up to an hour and a half and then eat lunch, which I usually bring. After a half-hour break, I resume walking for about an hour and a half, aiming to complete my walk by about 2 o'clock. This gives me ample time to get home, have tea, and get ready for the evening. This plan allows for a daily walk of about 12 to 15 km (7½ to 9½ miles). If you are not comfortable with kilometres, just think of a kilometre as equivalent to about 15 minutes of walking.

The book gives the distance of each day's suggested travel to the nearest half-kilometre and half-mile. It identifies each landmark by a code that measures its walking distance from the start of the route, so that you can easily see your progress. The code also allows you to look ahead and make decisions about whether to stop soon or carry on to a landmark ahead. For example:

| **Byrne Road** | 1.3 km | 0 hr 18 m | F33 |
| --- | --- | --- | --- |

shows that at Byrne Road, you have travelled 1.3 km (estimated travel time 18 minutes) since the previous landmark (which was Patterson Trail). You are on the Fraser route from Vancouver to Mission (F) and you are 33 kilometres from its start. The Burrard Loop landmarks begin with B and the western Horseshoe-Bay-to-the-USA landmarks begin with W.

If you prefer shorter walks, perhaps to allow more time to look around at points of interest, you can set a lower daily target of 9 km. To do this, read the description for possible stopping points close to the day's 9-km mark. The book tells you the location of bus stops along the routes, so that you can choose your own end-points to suit your needs. If you are driving, you will need to check the bus schedules, or call the appropriate transit agency to ask how to get from your planned end-point to the start. Be aware that buses are relatively infrequent in outlying areas and non-existent on Sunday on some routes.

## What the Route is Like

The routes are generally easy to walk, usually having little elevation gain and normally being well-surfaced. There are some scrambles into ravines or up banks, but they are short. The routes cross a number of bridges. I find that bridges offer fascinating views up and down the river, showing the activities on the water and its banks more clearly than a shoreline perspective. However, if you find traffic noise unacceptable or if you have no head for heights, you may wish to bus across instead.

Occasionally the route follows a road for some distance. If there is no sidewalk, I feel it is safer to walk on the left, facing the oncoming traffic. If the required road-walking takes less than fifteen minutes, I just bite the bullet and walk it. If the stretch is longer, I try to find ways to avoid it. I may end one day's walk just before the stretch begins and start the next one at the point where the asphalt ends. I don't insist on walking every piece of the route. Whenever the route follows the road for more than fifteen minutes, I alert you to the fact and suggest alternatives. Sometimes I suggest round-trip walks to enjoy the highlights of an area and avoid asphalt sections.

You will find it helpful to read the description of the day's walk before you start. This will alert you to situations such as the ones mentioned above, or to features, such as a set of steps, that you might want to avoid. Alternatively, you may be attracted to a potential side trip and be able to plan accordingly.

# What to Take

I do not presume to tell walkers what to wear or carry. I have a hiking companion who wears a short-sleeved T-shirt without a jacket, even in below-zero weather. Such choices are yours. However, my wife and I have walked the entire network, so you may find the following checklist useful. We agree on these items as necessities:

- **Hiking boots.** We wear hiking boots because we may come across muddy sections or seasonal streams. If you prefer to wear walking shoes, you may want to avoid light-coloured ones, which can get ruined.
- **Warm clothing and raingear.** Even on a fine summer day, the weather can change.
- **Sunscreen is always in our pack.** Many doctors recommend using it year-round.
- **The largest garbage bag we can find.** This item takes up almost no space and yet, cut down one long side and one short side and tied around your neck, it will cover your coat and pack and keep everything relatively dry. Nothing is waterproof in Vancouver—but you can try!
- **A hat.** We regard this as necessary in both cold and sunny weather.
- **A first-aid kit.** We include Band-Aids (for cuts), moleskin (for blisters), tape (for sprains), antiseptic ointment, antihistamine and ointment (for stings) and a pair of folding scissors.
- **Water.** One hot day without water will tell you to carry it always.
- **Lunch** and perhaps a piece of fruit.
- **Change for busfare and a bus timetable** for the area in case we decide to finish early.
- **A map or guidebook**—for example, this one!
- **A notepad and pen.** If we get separated, one can leave a note to tell the other what he is doing.

- **A change of clothes** in the trunk of our car. We rarely use them but it is comforting to know that they are available.
- **A seating pad** made from a gardener's kneeling pad, to keep comfortable and dry while eating lunch or resting.

Some of my companions consider a camera essential. Some take a flower or bird book. Some insist on mosquito repellent. You may have your own preferences to add to this list.

## Everything Changes

Despite my best attempt to give accurate descriptions, be aware that everything changes. I may indicate that there is a coffee shop, but do not rely on it; restaurants go out of business and new ones open up. I may make note of a certain building; if you can't find it, it may have been taken down. If the trail seems to have disappeared, see if you can find where the route resumes further on.

The website **www.greatwalksofvancouver.com** will post changes that affect the routing of the walks or access to them, but be aware that bus timetables change from time to time and check before you leave. If you note changes, you can also inform me at the website.

## Acknowledgements

I would like to acknowledge the Valley Outdoor Association, without whom these walks would not have been possible. A loyal band of followers accompanied my wife and me on each journey in this book. The memories of shared enjoyments on the trails are what hiking is all about.

I would also like to thank the professionals who turned my descriptions into book form. Jo Blackmore was an enthusiastic leader of the team. Andrew Johnstone provided an imaginative and efficient design. Editor Neall Calvert offered creative suggestions and identified my errors of fact. Editors of my previous books have all had their effect on changing and, I hope, improving my writing style.

# Walk
## the Fraser

ITS TRIBUTARIES AND ARMS

# Vancouver to Mission

The first eleven walks introduce you to the beauties of the Fraser River as you make a 140-km (85-mile) pilgrimage up the river from its mouth to Mission. They retrace Simon Fraser's path, starting at the plaque which records the place where he finally landed, at the mouth of the North Arm near UBC. They pass his statue at Westminster Quay and the cairn commemorating the site of the first Fort Langley—the place where he first realized he was near the ocean. They end at Mission's Westminster Abbey and the Grotto of Our Lady of Lourdes, a familiar landmark to early travellers up and down the river.

The Fraser River is one of the great rivers of the world. A federal-provincial program designated it a Canadian Heritage River to encourage preservation of its natural, cultural and recreational values. It was British Columbia's first transportation route and the lifeblood of its early residents, the Sto:Lo or river people. Early colonial settlements, such as British Columbia's first capitals of Fort Langley and New Westminster, took shape on its banks. While the river is celebrated in some of the small parks that dot its length, many British Columbians and visitors travel through the region barely glimpsing it. They miss much, because walking along it reveals a rich history and

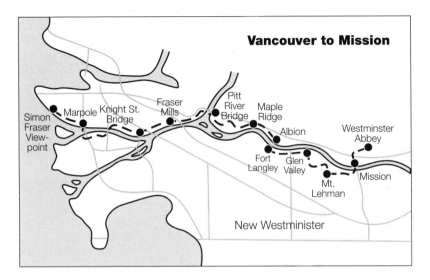

great views. The walks from Vancouver to Mission explore the river, with its fishing and waterborne commerce, and the nearby country-side, which ranges from industrial areas to farmland.

After you reach Mission, you have the time to explore a further 50 km (30 miles) of the Fraser River's other tributaries and outlets—something Simon Fraser didn't do. Up the Pitt River, you can enjoy mountain views from the dikes and climb High Knoll to enjoy its view over the Fraser Valley fields below. From New Westminster, you can cross the Fraser delta, taking a two-day walk that passes through a natural bog and a forest to reach Boundary Bay. Or you can walk along the dikes of the Fraser River's south arm to explore a little-known part of the river.

# Mouth of the North Arm

Today's 13-km (8-mile) walk passes through the southern half of Pacific Spirit Park to reach the banks of the Fraser River between Musqueam and Point Grey golf courses. It follows along the river's edge, then diverts through the horse-stabled Southlands area to pass around McCleery and Marine Drive golf courses. It rejoins the river at Fraser River Park before concluding at the south foot of Granville Street.

**Getting there:** If using transit, take a #41 UBC bus going west towards the university (it starts from Metrotown Station) and get off at the bus stop for Simon Fraser Viewpoint.

If driving, park near the foot of Granville Street (if you find nothing nearer, you can pay to park under Arthur Laing Bridge). Catch a northbound #98 Burrard bus on Granville Street at 71st Avenue, transfer to the half-hourly westbound #41 UBC bus on 41st Avenue and get off at the bus stop for Simon Fraser Viewpoint. A bus at 8:45 a.m. on Saturday takes just over 30 minutes.

## Simon Fraser Viewpoint                    0 km    0 hr    F0

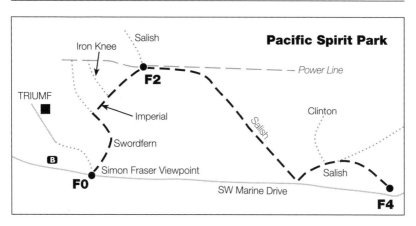

From the bus stop, walk east on the north side of the road until you are opposite the viewpoint and its parking lot. Cars really speed by here, so to take a closer look at the viewpoint, cross carefully to the divider and again to the viewpoint. You can see across the mouth of the Fraser River to the airport, the Gulf Islands and, on a fine day, the distant skyline of Vancouver Island. The water in the foreground is filled with log booms waiting to be towed to a mill. The Simon Fraser Memorial's plaque describes how Fraser's party landed here and encountered Musqueam warriors.

Go to the eastern exit of the parking lot, cross back to the divider and again to the far side. Follow Swordfern Trail into Pacific Spirit Park. As one of the trails in the park where bicycles and horses are not allowed, Swordfern Trail is normally firm and makes for good walking. In sunny weather, the leaves of the maple understory shine yellow in the spring and golden in the fall. The path leads to Imperial Trail, which used to be Imperial Road. Turn right and follow the trail, which forms the northern boundary of Ecological Reserve #74—a second-growth timber area set aside to allow study by university researchers. Cross Cutthroat Creek and, where the trail meets a power-line right-of-way, continue in the same general direction. Salish Trail joins from the left.

# Simon Fraser Viewpoint

In 1808, Simon Fraser set out to explore what he thought was the Columbia River, embarking with his party at Fort Fraser and travelling to Fort George and down to the river's mouth. At Lytton, he named the tributary river the Thompson, after David Thompson who explored the real Columbia River. Once in the Fraser Canyon, Fraser realized that his group could not continue by water during the June freshets, and they made their way overland to the Fraser Valley.

At a village near present-day Fort Langley, he learned from the natives that he was near the sea and tried to borrow a canoe. Despite a dispute over goods—which the natives took and Fraser considered stolen—the chief reluctantly agreed to lend Fraser his canoe and accompany him. At a Kwantlen village opposite New Westminster, Fraser learned that the people there were at war with the Musqueam, and the Fort Langley chief asked him not to continue. He rejected this request and, after a struggle, commandeered the canoe and went on, but was unable to follow protocol and announce his planned arrival and purpose. Because of this, the Musqueam treated him as an enemy when he arrived near the present Simon Fraser Viewpoint. Assisted by the newly-arrived Kwantlen pursuers, the Musqueam drove him off.

Fraser met with hostility everywhere as he returned upriver, and was lucky to escape with the borrowed canoe, leaving a blanket as payment. His disappointment was even greater when he took his bearings and found that he had not followed the Columbia after all. It was left to David Thompson to name the Fraser River.

*Source: "Simon Fraser—Explorer" by Barbara Rogers from **The Greater Vancouver Book**, edited by Chuck Davis. Vancouver, BC: Linkman Press, 1997.*

## Salish Trail                    1.8 km    0 hr 27 m    F2

Your first potential coffee-shop stop will be over an hour further on, so you may want a brief refreshment pause here. Then continue briefly along the power-line route, with dense clusters of salmonberry bushes and an occasional thimbleberry bush growing under the power lines on the left. The salmonberry bush has small leaves in groups of three; the berries are red or cream-coloured and can be tasty sampled at the tip of the tongue. Turn onto the continuation of Salish Trail where it is signed as leading off to the right. Pacific Spirit Park's forests are of varying ages; some parts of the park are alder forests, while others contain more mature second growth. The Salish Trail passes through typical second-growth timber and west coast underbrush. Huckleberry bushes grow out of the large cedar stumps close to the trail. Huckleberry bushes only grow where cedar trees also grow and frequently on the old stumps; alder forests have no huckleberries. Stay with the Salish Trail to the corner of 41st Avenue and Marine Drive, watching out for cyclists as they like this trail. Press either of the buttons to change the signal lights—the higher one is for horse riders.

## West 41st Avenue              2.4 km    0 hr 38 m    F4

Cross the road and continue onto the trail ahead, which is shared by pedestrians, cyclists and horse riders. Follow the shared trail as it parallels a residential street and then bears left to reach a paved road. Jog right and then left to pick up the trail again.

The route now leads around Musqueam Village. Musqueam Creek is on the left at first; the area is being restored to encourage the return of more salmon. This shared trail, nearly always muddy, is very popular with horse riders—the Southlands Riding Club was one of the groups that promoted and initially maintained the trail you will later follow around Point Grey Golf Club. At the first trail intersec-

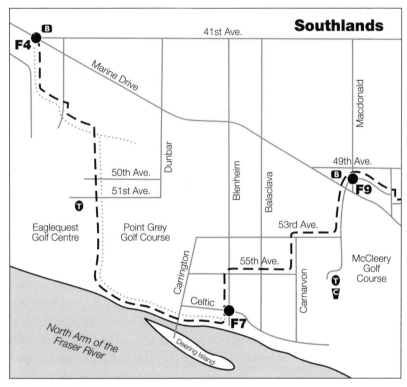

tion, bear right and head south towards the river. At the second road crossing, Eaglequest's Musqueam Golf Centre is on the right. It is operated by the Musqueam Nation and has a restaurant and washrooms in the clubhouse.

Continue along the path, with Musqueam Golf Course on the right and Point Grey Golf Course on the left. The end of the path offers the first good opportunity to enjoy a close view of the great river. Large rocks and a rough stone wall reinforce the riverbank outside the golf-course fence. Iona Island, which houses Vancouver's sewage treatment plant, lies opposite. Pleasure boats, fishing boats, tugs and barges make their way up and down the river, and planes land or take off at the airport a little further upstream. If it is not windy, the riverbank makes an enjoyable lunch spot. The trail continues east between the golf course and the river until it heads inland at an inlet, where you may see herons. It emerges at Carrington Street, with Deering Island and its residential development on the right. The BC Packers fishing company used to own the land and once moored their boats in the stream here. One of the old buildings is visible just ahead. Continue directly across the street, following along the path. The protected green areas on the right help compensate for wetlands removed during the nearby residential development. You emerge onto Blenheim Street; turn left and continue to the nearby intersection with Celtic Avenue.

## Musqueam and Cutthroat Creeks

A century ago the city of Vancouver contained over 50 salmon spawning streams. Now only Musqueam Creek and its tributary, Cutthroat Creek, remain. The rest are buried beneath pavement and landfill or have disappeared.

As recently as twenty years ago, hundreds of salmon returned to spawn in Musqueam Creek. Willard Sparrow, a Musqueam who has lived near the stream all his life, recalls, "There were so many coho and chum you could hear the salmon spawning in the creek before you could see them."

In 1997, only 12 coho and chum salmon completed their journey home. That year, the Musqueam First Nation and David Suzuki Foundation joined in the Musqueam Watershed Restoration Project to repair ecological damage to the watershed caused by development, and to enable Musqueam and Cutthroat Creeks to once again support a large salmon population. Salmon are returning and further rehabilitation continues upstream, but it is uncertain to what extent the numbers will rebuild.

*Source: "Vancouver's Last Wild Salmon Stream." Vancouver, BC: www.davidsuzuki.org/Campaigns_and_Promises/Local_Initiatives/ Last_Wild_Salmon_Stream/default.asp, July 2001.*

## Celtic Avenue 2.7 km 0 hr 38 m F7

Continue north on Blenheim Street through the traditional equestrian community of Southlands. Although recent "monster houses" have started to break down the traditional house-and-barn neighbourhood pattern, planners zoned this area into 4-acre lots to prevent subdivision and retain the neighbourhood's horsy character. Turn right onto West 55th Avenue, a road with a wide grass strip at the edge that makes walking easier for horses (and for pedestrians too). At Carnarvon Street, turn left and go around the Southlands Riding Club by turning right on West 53rd Avenue and continuing to Macdonald Street. If you want to detour one block to the right, the McCleery Golf Course is public and the bright new 1996 clubhouse has a restaurant and washrooms. It makes a good lunch stopping place. The golf club is named after the pioneer McCleery farm, which was located here.

Go up the hill to busy South West Marine Drive, a street carrying heavy traffic to and from the university. There is no crosswalk, so cross carefully and continue up to West 50th Avenue. (If you want to

## McCleery Farm

Samuel and Fitzgerald McCleery settled in the area in the 1870s. Fitzgerald and Mary McCleery built their pioneer farmhouse here in 1873 on lands which are now part of the golf course. It was the first building on this part of the river and served as a stopping-off point for refreshment for people travelling between Victoria and New Westminster. It was also the first place of divine worship in Vancouver, being called St. Patrick's Cathedral, and later became a school.

*Source: Vancouver, by Eric Nicol. Toronto: Doubleday, 1970.*

end your walk, go to the bus stop on this side of West 49th Avenue for a #49 bus to Granville Street and Metrotown Station. The bus on the other side goes to West 41st Avenue at Dunbar Street.)

## West 50th Avenue        1.6 km    0 hr 23 m    F9

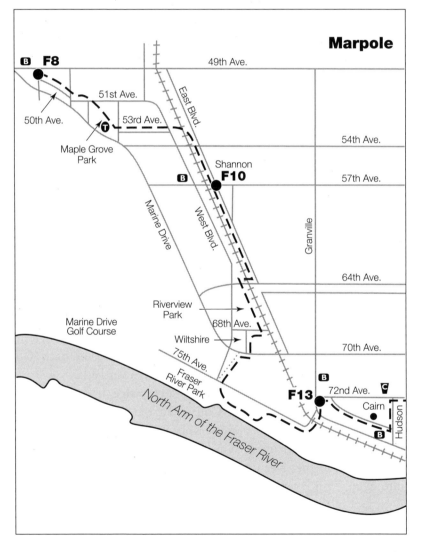

Proceed east on 50th Avenue for one block, then down to 51st Avenue and east to Maple Grove Park, a small play area for local residents, with washrooms that are not often open. Angle across the park to 53rd Avenue and follow it east to the Arbutus railway line. The Vancouver–Lulu Island Railway's interurban trains used to run on this line from Vancouver to Marpole and across the Fraser River to Lulu Island and Steveston. The Canadian Pacific Railway owns the line now but trains rarely use it. Cyclists would love it for a cycling route and civic officials enviously eye it for a Light Rapid Transit line.

Walk one block to the right down West Boulevard, cross the boulevard at the divider and cross the railway on the gravel path at West 54th Avenue. Turn right, and after one block reach the small shopping area of Shannon, named after the former railway station at this point. The new natural-foods grocery store offers a wide variety of snacks and drinks.

## Shannon                           1.7 km    0 hr 24m    F10

Follow the rail corridor and continue straight on where West Boulevard veers off to the right and East Boulevard joins on the left. At West 64th Avenue, jog right, then left, to enter Riverview Park. Keep to the left-hand edge of the park and enter the lane at its end. Turn right on West 68th Avenue and left on Wiltshire Street to reach busy South West Marine Drive. Cross the road; if necessary, detour one block left to the traffic signals, cross there and come back. Go right and take steps on the left down to Fraser River Park.

Boardwalks and paths along the water's edge lead west until stopped by Marine Drive Golf Course. At the riverbank, there are picnic tables, benches and notices explaining the area's biology and history of human settlement. When you are ready to go on, head east, staying close to the river until you reach private parking areas. Exit onto West 75th Avenue and follow it as it bends and reaches the south foot of Granville Street.

## South foot of Granville          2.6 km    0 hr 37m    F13

**Getting home:** The #98 bus goes express from Granville & 71st Avenue to downtown Vancouver, stopping only to make connections to other routes at the major cross streets. In the opposite direction, the bus goes express to Richmond.

**Fraser River Park**

# Industrial North Arm

Today's 13-km (8-mile) walk crosses Oak Street Bridge from Marpole to the south side of the river and heads east along the dikes. On the way, it offers views of the industrialized areas on the opposite shore. The route then crosses Knight Street Bridge and follows a seawall on the north side of the river.

**Getting there:** If using transit, take a bus to the south end of Granville Street and make your way to its east side at 72nd Avenue.

If driving, park on Elliott Street between South East Marine Drive and the river. Take the westbound #100 Airport bus from the north side of South East Marine Drive to Granville Street at 70th Avenue. Cross the road at the signals and walk south to 72nd Avenue. A bus at 8:57 a.m. on Saturday takes just over 15 minutes.

**South foot of Granville**             0 km    0 hr    F13

Marpole has coffee shops on Granville Street or Hudson Street if you want a drink before you start. Head east along 72nd Avenue and veer right onto 73rd Avenue to follow the edge of Marpole Park. Where it ends, a cairn commemorates the Great Midden.

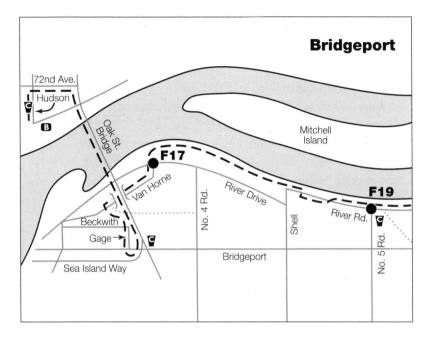

At Hudson Street, turn left for two blocks to West 72nd Avenue and turn right to reach Oak Street. After a jog left to the Oak Street Bridge sidewalk, turn right and prepare for a 25-minute walk across. Downstream you can see the marina at Bridgepoint, the site for the planned Richmond Casino. A mix of warehouses greets you below as you cross the south riverbank. As soon as the bridge ends, take the path to the right to nearby Bridgeport Road, go left and cross at the crosswalk. If you want a refreshment break, there is a fast-food coffee shop three minutes to the right.

Continue north on Gage Street, passing the Holiday Inn. At the end of the street, go through the gap in the chain-link fence facing you and follow the trail to a cleared area under the bridge. Turn slightly left on the dirt track and reach a footpath. This was once a Canadian National Railway track and is now a municipal trail. Turn left and arrive at Van Horne Way. Follow this street to the right through an industrial area until you reach River Drive, with Fraser River Terminals at the north west corner.

# Marpole

The Coast Salish lived and thrived by the river. They sat here looking out to sea before the Fraser River carried down enough silt to extend the delta westward. Settlement dates back to the last Ice Age, some 10,000 years ago. In the early 1930s, UBC researchers found many 2,000- to 3,000-year-old artefacts in a two-hectare midden (refuse heap) buried under the roots of 1,000-year-old trees.

Nobody lived here in 1865 when the first European registered land. Harry Eburne arrived in 1875, worked briefly at McCleery Farm and then established a general store. The community of some 20 people became known as Eburne. In 1891, after the North Arm bridges were built, Harry Eburne moved his store to the south side of the river. In 1894, his post office was officially named Eburne. For the next 20 years, "Eburne" referred to the community on the south side and "Eburne Station" to the community on the north side. As many as 11 canneries operated in the area. In 1916, the northern community adopted the name Marpole to avoid confusion.

*Source: **Marpole—Heritage of 100 Years** by Peg McNamara. Vancouver, BC: Marpole-Oakridge Area Council, 1975.*

---

**River Drive**                              4.6 km      1 hr 13 m      F17

---

Continue on the extension of Van Horne Way, keeping to the narrow strip of road to the right of the yellow line, to reach the shoreline. You are now back on the Fraser River, this time on the south side of the North Arm. The western tip of Mitchell Island appears opposite and its industrial character becomes apparent as you proceed east along the dike path. Pleasure boats, fishing boats, tugs and scows will likely be plying the river, and airplanes will be landing or taking off in fairly quick succession. This section of dike ends at the corner of Shell Road and River Road.

Stay on the north side of River Road until you are clear of the corner, then cross carefully. Follow the sidewalk until you see a parking area on the opposite side, just past the last building on the bank. Cross back to the bank when it is safe and follow the dike path toward Knight Street Bridge, which you can see ahead. There is a coffee shop in the commercial area at the end of No. 5 Road.

## No. 5 Road   2.0 km   0 hr 31m   F19

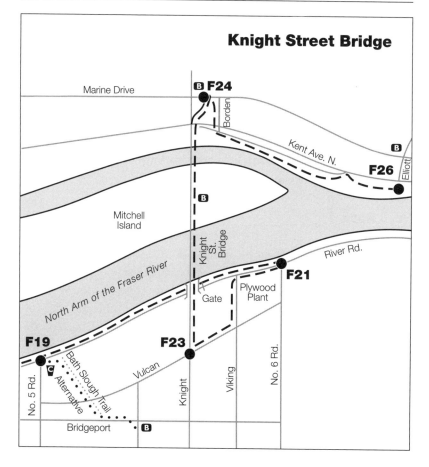

If you prefer not to walk across Knight Street Bridge or make the informal scramble up to it, cross here to the south side of River Road and take Bath Slough Trail where it leads off to the right, just east of No. 5 Road. Follow the trail until it reaches busy Bridgeport Road, turn left to the traffic signals and cross to the bus stop on the south side. A bus will take you across Knight Street Bridge to South East Marine Drive.

If you intend to take the informal trail, continue walking on the north side of River Road. Interesting yachts and other vessels are likely on view across the river at Arrow Marine. Just before you reach a cluster of cottonwoods before the bridge, there is a good beach at low or medium tide. You may want to have lunch here, overlooking the river. If it is raining, you can sit under the bridge to eat and keep dry.

Continue past the gate and follow the dike road. You can take Viking Way road on the right but I prefer to first continue to the end of the dike. Here a path leads through a culvert under Richmond Plywood's jack ladder to a path on the other side, emerging at No. 6 Road. You can sit on the concrete abutment and look at the river and its marine traffic. Gravel trucks, barge-loading and other industrial activities may be busy on the other side.

### No. 6 Road                    2.0 km    0 hr 29m    F21

After enjoying the view, retrace your steps past Richmond Plywood and take Viking Way on the left at the side of the plywood plant. Where Viking Way meets Vulcan Way, cross Vulcan Way and turn right to reach a point under the bridge. The informal trail follows the west side of the swath of grass under the bridge, reaches the bridge structure, crosses to its east side and goes up the path (well-worn by bicycle use) to the sidewalk above.

## Knight Street Bridge South     1.1 km    0 hr 16 m    F23

The walk across the bridge is noisy but well-protected from traffic. It offers interesting upstream views of the Richmond River Road bank on the right and Mitchell Island industries on the left. After some 15 minutes, you descend to Mitchell Island and a bus stop, where a bus could take you to South East Marine Drive. However, seven more minutes of walking does the same, as you cross the span to the mainland and take the exit ramp to the right leading down to South East Marine Drive. If you want to end your walk, the #100 bus goes east to New Westminster; in the other direction, it goes to Marpole. The #22 bus into Vancouver stops on the north side under the bridge.

**The Industrial Fraser River near Knight Street**

35

## Knight Street Bridge North     1.7 km    0 hr 24 m    F24

Turn right on South East Marine Drive and almost immediately right again down Borden Street, cross the railway tracks at its foot and turn left for two blocks. Then turn right and pick up a seawall along the river. The eastern tip of Mitchell Island lies opposite, stacked high with shipping containers. Where the seawall passes the new housing development and curves left to rejoin the road, take the riverside path that leads off to the right. It closely follows the river; log booms are usually moored nearby. Where the path passes a metal frame and curves right to a flat open area with a children's playground, turn left to find a Vancouver Park Board map of the area. Elliott Street is opposite.

## Elliott Street     1.8 km    0 hr 26 m    F26

**Getting home:** Walk five minutes up Elliott Street to South East Marine Drive. The #100 bus goes east to 22nd Street Station, and west to Marpole for bus connections to Richmond, Delta and Vancouver.

# North Arm Parks

Today's 12½-km (8-mile) walk starts along the riverbank through Riverfront Park and detours into Everett Crowley Park, an area that the City and volunteers are restoring after its previous use as the Kerr Road Dump. It then returns to the river's edge to reach Fraser Foreshore Park. It turns inland, travelling up 200 steps at the edge of magnificent Byrne Creek Ravine to reach Edmonds Station. It then follows BC Parkway—the pedestrian and cycle route in the SkyTrain corridor—to 22nd Street Station at the north end of Queensborough Bridge.

**Getting there:** If using transit, take the #100 bus, get off at Elliott Street and walk five minutes downhill to the riverbank.

If driving, park somewhere near 22nd Street Station, take the #100 Airport bus, get off at Elliott Street and walk five minutes downhill to the riverbank. A bus at 9:12 a.m. on Saturday takes about 15 minutes.

## Elliott Street 0 km 0 hr F26

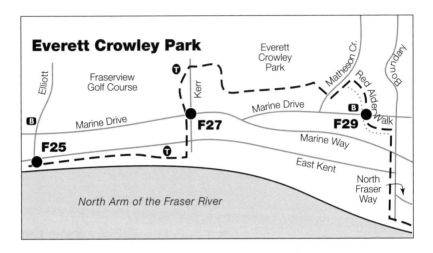

Follow the path eastward to the left, passing the waterside offices of Northland Navigation. Tugboats and other vessels will be moored at the edge of the dock. A large floating barge housing a fishing lodge may be moored in the winter months; it is towed to the Queen Charlotte Islands in the summer. Follow the path to a playground area with picnic tables and toilets. You may want to take a brief break here. The walkway continues to Kerr Road, where you turn left and ascend the hill to South East Marine Drive.

## Kerr Road 1.4 km 0 hr 20 m F27

Cross the intersection on the west side and find a footpath leading from the corner, part of Perimeter Trail which goes around Fraserview Golf Course. Follow it up the hill for about five minutes, passing a building with washrooms on the left. This facility serves golfers as well as walkers and is likely open. Continue briefly on the bark-mulch path across the driveway and emerge onto Kerr Road. There is no crosswalk, so cross carefully to the entrance of Everett Crowley Park.

# Northland Navigation

Northland Navigation is a historic name in BC shipping. The company started life in 1942 as the British Columbia Steamship Company, operating a single vessel in local coastal waters. It changed its name to Northland Navigation in 1952 and began to expand its passenger service up the BC coast. In 1958, it took over the Canadian Pacific steamer service on Vancouver Island's west coast, acquiring the Princess Norah and renaming her Canadian Prince. In 1959, it bought the Union Steamship Company. The company's fleet became the major shipping line delivering goods and passengers to BC's coastal communities. In the 1960s, the rise of the government-run British Columbia Ferry Corporation and increasing use of air freight cut into the business. In the 1970s, a change in government ended its subsidy, and in 1976, Northland Navigation withdrew from passenger service to concentrate on the freight and charter business that it still operates.

Source: "Northland Navigation" in *Encyclopedia of British Columbia,* edited by Daniel Francis. Vancouver, BC: Harbour Publishing, 2000.

Enter the park and follow the trail straight ahead to a T-intersection with a paved trail. Turn right and go straight on, ignoring a trail that bears left at the foot of "Mount Everett." The paved trail leads to the first of three viewpoints overlooking the river and flat agricultural lands on the far side. On a clear day, you can see Mount Baker to the south east and the Gulf and San Juan islands to the south west.

Return to the path and follow it east along the escarpment. A sign at the middle viewpoint directs your attention to Mount Baker in Washington State. At the end of the escarpment, the main trail curves left to head back into the park. Ignore this route and head downhill along a trail through brambles, marked by a rock at the top and townhouses below. The trail reaches a paved path, which leads to the right and descends to Matheson Road. Walk uphill to be clear of the corner, cross carefully and continue on the path that leads off beyond the bus stop, bypassing the houses on the right. Continue bearing right and follow Red Alder Walk to South East Marine Drive. If you want to end the walk, the #100 bus on this side of the road goes to Marpole for connections to Richmond, Delta and Vancouver. On the other side, the #100 bus goes to 22nd Street Station.

## Everett Crowley Nature Park

Everett Crowley Park consists of 40 hectares of grassland, forest, ponds and creeks connected by five kilometres of trails. In the 1880s, the area was farmed, logged and quarried. Later, the city's Kerr Road Dump filled the ravine. In the 1970s, the Vancouver Parks Board considered various uses for the property—a golf course, botanical garden, orchard, pioneer farm, miniature railway and trout-stocked pond. Eventually, the idea of a nature park located south of the Champlain Heights subdivision took hold. It was named Everett Crowley Nature Park after a former parks board commissioner.

The ecological restoration of the park is still underway. Vegetation consists mostly of opportunistic brambles, buttercups and broom—all introduced species—but native ocean spray bushes sport white plumes in April and May. Workers liberally apply bark-mulch to discourage brambles and permit the return of native plants.

*Source: "Everett Crowley Park." Notice board at Everett Crowley Park. Vancouver, BC: Vancouver Parks Board, 2000.*

## Red Alder Walk    1.9 km    0 hr 27 m    F29

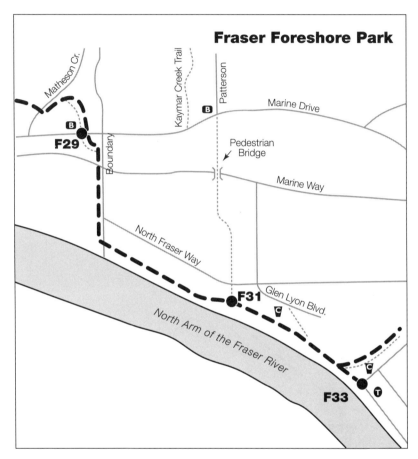

Cross South East Marine Drive at the crosswalk, descend the steps and follow the path down and left to Boundary Road. Continue downhill to Marine Way. Cross and follow Boundary Road over the railway tracks, keep right at the next intersection and continue to the river. Turn left—this is where you enter Burnaby—and follow the riverside path past a gate. Where the bark-mulch path bends, Patterson Trail leads in from the left, having crossed Marine Way on a pedestrian overpass.

## Patterson Trail          2.0 km      0 hr 30 m      F31

Continue on the riverside trail, which now enters Fraser Foreshore Park, with Richmond's River Road and its agricultural lands across the river. The industrial park on the left is expanding; there is a café near the trail, open Monday to Friday. The trail crosses a small stream and continues to the foot of Byrne Creek and an area offering picnic tables, some sheltered in case of rain. Just past these tables the trail reaches seats, a playground area and washrooms at the foot of Byrne Road. A restaurant in the industrial area just up Byrne Road and to the left is open Monday to Saturday from 3:30 a.m.

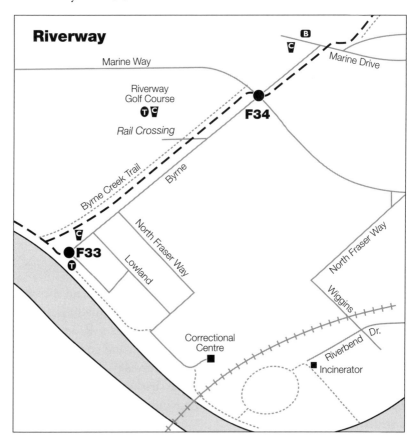

## Byrne Road                1.3 km    0 hr 18 m    F33

Burnaby has recently extended Fraser Foreshore Park for a further two kilometres beyond this point and it is worth exploring on another occasion. However, the Byrne Creek Ravine route is more attractive, so double back along the riverbank from Byrne Road to the creek and follow the dike path inland on its east side. This path leads to an active railway line serving industries along the river. Across the tracks is the Riverway Golf Course clubhouse, which has a coffee shop, washrooms, and a fireplace to revive your spirits if you are cold or wet. The dike trail continues north on the east side of the creek to reach Marine Way. Turn right, stay as far away as possible from the busy traffic and go to the nearby Byrne Road signals.

## Marine Way               1.8 km    0 hr 29 m    F34

Cross both sets of signals to the far corner of the intersection and follow the path on the right side of Byrne Road, cross Byrne Creek and continue to Marine Drive. Cross Byrne Road at the signals, turn right and cross Marine Drive, then continue left over a crosswalk. If you want to end the walk, buses stop a short distance to the left, connecting to Marpole and Metrotown and 22nd Street Stations. The route continues uphill on a sidewalk to the right and soon reaches Byrne Creek Ravine Park's entrance on the left.

I enjoy walking this magnificent ravine at any time of year. The steep walls of the ravine, the high trees and the stream running below give an air of peace and a glimpse of nature amid the busy city life which is so near. You walk up 200 steps from bottom to top, getting aerobic exercise as you enjoy the ambience. The path reaches its high point at a residential street and continues around the edge of the ravine to a tennis court. Beyond the court, keep as close to the treed edge of Ron McLean Park as the dampness of the grass permits. In due course you will reach a footpath between a townhouse complex and the treed ravine, which joins to the BC Parkway that follows the

**Burnaby Foreshore Park**

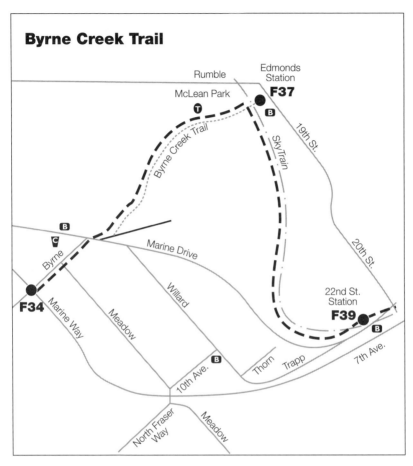

## Byrne Creek Trail

SkyTrain line. (A left turn here would get you, in 4 km, to Metrotown Station—B111 of the Burrard Loop.)

| Edmonds Station | 2.2 km | 0 hr 40 m | F37 |
|---|---|---|---|

Follow BC Parkway to the right as it rises to a clear area, with a BC Hydro high-rise on the left. As the path continues, clear views of the whole Fraser River estuary open up on the right, with Alex Fraser Bridge prominent below. SkyTrain's maintenance yards lie on the other side of the tracks as you proceed. The footpath curves around and enters New Westminster, skirting the edge of the Schara Tzedeck Cemetery. (If you want to look around the cemetery, divert down 23rd Street to Marine Drive and turn right to find the entrance.) A Holocaust memorial on the grounds lists the names of the World War II concentration camps. I found the memorial especially moving when I visited on November 11—Remembrance Day—some years ago. Continuing on, the footpath reaches 22nd Street Station.

## 22nd Street Station                    2.0 km    0 hr 28 m    F39

A walk to Boundary Bay starts here (the Queensborough-to-Mud-Bay-Park route—FD0 to FD22), connecting to a walk along the Fraser River's south arm that will eventually lead to Massey Tunnel (FS0 to FS13).

**Getting home:** SkyTrain connects to the rest of the region. In addition, several local buses leave from stops outside the station, including the #100 that serves Marine Drive and the nearby areas you have explored.

# Through New Westminster

Today's 13½-km (8½-mile) walk follows SkyTrain from 22nd Street Station to a popular seawall leading to New Westminster Quay. It passes through Queen's Park and down a ravine that used to be part of the former BC Penitentiary grounds. It passes through Sapperton Landing Park, offering sweeping views over the Fraser River. It continues to Royal Columbian Hospital, crosses the Brunette River and climbs to Coquitlam Golf Academy, a new golf course on a former regional landfill. It then descends to Fraser Mills.

**Getting there:** If using transit, take SkyTrain to 22nd Street Station and pick up the trail on the south side.

If driving, park in the Park-and-Ride on the south side of King Edward Street just east of the Trans-Canada Highway. Cross Lougheed Highway at the traffic signals and cross King Edward Street to reach the bus stop on the east side of Lougheed Highway. Take any bus to Braid Station and travel four stops on SkyTrain to 22nd Street Station. The trip takes about 20 minutes.

## 22nd Street Station                                     0 km   0 hr   F39

Exit 22nd Street Station at the bus stops, turn left, walk down the path to 20th Street, cross carefully, and go slightly left into Grimston Park. The shortest route is a wide, paved cycle path leading downhill to the right. However, you may first prefer to enjoy the view from the

47

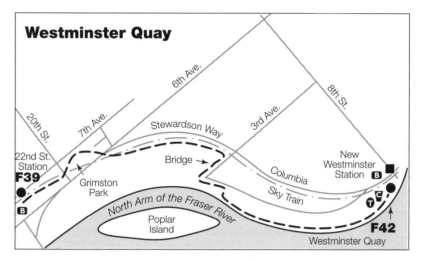

**Westminster Quay**

top of the hill. To do this, follow the path across the grass to the left and up beside the lane to reach the top of the park between a paddling pool and a children's playground. A small building with washrooms may be open.

From the playground, walk along the path in front of the seats on the right. You can pause to enjoy the view over the Fraser River, sweeping from Mount Baker to the Gulf Islands. After passing the last seat, follow the path down to the grass and head for the corner of the park below you to the left. Exit the park and cross Stewardson Way at the traffic signals.

Follow the pedestrian path down the hill, passing the Scott Paper plant. There are views of industrial New Westminster and then of Westminster Quay's residential units, built on former railway and industrial lands. Where the path reaches 3rd Avenue, turn right and take the bridge over the railway. Follow the road briefly left and turn right as soon as possible into the residential development to reach the promenade at the river's edge. This is a delightful section of the walk and you will probably find many others enjoying it with you. The walkway passes the old rail-and-road bridge that once crossed from here to Queensborough and reaches the Public Market at Westminster Quay, which has stores, coffee shops and washrooms.

## Westminster Quay     3.7 km    0 hr 52 m    F42

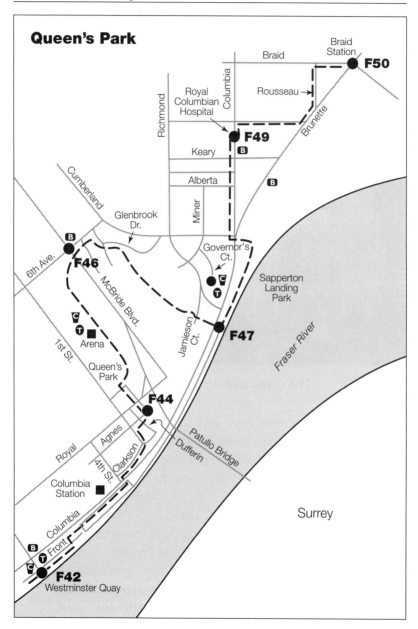

49

**The Casino at Westminster Quay**

Continue on the waterfront past the market, taking the time to look at the statue of Simon Fraser outside, commemorating his voyage down the river bearing his name. Then pass the casino, which is located in a moored paddlewheeler; there may be moored freighters at the river's edge. New Westminster is a city of bridges; from here, you can see SkyBridge, Patullo Bridge and, beyond it, a railway bridge that serves four railways. When you reach the fence at the edge of the parking area, go inland and cross the railway and the street at the Stop sign and continue up the hill to Columbia Street. Turn right, pass Burr Theatre honouring New Westminster actor Raymond Burr (Perry Mason and Ironsides of TV fame) and reach 4th Street. Cross

Columbia Street, walk half a block up the east side of 4th Street right onto Clarkson Street. With the SkyTrain line on the right, follow it to the end and take the path to the left into Albert Crescent Park. Angle across it and if you want to rest, you can sit on the grass or on a bench and enjoy the view. Take Albert Crescent uphill on the left for one block, turn right onto Agnes Street and continue to Dufferin Street.

## Agnes and Dufferin                    1.9 km     0 hr 28m     F44

Head left up Dufferin Street to Royal Avenue and cross at the traffic signals. Continue north on the grass of Queen's Park to reach a raised bank, scramble up, and take the path leading to the right. Pass through a treed area of Douglas firs, cedars and maples overlooking a fitness track below on the right. Continue past the Bernie Legge Repertory Theatre and emerge at a road. A concession and washrooms may be open in the arena opposite.

Continue north on the road beside the arena and pass between two gates, where a plaque marks the 1960 New Westminster centennial. Picnic tables are available on the left if you want a snack. Where the road divides, bear right down the hill and pick up Queen's Park Millennium Trail continuing downhill to the McBride Boulevard traffic signals.

## McBride Boulevard                     1.4 km     0 hr 20m     F46

Cross McBride Boulevard, head east on 6th Avenue and turn right on Glenbrook Drive. Bear left at the first fork and then stay on the right-hand side of the road. Follow the edge of the ravine and find a post marking a steep slope which you scramble cautiously down to reach a path at the bottom. This path leads gently down a peaceful rural gully in the old penitentiary lands. At the ravine's foot, take the central path that leads straight on, ignoring the road curving off to the left and the path on the right that crosses a bridge. A case on the right displays the BC Penitentiary bell, which was cast in West Troy,

**A City of Bridges: SkyTrain over Golden Ears**

New York, in April 1895. It used to call in the prisoners after a day working in the fields. The building behind it is a community centre.

At this point you can consider a short detour to see a heritage building that was part of the BC Penitentiary. If you want to do this, turn left up the hill to Richmond Street and if you are comfortable crossing here, do so, or else detour via the nearby signals. Then follow the road into the housing development (signed as leading to 48 Richmond), observe the Private Property signs and stay on the road and pathways. Climb the footpath at the road's end and follow around and down to Governor's Court, where you will find the heritage building, with offices, a café and a balcony offering a great view up and down the Fraser River.

After the detour, if any, come back and cross opposite the community centre. Follow the path downhill to reach Columbia Street, turn right and reach the traffic signals.

**The Former BC Penitentiary**

## Columbia Street        1.4 km     0 hr 20 m     F47

Cross at the signals and make your way carefully down the short, busy, pedestrian-unfriendly section of Front Street and heave a sigh of relief as you turn left into Sapperton Landing Park. The riverbank walk offers views across the river, which is wide and usually busy with tugs, boom boats, fish boats and pleasure craft. You can go out on the pier and enjoy lunch at picnic tables; there are nearby toilet facilities. At the end of the park, come up and cross the main road at the pedestrian-activated crossing at Cumberland Street. Turn right and walk up the hill into an area of New Westminster known as Sapperton, named

---

# Royal Columbian Hospital

In February 1862, a public meeting in the New Westminster courthouse led to the construction of BC's first hospital. A chain-gang from the jail cleared the land at 4th and Agnes Streets. The 20-bed hospital opened in October 1862, accepting all but maternity patients, children, the incurable and the insane.

In 1889, the hospital moved to a three-storey wooden building at the present site in Sapperton. In 1901, the BC legislature incorporated the Royal Columbian Hospital. The facility amalgamated with the Women's Hospital, established in 1893 by the Women's Christian Temperance Union, and established a school of nursing that operated until 1978.

In 1912, the cornerstone was laid for a new brick structure which has evolved over the years to the present large hospital. A small green area east of Columbia Street, just north of the hospital, displays this cornerstone and some of the original bricks.

*Source: "Royal Columbian Hospital—History" by Kathleen Harris. New Westminster, BC: February 2001. Reprinted on the Simon Fraser Health Region website (www.sfhr.com), January 2002.*

---

for the "Sappers" or Royal Engineers based here in the early days of the province. You pass stores including coffee shops and cross at the signals at Keary Street to reach Royal Columbian Hospital.

## Royal Columbian Hospital        1.8 km      0 hr 26 m      F49

Turn left, pass the hospital and enter the small park on the right to see the low brick hospital memorial and its commemorative plaque. At Sherbrooke Street, go downhill to Brunette Avenue, turn left and left again onto Rousseau Street and follow it to Braid Street. These streets are in a quiet residential area on a hillside with views of the river and the Fraser Valley. Turn right down busy Braid Street to the signals at Braid Station.

## Braid Station        1.4 km      0 hr 20 m      F50

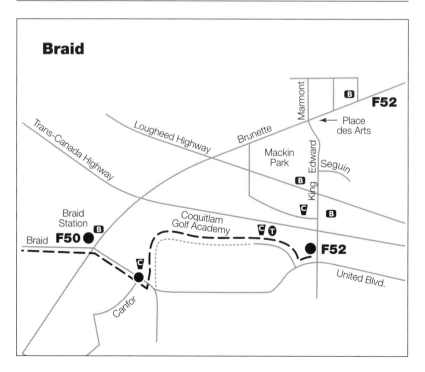

Cross Brunette Avenue and continue along the sidewalk on the right-hand side of Braid Street to reach a one-lane bridge over the Brunette River. Cross the road when it is clear, continue briefly and reach a road angling up on the left and passing an active landfill operation. This road almost immediately enters Coquitlam and becomes the four-lane major Braid Street Connector leading to United Boulevard. A sign at the road's entrance (still in New Westminster) says Private Property and Enter at Your Own Risk; but hundreds of cars a day do just that. You can do the same, at your own risk, if you want. I prefer to start up the hill for a few metres and turn left behind a chain-link fence to follow a road leading left. This road carries faded signs (from the days when vehicles used it) cautioning of the dangers of emissions from the landfill, including methane emissions (where vehicle sparks could create explosions). The road turns right and passes behind the landfill site to reach the Coquitlam Golf Academy at the top of a hill. The golf course is an oasis of green amid the surrounding industry and its clubhouse allows a refreshment break and use of its washrooms. Then go downhill to United Boulevard and continue to the traffic signals at King Edward Street. This is the start of the old community of Fraser Mills, which was once a separate municipality from Coquitlam.

## King Edward Street      1.7 km     0 hr 26 m     F52

**Getting home:** Go left to the first signal, cross King Edward Street, turn left and cross Lougheed Highway. Then cross back over King Edward Street to the bus stop on Lougheed Highway. Any bus will go to Braid Station for SkyTrain connections throughout the region.

# Fraser Mills

The community of Fraser Mills was originally called Millside. It was located in dense forest, separated from New Westminster by five kilometres of rough trail. The company town served the Ross Maclaren Sawmill, built in 1889, which became Fraser River Sawmills in 1906, and later Canadian Western Lumber. The Chinese, East Indian and white workers lived in separate parts of town. Racial tensions reduced the mill's productivity so, in 1909, the company directors consulted with the Oblates of Mary Immaculate in New Westminster to help recruit workers from Quebec (French Canadians were known for their expertise in the lumber business). The company offered them 25 cents an hour for a 10-hour day, 6-day week, plus financial assistance with their housing.

One hundred and ten workers arrived in 1909 and more francophones followed in the next few years, reducing the mill's reliance on coloured workers. Canadian Western Lumber offered each family a one-acre lot in an area about two kilometres north of the company town—an area now known as Maillardville. (The original 1891 Fraser Mills Station has now been moved there as a heritage building.) Each lot cost $150, payable through $5 monthly salary deductions. The company also promised the necessary lumber to build homes and construct a church, rectory and school. The first school was set up over the general store. When the first teacher left in December 1909, the Sisters of Child Jesus in New Westminster took over the teaching duties, travelling on the tram to Sapperton and walking from there.

*Source: "A 75-Year Chronicle—Maillardville," by Tony Paré et al. Maillardville, BC: 1984. Reprinted on www.maillardville.com/ english_smu/eng_history_75years.htm, July 2001.*

**Welcome Sign by Original Fraser Mills Station**

# Mouth of Pitt River

Today's 13½-km (8½-mile) walk starts at Fraser Mills, passes through an industrial park to Maquabeak Park under Port Mann Bridge and follows the Fraser and Pitt River shores to Pitt River Bridge. On its way, it passes the mouth of the Coquitlam River and offers views over the wide confluence of the Pitt and Fraser rivers.

**Getting there:** If using transit, take a #158, #159 or #169 bus (which start from Braid Station), get off at King Edward Street and walk along it to pass under the Trans-Canada Highway.

If driving, take Lougheed Highway to the traffic signals just east of Pitt River Bridge. Turn north onto Dewdney Trunk Road and almost immediately left onto a side road. Drive to the crash barrier by Lougheed Highway and park nearby. The #701 Coquitlam Station bus leaves from the bus stop on the other side of the crash barrier. Take the bus to Coquitlam Station, transfer to the next Braid Station bus, get off at King Edward Street and walk along it to pass under the Trans Canada Highway. A bus at 8:44 a.m. on Saturday, transferring to the #169 bus, takes about 35 minutes.

## King Edward Street 0 km 0 hr F52

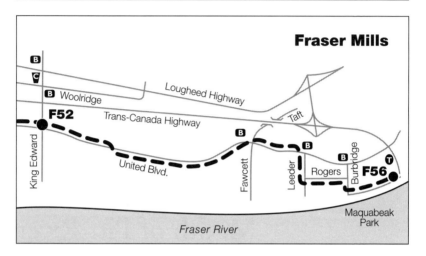

If you want a coffee before you start, a fast-food outlet is located just down Woolridge Street, north of King Edward Street at the freeway underpass. Walk along King Edward Street to United Boulevard and follow the road through the commercial development of Fraser Mills. The street is lined with warehouse-type buildings where retailers sell carpets, furniture and the like.

It looks tempting to take one of the streets on the right and follow it down to the Fraser River, but I recommend against it. There are viewpoints but no waterfront walkway or through-route; it is a significant detour and you must return to United Boulevard in the end. Where the commercial development ends, follow the road as it bends towards the Trans-Canada Highway and then away, paralleling an off-ramp. Turn right on Leeder Street, turn left on Rogers Avenue and right onto Burbridge Street. Follow this street, which curves to parallel the river and ends in Maquabeak Park, where there are washrooms and picnic tables. Take a break, enjoy the river, and wonder where everybody is going on Port Mann Bridge overhead.

## Maquabeak Park · 4.0 km · 0 hr 56 m · F56

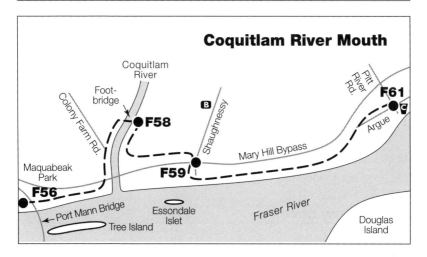

**Coquitlam River Mouth**

Continue under the bridge and follow the path until it reaches the Coquitlam River, where the trail bends left under the road bridge. On the right, a small track leads to an attractive beach where the Coquitlam River flows into the Fraser River—another good spot for a break. Tree Island lies downstream, Canadian National Railway's Port Mann rail yards are opposite, and the tip of Douglas Island is on the left.

Continue along the track under the Mary Hill Bypass bridge, following the bank of the Coquitlam River. Pass a gate and bear right on a track which the Kirkwitlum Indian Nation allows pedestrians to use through their reserve. Soon the route passes a yellow gate and enters Colony Farm Regional Park. This whole area was once part of Home Farm, which served Riverview Mental Hospital; you can see an old silo across the river on the park's eastern boundary. The area is favoured by birders and cyclists, and you will probably meet both. Where the path meets a footbridge, you cross to enter Port Coquitlam. (Burrard Loop comes in from the left—B84—having crossed Mary Hill, which you see ahead.)

## Coquitlam Footbridge          1.8 km   0 hr 25 m    F58

Follow PoCo Trail to the right, with the Coquitlam River flowing downstream beside you. As the trail approaches Mary Hill Bypass, it swings left at the south edge of the park, an area alive with buttercups and horsetail in the spring. Where the trail ends at the corner of Shaughnessy Street and Mary Hill Bypass, cross the bypass at the signals and continue to the riverbank.

If you want to end the walk, the half-hourly #159 bus leaves for Vancouver from the bus stop on the west side of Shaughnessy Street and for Port Coquitlam at the stop on the east side.

## Shaughnessy Street          0.9 km   0 hr 13 m    F59

The route stays close to the foreshore, passing through land that contained major gravel pits and is now being developed as part of the Mary Hill residential area. New houses were being built on Mary Hill in 1957, when I arrived in Vancouver, and new houses are still being built there today, as well as on the river side of the bypass. Surrey lies on the opposite side until Douglas Island appears. Douglas Island was provincial land until it was given to the Greater Vancouver Regional Parks District as a Legacy Park, one of many donated to remember the 1994 Commonwealth Games in Victoria. Logs are boomed against its shore and boom boats often manoeuvre the logs in or out of their mooring places. The route continues on Argue Street to Pitt River Road.

## Pitt River Road          2.4 km   0 hr 34 m    F61

The route crosses Pitt River Road and continues on Argue Street, close to the river. If you go to the edge of the paved area by the stores on the right, you can enjoy a clear view of the Pitt and Fraser River confluence. Continue on the road and pass a yellow gate onto a dike path. Industrial plants line the landward side, so you may prefer to

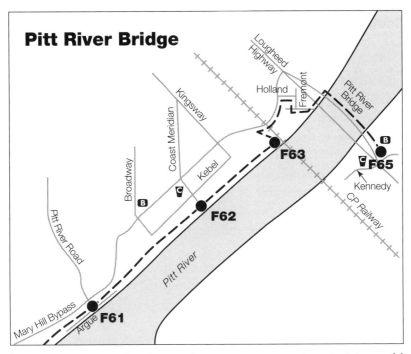

keep your eyes on the river and upstream mountains. In May, wild roses bloom below.

At the next yellow gate, you reach Coast Meridian Road. You can have a lunch break sitting on the benches to the left, or visit the coffee shop, open weekdays, in a service station for truck drivers in the plaza up the road.

### Coast Meridian Road       1.2 km    0 hr 17 m    F62

As the dike path continues, the fronts of industrial buildings are on the left and the river on the right. The distant Canadian Pacific Railway gets slowly closer as you make your way towards it. Just before the path reaches the rail bridge, it bends sharply to the right. This ends the walkable part of the dike on the south side of the bridge. (If you were to proceed, you would pass under the rail bridge and then be blocked by a sawmill.)

## South Dike                    1.1 km    0 hr 15 m    F63

Turn left and follow the trail to the main road. Turn right, follow the sidewalk under the rail bridge, turn right onto Holland Street, right onto Fremont Street and left onto the dike, passing a restaurant pub on the way.

Looking at the waterfront from the dike, the berths and small community indicate that this was the terminal of the ferry that carried traffic across the Pitt River before a road bridge was built in 1912. (On the other side of the river, Ferry Slip Road leads to the eastern terminal.) Continue on the dike, follow the trail under both spans of Pitt River Bridge and emerge onto the dike path on the north side.

Go to the sidewalk and cross the bridge. Make sure to stop halfway and take in the view to the north. The snowy mountains, brooding peak of Golden Ears and flat marshlands bordering the Pitt River surely encapsulate the beauty of this part of the world. Follow the path—protected from the traffic by a crash barrier—downhill towards the traffic signals at Dewdney Trunk Road. You have entered Pitt Meadows.

## Pitt River Bridge East         2.1 km    0 hr 30 m    F65

**Getting home:** The #701 Coquitlam Station bus stops at the north-side bus stop and connects to regional bus services. The #701 bus to Maple Ridge stops on the south side.

# Alouette River to Maple Ridge

Today's 12-km (7½-mile) walk follows the Pitt and Alouette River dikes along the route that the Municipality of Pitt Meadows selected for the Trans Canada Trail. They have provided interpretative panels, picnic tables, seats and toilets. The route offers wide, sweeping views of the Pitt River area and passes berry farms, greenhouses and small mixed-livestock farms along the Alouette River.

**Getting there:** If you are arriving by transit, take the #701 bus to the first stop east of Pitt River Bridge.

If you are driving, park near the intersection of Dewdney Trunk Road and Laity Street (213th Street). Take the #701 bus on the north side of Dewdney Trunk to Pitt River Bridge. A bus at 8:53 a.m. on Saturday takes just over 15 minutes.

From the bus stop, walk on the north side of Lougheed Highway and reach the dike gate on the eastern side of the Pitt River. (If you want to have a coffee and use a washroom before you start, first visit the service station on the south side of Lougheed Highway.)

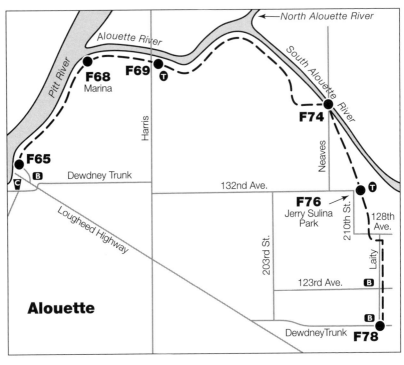

## Pitt River Bridge East      0 km    0 hr    F65

The first fields on the right are barren but cranberry, red currant and blueberry plantations soon appear. Burke Mountain dominates the landscape ahead across the river. In April, you may see geese arriving to breed and, in October, you may hear their honking as they gather to fly south in skeins. You can rest and enjoy the view from a bench outside Pitt Meadows Marina, where the Alouette River joins the Pitt River.

## Pitt Meadows Marina      2.5 km    0 hr 35 m    F68

The dike path now follows the Alouette River, and has interpretative notices describing the river, waterfowl, salmon and raptors. Benches, sometimes decorated with flowers on them or planted below, commemorate the lives of various local people. Berry farms continue on the right. You may see walkers on the opposite side using a dike path which leads further up the Pitt River. It continues for four kilometres and has beautiful mountain views, until it stops at a gravel pit.

About 20 minutes from the marina, a Harris Road staging area provides picnic tables, a toilet and parking for cars and bicycles. This landscaped spot is a pleasant place for a break. (The walkers on the opposite dike may well have parked here.)

## Trans Canada Trail

The Trans Canada Trail opened on September 9, 2000. It will span 16,000 km across Canada, from the Pacific and Arctic Oceans to the Atlantic. In various parts of the country the trail is shared by walkers, cyclists, horse riders, skiers and snowmobilers, but in the Lower Mainland the trail accommodates walkers, cyclists and horse riders only. Moreover, west of Fort Langley walkers and cyclists follow a route from Horseshoe Bay to Fort Langley, crossing Burrard Inlet on SeaBus. Horseriders follow a different route, since SeaBus does not welcome horses and horses don't have any great love of SeaBuses.

To mark the official opening of the trail, runners filled bottles of water from each of the three oceans bordering Canada— tha Arctic at Tuktoyaktuk, NWT, the Pacific at Victoria, BC and the Atlantic at St. John's, Nfld. From February to September, 5000 carriers relayed these bottles to Ottawa, where they were poured symbolically into an especially constructed Trans Canada Trail Fountain on September 9, 2000.

The Trans Canada Trail Foundation (www.tctrail.ca) coordinates the efforts of trail-builders throughout the country, raising funds by symbolically selling metres of trail and giving donors the opportunity to have their names inscribed in a pavilion of their choice along the trail.

## Harris Road                1.4 km    0 hr 20 m    F69

The path continues along the dike, curving with the bends in the river. You again will see walkers on the opposite bank, where a dike path provides a one-hour round-trip from the north side of Harris Road bridge. After the confluence with the North Alouette River, continue along the South Alouette River towards its Alouette Lake headwaters. In the north, a wall of mountains marks the eastern edge of Pitt Lake. The nearest of these mountains defines the eastern edge of Pitt Polder, which was reclaimed from marshland by Dutch settlers in the early 1950s. If you were to climb over the mountain barrier, you would reach Malcolm Knapp Forest, UBC's research forest.

Along occasional roads to the right you will see a greenhouse and possibly horses, sheep and the odd llama or ostrich. The path makes a final sweep south to an impressive stand of cottonwoods before turning left to Neaves Road. When I walked here one hot summer day, the trees provided some welcome shade.

## Neaves Road                5.0 km    1 hr 10 m    F74

Cross Neaves Road when it is clear and stay on the dike path following the south side of the river. The path curves and reaches small Jerry Sulina Park, named after a municipal administrator. It has a toilet and a small parking area. Because it is located at the corner of 132nd Avenue and 210th Street, close to an urban part of Maple Ridge, you have probably been meeting many walkers and dogs.

## Jerry Sulina Park           1.3 km    0 hr 18 m    F76

A 10-minute walk takes you to the end of the dike at 128th Avenue, where Trans Canada Trail signs point left and then right up Laity Street. Pastures lie on the right and houses at the outskirts of Maple Ridge appear on the left. At 124th Avenue, a Trans Canada

Trail sign points to the left. However, continue for four blocks down Laity Street to Dewdney Trunk Road to end today's walk.

**Dewdney Trunk Road**　　　　　2.0 km　　0 hr 28 m　　F78

**Getting home:** The westbound #701 bus goes to Coquitlam Station, connecting to points throughout the region.

**Golden Ears from the Alouette River**

# Maple Ridge to Fort Langley

Today's 13-km (8-mile) walk heads south on Laity Street to St. John the Divine, BC's oldest active church. It then follows River Road before dropping into Port Haney and the West Coast Express railway station. It continues along the Fraser River Heritage Trail, passing Thomas Haney House and the Maple Ridge Museum, and going through the Thomas Haney campus of Douglas College to 232nd Street. At the foot of the hill, it enters Kanaka Creek Park and follows the creek, whose oxbows lead to the Fraser River. The route follows a riverbank trail to Kanaka Landing, continuing to River Road and the Albion Ferry. It crosses the river by ferry and continues briefly to Fort Langley.

**Getting there:** If using transit, take the #701 Haney Place bus and get off at Laity Street.

If driving, park by the Albion ferry, take the infrequent #722 bus to Haney Place, change to the #701 Coquitlam Station bus and get off at Laity Street. A bus at 9:05 a.m. on Saturday takes 40 minutes, including a 17-minute wait at Haney Place which might permit a quick coffee or washroom stop in the mall. The next #722 from the ferry is three hours later.

## Dewdney Trunk Road · · · · · · · · · · · · · · · · · 0 km · · · 0 hr · · · F78

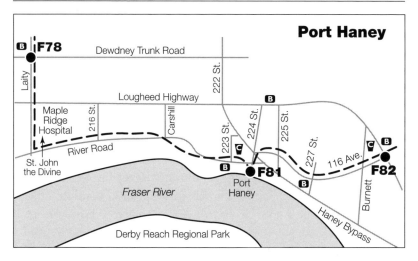

Walk south along the residential Laity Street to reach the traffic signals at Lougheed Highway. Cross and continue south, passing Maple Ridge Hospital on the left. Continue to River Road; St. John the Divine, BC's oldest active church, lies just round the corner.

From here, walk 20 minutes east on the north side of River Road. Where the pedestrian walkway ends at Carshill Street, cross the busy River Road carefully and follow the sidewalk that departs from the road, separated by a buffer of greenery. At the bottom of the hill, the road parallels the railway, with the river beyond. When you reach the West Coast Express station, you can detour one block north on 223rd Street to St. Andrew's Presbyterian Church, a heritage building flanked by a manse and a Masonic Hall. Return to River Road and continue to the Port Haney wharf, stopping off at the coffee shop on the left, if you want a refreshment break.

# St. John the Divine

!n November 1858, James Douglas became governor of the crown colony of British Columbia. He selected the area of the then-fort, four kilometres downstream from present-day Fort Langley, to be his capital, naming it Derby. The Anglican Church sent Reverend William Burton Crickmer, who arrived in February 1859. Under Colonel Richard Moody's direction, the Royal Engineers built the church of California redwood, as there were no local sawmills. They followed Reverend Crickmer's plans, based on St. John's Church in Deptford, London—his first curacy. The boom at Derby was short-lived, however, as Colonel Moody recommended against retaining Derby as the capital and proposed New Westminster instead.

July 17, 1859 is the date of the first entry in the church registry and January 8, 1860 the last. Reverend Crickmer was sent to Yale, and the bishop petitioned Douglas to move the church and parsonage there. Douglas replied that a move 70 miles upstream against the current would be impossible. The church remained at Derby for just over 20 years, used by visiting clergy and others. Pioneer Thomas Haney and his wife occupied it for six months in 1876 while their house was built in Maple Ridge.

In 1881, the townsite of Maple Ridge began to boom with the coming of the railway. The Anglican Fraser River Mission established a committee under Magistrate John Laity to bring the church from Derby to Maple Ridge. Crews floated it across the river on a raft of its own timbers, and bull teams and windlasses hauled it on rollers up the 30- to 40-degree slope to the corner of present-day River Road and Laity Street. The first service took place in 1882. A century later in 1983, construction crews moved the church 30 metres east on rollers to its present site and added a lounge, kitchen and nursery.

**St. John the Divine Church**

*Source: "Parish History; St. John the Divine Anglican Church." Maple Ridge, BC: Pamphlet supplied by Reverend Charles Balfour, Rector, 2000.*

# Port Haney's Heritage Buildings

In 1874, the provincial government established Maple Ridge, stretching from Stave River in the east to Pitt River in the west. In 1876, pioneers Thomas and Ann Haney arrived and built a home near the centre of town in present-day Port Haney. Descendants lived in the Thomas Haney House until 1979, when the family donated it to the people of Maple Ridge. It is furnished in its original style and is open to the public on Wednesday and Sunday from 1 to 4 p.m.

Thomas Haney founded the town of Port Haney in 1882, centred around his brickworks, the railway station and the wharf. In 1888, he donated land to the Presbyterian Church for St. Andrew's Church, a brick-faced structure that still stands on 116th Avenue. The congregation joined the United Church in 1926. In the 1930s, they added a steeple to house a bell from the Methodist Church, which had closed. Services continued until 1956.

The Bank of Montreal built a Port Haney branch in 1911, with upstairs living quarters for the manager. It has operated as the Billy Miner Pub since 1981. Bill Miner engineered Canada's first train robbery at nearby Silverdale in 1904, stealing $1,000 in cash and $6,000 in gold and bonds. A second robbery attempt at Monte Creek, near Kamloops, only netted him $15 and he was captured within a week and sentenced to life in the BC Penitentiary. He escaped to the United States, continued robbing trains, and died in Georgia after spending time in jail there.

During Port Haney's first 40 years, a post office operated out of various retail businesses in town. In 1932, it moved to its own quarters in the building next to the pub, which is now a residence. It operated until 1939, when businesses moved to the upper town centred around Lougheed Highway.

Maple Ridge Museum is housed in the 1907 home of the manager of Haney Brick & Tile Co., which operated on the property from 1907 to 1977. It displays objects from the local First Nations heritage and the community's pioneer past, and contains community archives, documents and photographs. A 1944 wooden caboose is displayed outside. The museum is open Wednesday and Sunday from 1 to 4 p.m., with extended summer hours.

The other building on the site now serves as the Maple Ridge Arts Council office. It was originally the offices of Haney Brick & Tile Co., built in 1930, using brick, tile and cement.

*Sources: "Port Haney—Heritage River Walk." Maple Ridge, BC: Pamphlet of the Maple Ridge Historical Society, 1999. "The Bill Miner Story." Maple Ridge, BC: Pamphlet of the Billy Miner Pub, 2000.*

**The Fraser River from Port Haney Wharf**

## Port Haney 3.0 km 0 hr 44m F81

Cross the railway tracks and go to the wharf, which offers a wide view of the Fraser River. Derby Reach Regional Park occupies the opposite shore. Across the street from the wharf are two historic buildings, originally the 1911 Bank of Montreal and the 1932 post office. One is now a pub/restaurant and the other a private residence.

To continue, cross the road to Fraser River Heritage Walk, a pedestrian way that links local heritage sites. Go through the tunnel to the foot of 224th Street and take the gateway on the right leading to a path past Thomas Haney House. This path winds downhill to Brickwood Park. Continue downhill along the sidewalk and cross 227th Street. The path rises, with Jim Hadgkiss Park on the right. You can see Maple Ridge Museum near the bypass. Continue across 226th Street and follow the footpath to Lougheed Highway. There is a restaurant near this corner and there are several fast-food restaurants one or two blocks to the left, on the south side of the highway.

**Thomas Haney House**

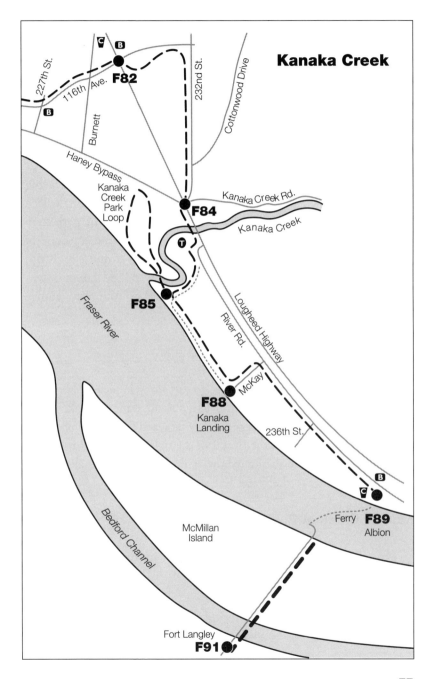

Kanaka Creek

## Lougheed Highway    1.7 km  0 hr 26 m  F82

Cross the highway at the pedestrian-activated signals to the far corner adjacent to the playing fields. Pass through a gate in the chain-link fence to enter the grounds of Telosky Stadium and go to the far corner of the grassed area. If teams are playing, keep close to the fence by Lougheed Highway. When I visit, there is rarely anyone playing and I follow the path in and cross the field towards the tallest tree at the far side, keeping parallel to the highway but between the playing areas of the fields. At the trees, a small paved path leads left, with a steep drop-off to a ravine just visible through bushes. The path soon bends towards some buildings on the Thomas Haney campus of Douglas College. Stay on the grass and follow it around to 116th Avenue, turn right and right again, and follow 232nd Street downhill to a major intersection with Lougheed Highway and Haney Bypass.

## 232nd Street Foot    1.4 km  0 hr 23 m  F84

Cross the highway and the bypass, go east along Lougheed Highway, cross Kanaka Creek, and turn onto River Road. Enter Kanaka Creek Park; you will find washrooms and picnic tables to the right. Follow the trail into the park towards the river. On the right, a viewing tower with decks provides views over the oxbow at the mouth of Kanaka Creek. The trail continues to the Fraser River's edge.

## Kanaka Creek at River    1.0 km  0 hr 16 m  F85

From here, turn right and follow the path across Kanaka Creek on an imposing bridge, where a sign tells of the Hawaiians—or Kanakans in the Chinook language—who worked in a nearby sawmill. Stay on the path at the river's edge; picnic tables and toilets make this a good lunch stop. Where you reach a wide path leading

**Kanaka Creek**

inland, take it and go right where directed by a sign (straight-on leads to the railway and an emergency exit for vehicles to Haney Bypass). The path leads through the woods and returns to the Kanaka bridge and the point where you started the loop.

Continue east along a wide path. Derby Reach Regional Park lies across the river at the original Fort Langley site. The river path is especially attractive in spring, when sticky cottonwood buds smell sweet and the green beads of fruit ripen and split, releasing the cotton. Cherry trees flower from April to June and bleeding hearts and lily of the valley abound. Watch out for stinging nettles at the trail edge. The trail narrows after it leaves the park and brambles proliferate across the path at ground level, threatening to trip you. At its end, pass on the river side of a gate to Mackay Avenue and Kanaka Landing.

**Ferry Approaching the Dock at Albion**

**Fort Langley Merchants in Historic Garb**

## Kanaka Landing 3.0 km 0 hr 44m F88

Turn left, go along McKay Avenue and turn right along River Road. You pass a pole company, a house-moving company and other river-based industries. Watch for vehicles turning onto 236th Street, which leads to Maple Ridge's recycling plant. The Albion Ferry terminal has washrooms and a restaurant, patronized mostly by people with several sailings' wait. The continual activity of loading and unloading, and the manoeuvring of ferries in their journey make an interesting spectacle. If you want to finish the walk here, the infrequent #722 bus leaves from a stop across the street. A bus at 2:51 p.m. on Saturday will get you to Coquitlam Station just before 4 o'clock. The next bus is three hours later.

## Fort Langley

The original Fort Langley was built in 1827 on what is now a heritage area in Derby Reach Regional Park. The fort remained at this site for 12 years until Hudson's Bay Company chief trader James Murray Yale wanted to expand the farming activities. Accordingly, he built a new fort upstream in 1839, close to present-day Fort Langley. On the night of April 11, 1840, a fire broke out in the smithy and soon spread to other buildings and the stockade. By morning, only hot ashes and charred stumps remained. Yale immediately set about rebuilding nearby, and a new and larger fort was completed within months. It was enlarged slightly some years later to become one of the company's largest outposts.

In November 1858, James Douglas became governor of the crown colony of British Columbia. He selected the site of the original Fort Langley as his capital and renamed it Derby, after Edward Stanley, Earl of Derby and Prime Minister of England. However, Royal Engineers commander Richard Moody decided that Derby was vulnerable to American attack and recommended that the capital be further downstream. The site that was eventually selected became New Westminster.

Source: *Fort Langley, Birthplace of British Columbia,* by *B. A. McKelvie. Victoria, BC: Porcépic Books Limited, 1991.*

| **Albion Ferry** | 1.7 km | 0 hr 24 m | F89 |
| --- | --- | --- | --- |

To reach Fort Langley, cross on the free ferry and take a 20-minute walk into town along Glover Road. Fort Langley is an attractive place, with interesting stores, restaurants and historic buildings in addition to the well-known fort. A tourist information office in a store by the railway crossing supplies pamphlets on historic houses, stores, galleries, restaurants and the sights of Fort Langley. (Fort Langley is also the end of the Peace-Arch-to-Fort-Langley walks at WS41.) The fort itself, at the end of Mavis Street, is a National Historic Site and well worth a visit.

## Fort Langley Station        1.2 km    0 hr 21m    F91

**Getting home:** You can catch a C62 bus on 96th Avenue at Glover Road in Fort Langley and transfer at Walnut Grove to the #501 bus to Surrey Central Station. A bus at 3:21 p.m. on Saturday will get you to Surrey Central Station at 4:10 p.m.

# Glen Valley

The next section of the walk passes Fort Langley airport and a government landing dock to reach Two-Bit Bar, the first of several small enclaves that make up Glen Valley Regional Park. The route continues along the Fraser River, passing through Poplar Bar Park with its fishing bar, and reaches Bradner Road. You can detour further to just beyond the next fishing bar at Duncan Bar, but the route then dead-ends and the next section of the walk resumes from Bradner Road.

There is no bus service immediately east of Fort Langley, so to continue to walk one-way you will need to leave one vehicle at the end and car-shuttle. This provides you with a walk, much of which is along busy 88th Avenue. I once walked it on a November weekday when the road was pleasantly quiet; if you can find a similar calm spell or if you are comfortable walking the road, by all means do so. The one-way distance is 12½ km (7½ miles) to Bradner Road or up to 2 km longer if you choose to extend it to Duncan Bar.

However, I must admit that I prefer to drive slowly along 88th Avenue, enjoying the Fort Langley to Two-Bit Bar section from my car. I then enjoy the highlights of the following Fraser River stretch by walking to just beyond Duncan Bar and back. This provides a 13-km (8-mile) round-trip walk that can be done with just one vehicle.

**Getting there:** If you are car-shuttling, drive in two vehicles and park one at the intersection of River Road and Bradner Road (or further east on River Road to Duncan Bar if you want). Then drive in the other vehicle to Fort Langley and park by the fort near the picnic tables. Walk west down the road to Glover Road by the railway station.

If you want to see only the highlights of the Fraser River section, drive east on Mavis Avenue from Fort Langley Station, turn left onto 88th Avenue below the fort and follow the road to 272nd Street. Turn left and park on the left in Two-Bit Bar (F99) and follow the directions from there.

**Fort Langley Station**        0 km    0 hr    F91

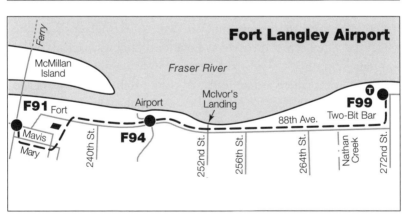

If you want a coffee stop, you can choose from a number of restaurants in Fort Langley. Starting from Fort Langley Station, walk two blocks south along Glover Road and head left along Mary Street. At the first corner you will see St. George's Anglican Church, which opened in 1901 and still serves its parishioners. The wrought-iron cross attached to the church's west gable commemorates a Hawaii-born Hudson's Bay Company employee. The cross formerly stood in the original cemetery which was situated just north of the church. Continue along the road to a large swath of grass in front of the fort's south stockade. Cross the grass to the fort's eastern edge and follow the narrow path between the fort and its fence. This path offers a panoramic view over the farms on the flatland. It leads to a yellow gate at 88th Avenue, where you turn right. This road is normally busy, so be careful if you cross it to face the oncoming traffic. A sod-growing area appears on the left and, a little further on, opposite Armstrong Road, the Fort Langley Airport entrance. The airfield is usually quiet, as pilots of small airplanes tend to use airports nearer to Vancouver. There may be vessels moored, including a fishing lodge that is towed to a coastal destination in the summer.

## Airport Entrance                         2.9 km    0 hr 41m    F94

Continue on 88th Avenue and cross West Creek to 252nd Street. If you detour to the waterfront, you will reach McIvor's Landing, which has views across the river to Lougheed Highway traffic passing through Whonnock. The road passes 256th and 264th Streets to Nathan Creek, where a dike leads off to the right. Many years ago, while looking for a possible off-road route, I walked almost to the end of the dike. When I saw the owner of a nearby house, I asked if I could cross his property to the road. With a friendly smile he said that I could, but that if I came again he would shoot me. I took this as a hint that he disliked trespassers and I have not gone back. Continue on the road to 272nd Street, turn left and, just before the road reaches the river, turn into Glen Valley Park's Two-Bit Bar.

**Two-Bit Bar**     5.9 km     1 hr 23m     F99

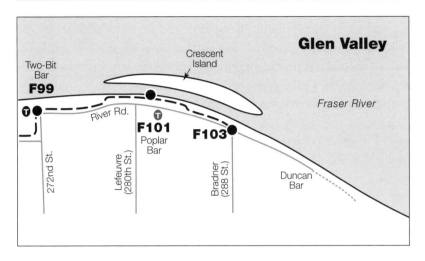

This is where to park and start walking if you have omitted the road walk. The heritage Hassall House, built in 1917, is still private property. Walk west of the house to enjoy the river view and take a break; there is a toilet. Walk along the grass strip between the river and the fence at the back of the house to return to River Road.

Walk along this normally quiet road. Trees at the edge of the river prevent a good view, but it is interesting to see half a dozen grown-over car bodies along the first kilometre between the road and the river. After a bend in the road and a sign indicating that you have entered Abbotsford, take the trail leading left into Poplar Bar park. A boardwalk and bark-mulch path leads to an open park site with picnic tables and a toilet. Long, thin Crescent Island starts in the channel here and extends three kilometres east.

**Poplar Bar**     1.5 km     0 hr 21m     F101

Continue on the trail, taking either path where the trail forks, and reach River Road in about a kilometre. Continue to Bradner Road.

## Bradner Road 2.1 km 0 hr 29m F103

Your next day's route to Olund Park and Matsqui Trail lies up the hill, but you can explore 2.8 km further by continuing along River Road. Openings appear from time to time on the left, with paths leading down to the shore. These spots are popular with fishers of the protected sturgeon, even though any fish that are caught must be released. The waters immediately upstream and downstream from Mission are one of its principal habitats. The paved road ends at Duncan Bar, just under two kilometres from Bradner Road. You can continue further by passing the yellow gate and following the track on the River Road right-of-way to a railway, where a hut bears a Glen Valley sign. This is the busy main line of the Canadian National Railway (CNR). The Canadian Pacific Railway used to run all its trains on the north side of the Fraser River and CNR all its trains on the south side. However, the railways now co-operate, so that long-distance westbound trains use the south side and long-distance eastbound ones the north side. After this point, there is no further way on and you must return to your vehicle.

# Mount Lehman

Today's walk starts from the foot of Bradner Road and winds uphill to a small community hall. An 8-km (5-mile) stretch of moderately quiet road leads to a historic cemetery and the community of Mount Lehman. A well-graded trail then makes its way down a ravine to Lehman's Landing, where riverboats served this community for many years. The route continues to Olund Park and the start of Matsqui Trail.

You can again choose between a one-way 13½-km (8½-mile) walk involving significant stretches of paved road or a round-trip 10-km (6-mile) walk of the highlights.

**Getting there:** For the one-way walk, drive in two vehicles to Olund Park off Harris Road, opposite its intersection with Olund Road. Then take one vehicle to the foot of Bradner Road, find somewhere to park off River Road (probably just east of Bradner Road) and start walking from there.

For the highlights-only route, park by Mount Lehman Cemetery (F111) on Taylor Road just east of Ross Road.

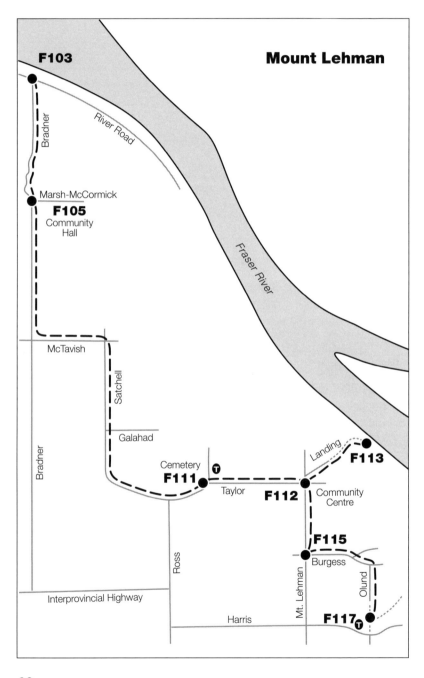

## Bradner Road            0 km    0 hr    F103

Cross the railway and head up the hill. The paved road soon changes to a winding dirt road with glimpses over the valley. The community hall at the top is unlikely to be open, but you may find a spot to sit and rest after your exertions.

## Community Hall            1.8 km    0 hr 30m    F105

The walk continues on the roadway to Mount Lehman. Go south on Bradner Road, east on McTavish Road and south on Satchell Road, which curves east to join Taylor Road and reach Mount Lehman Cemetery. This is where you should park for the start of the round-trip walk.

## Mount Lehman Cemetery        5.7 km    1 hr 20m    F111

A portable toilet outside the cemetery fence is marked Women, although both sexes use it. The graves against the western edge of the cemetery have the most historical interest, with some dating to the late 1800s. Mounted on an old stone is a new marble pillar marked Lehman, bearing the names of several family members, including the original Thomas and Lucy Hannah Lehman; Hannah Creek flows in the ravine behind. Small headstones commemorate two babies. The oldest grave I could find was that of a two-year-old McCallum baby who died in 1884.

Continuing east on Taylor Road, you pass Taylor's Manzana apple orchard on the right and reach Mount Lehman's school and a community centre with a hall, playing field and park. You can find a picnic table behind the hall and another one a little further on.

## Mount Lehman Community Centre  1.2 km  0 hr 17m  F112

Head north on Mount Lehman Road (marked by a No Exit sign) and turn right down Landing Road, which soon turns into a track. At the head of the ravine, you will find a picnic table and a notice board giving details about the early farming community and the boat service at Lehman Landing. The track winds downhill and ends close to the railway and the river. An unofficial trail leads down to the rails of the old siding. Across the tracks, a steep, rough trail leads to log-boom storage on the river; don't go, as the rail line is very busy and a fall could be fatal.

## Lehman's Landing  1.3 km  0 hr 17m  F113

Head back up the track, retrace the route to the community centre and continue along Mount Lehman Road to Burgess Avenue. Another settlement concentrated here when BC Electric Railway established its Mount Lehman Station. The present settlement has a fire station, insurance agency, auto repair shop and credit union, but no café.

## Burgess Avenue  2.0 km  0 hr 30m  F115

Go east along Burgess Avenue until it forks, bear right, cross the railway and go south along Olund Road. At its end, continue on the bark-mulch trail that heads downhill a short distance before reaching an intersection. Matsqui Trail on the left leads down to the Matsqui Dikes and is part of the Trans Canada Trail. The next walk follows that route.

# Lehman's Landing

At the end of the 19th century, the south side of the Fraser River had no railways and few roads. Riverboats provided transportation for the early farming communities; Lehman's Landing served the Matsqui community on the Mount Lehman escarpment. The riverboats *Rowena, Defender, Royal City, Royal Queen, Fairy Queen, Sampson V, Beaver* and *Skeena* provided weekly service, shipping farm produce from Matsqui to New Westminster. Mount Lehman built a school in 1884 and the BC Electric Railway came through in 1908. The Canadian National Railway came later, following the Fraser riverbank.

*Source: "Lehman's Landing." Notice board at Lehman's Landing trailhead, Abbotsford, BC: Matsqui Centennial Society, 1992.*

**Matsqui Trail Turn**                    1.5 km      0 hr 24m      F117

Continue for 200 metres further to reach the entrance of Olund Park, with a notice board and a unisex toilet.

**Getting home:** Rejoin your vehicle if you parked it here. If walking the round-trip, retrace your steps to the cemetery.

# Matsqui Trail

Today's 15-km (9½-mile) walk starts with a 5-km quiet road walk through Fraser Valley farmlands to reach the head of Matsqui Trail, where you ended last time. Matsqui Trail then leads through woods at the side of the Coligny Creek ravine and through Matsqui Nation Reserve to the Fraser River. It continues along the dikes of Matsqui Trail Regional Park and across the bridge to Junction Mall on the outskirts of Mission.

**Getting there**: If you want to use transit, City Link bus service connects Vancouver and Abbotsford. You can catch the bus from Main Street Railway Station in Vancouver at 9:15 a.m. (or from New Westminster or Guildford later) and arrive at Sevenoaks Mall in Abbotsford at 10:45 a.m. You can have a coffee and use the washroom in Sevenoaks Mall before catching the 11:15 a.m. bus from the bus exchange one block to the right from the nearby traffic signals. Take the #1 Crosstown bus via Blueridge; there are several #1 Crosstowns, so watch for the Blueridge one. Get off at Townline and Blueridge 15 minutes later.

If you are driving from Vancouver along Lougheed Highway, turn right at the entrance to Mission, where the sign points to Abbotsford via Highway 11. Take the first exit almost immediately and follow the Shopping Centre signs to Junction Mall. At present there is no posted parking restriction, so you can find a place out of the shoppers' way and go to the bus stop in the centre of the mall's parking area.

If you are driving from Abbotsford on Highway 11, do not turn off at the first Mission exit but keep left. Take the next exit on the right, following the Shopping Centre signs. As noted above, there is no posted parking restriction, so find a place out of the shoppers' way and go to the bus stop in the centre of the mall's parking area.

Catch the #11 Valley Connector bus to Abbotsford Bus Exchange and transfer to the #1 Crosstown bus via Blueridge; there are several #1 Crosstowns, so watch for the Blueridge one. Get off where the bus turns into Blueridge from Townline Road. A bus at 9:48 a.m. on Saturday takes just under 45 minutes to Townline Road, including transfer time.

## Townline and Blueridge                                         0 km    0 hr

When it is clear, cross Townline Road and head downhill. A painted path leaves adequate room to walk facing oncoming traffic. The quiet road is flanked by fields, although these are probably destined for housing in the not-too-distant future. The road becomes even quieter after you cross busy Downes Road at the foot of the hill. It narrows and climbs to the top of a small hill, where Polar Avenue branches off on the left. Now you are definitely in farmland; the new subdivisions of Abbotsford are well behind you. The road drops towards the valley floor, with views of mountains to the north and fields in the valley. It winds its way down, losing its paved surface for a while, and reaches Olund Road at the bottom.

Turn left and follow the road through pasture land. Cross McLennan Creek, although you will continue to hear it in a channel behind the hedge as you walk. A house on the hill to the right enjoys

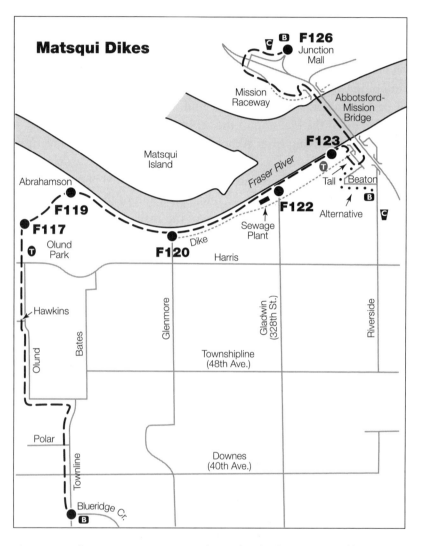

views over the attractive territory through which you are walking. The road soon bends right and climbs to pass this house at the top of the rise. From here, you follow a ridge with a panoramic view to the many humps of Sumas Mountain in the east. I have observed that a white rail fence usually means horses and that seems to be true here. (Horses are kept behind white fences and cattle behind plain wooden ones.) At the end of the ridge, the road jogs where Hawkins Road leads off to the left, then continues downhill to busy Harris Road. Cross the road carefully, enter Olund Park and bear immediately left to find the Fraser Valley Regional District notice board; there is a toilet and parking. A bark-mulch trail continues north, leading to an intersection. Follow the Trans Canada Trail sign to the right onto Matsqui Trail.

**Matsqui Trail Turn**            5.2 km      1 hr 13m      F117

The next stretch of the walk follows a path through trees to the edge of the Fraser River. I find this the most enjoyable section of the day's walk; it is varied, remote, and opens up from time to time to wide views. The trail continues through fields and then drops down Coligny Creek's ravine, where the Matsqui Nation has agreed to the trail passing through their reserve. The trail soon crosses the creek and arrives at a railway crossing. Cross the Vancouver-to-Chilliwack tracks of the Southern British Columbia Railway, the successor company to the BC Electric Railway. As the trail continues, the ravine becomes deeper and steeper on the left side. An owl once flew from the bushes and settled on a branch to watch me; I held on to my hat and walked cautiously past. Where the Fraser River starts to show through the trees, a picnic table appears on the left. I find this a convenient place to break for lunch, although there is no toilet. You can see a board identifying Abrahamson Station on the Canadian National Railway track below. You will almost certainly hear a train or two during your break.

**Abrahamson**            2.0 km      0 hr 28 m      F119

One of the requirements of the Trans Canada Trail is that it serve walkers, cyclists and horseriders. Organized parties of horseriders use this section, as you can see by the well-manured trail (no poop-and-scoop regulations for horses yet). You will also almost certainly meet cyclists on this popular trail.

After crossing a wooden bridge over a swampy area and a subsequent rubber-surfaced bridge, the trail passes under the railway at a creek, emerging at a road leading to a shingle mill at the river's edge. Go right on the Trans Canada Trail to a stop sign and cross the road. In five more minutes, you leave Matsqui Nation Reserve and reach some large cottonwoods and a farm at Glenmore Road. Cars may park here, at the original western end of the Matsqui Dike Trail.

| **Glenmore Road** | 1.3 km | 0 hr 19 m | F120 |
|---|---|---|---|

Continue on the dike path, with the river clearly in view on the left and Matsqui Island forming the far shoreline. Where a sign tells horse riders to go left to a riverside trail, follow it and continue past the sewage treatment plant; the odour can be strong at times. A wooden bridge leads over Matsqui Slough outlet and the trail turns left. At the next corner, a wooden bench on the left provides a resting place with a downstream view towards the shingle mill that you passed earlier. Once, when I came by, a man was fishing for sturgeon. He caught one about 50cm long as I arrived, landed it, measured its length and released it. The trail continues briefly along the riverside and emerges at the foot of Gladwin Road.

| **Gladwin Road** | 1.9 km | 0 hr 27 m | F122 |
|---|---|---|---|

A Trans Canada Trail sign indicates that you should return to the dike, but I prefer to stay on the horse-free riverside trail all the way to the Abbotsford-Mission Bridge (the Trans Canada route also leads there). Sections of the riverside path may be underwater during the spring freshet in May or June, but the trail is normally open for the rest of the year. It offers broad views across the river, and the city of Mission unfolds as you approach. The trail first reaches some campsites and then an open grassy area with picnic tables and parking; toilets are up on the dike.

## Matsqui Dikes Park          1.2 km     0 hr 17 m     F123

Continue east on the dike, pass the house and yard on the right
and turn right down the horse trail at its side. Turn briefly right and
then left along Tall Road, which parallels the Abbotsford-Mission
Bridge above you. Follow the road to where it meets a railway line.
Your route now depends on whether you are willing to use informal
trails to scramble up to, and down from, the bridge.

If you want to end here, follow the road to the right, bear left to
cross the railway and turn left onto Beaton Road to reach busy
Riverside Road. You can catch a #11 Valley Connector bus to
Abbotsford from the bus stop on the right, or cross carefully to the
bus stop outside Matsqui Village Park, where a #11 bus goes to
Junction Mall. While you wait, you can visit a coffee shop one block
to the right.

To continue, scramble up to the Abbotsford-Mission Bridge, using
the trodden grass on the left. You rise steeply to reach a wide safe
pedestrian path on the bridge, separated from traffic by a barrier. The
bridge crosses Matsqui Trail; you will be able to trace some of the route
that you have walked. Further across the bridge, a view of the wide
river appears to the west. This is a great vantage point from which to
appreciate the size and majesty of the Fraser River. Matsqui Island lies
straight ahead, with the river dividing around it.

Where the bridge crosses the north shoreline, you will see a paved
dike path at the river's edge below. A short distance later, the sidewalk
ends and you are left to find your own way at the road edge. I find
continuing at this road edge unacceptably unpleasant and, if there
were no alternative, I would take the bus across instead. However, at
the end of the sidewalk, I step onto the grass on the left-hand side,
make a U-turn and take a brief, steep scramble back towards the river,
staying under the western edge of the bridge to pick up the dike path
below. (If you don't like this, go back over the bridge and pick up the
bus on Riverside Street.)

Turn right, away from the bridge, and follow the path to a road at the Mission Raceway entrance. This used to be a pleasant walk through trees, but it has been logged recently and is presently less attractive. Continue along the left side of the road to the traffic signals, cross at the crosswalk, take the bridge across Highway 11 and turn right, down to Junction Mall.

**Matsqui Dike Trail Riders**

## Junction Mall        3.5 km    0 hr 50 m    F126

**Getting home:** If you came by transit, you can return to Abbotsford on the half-hourly #11 Valley Connector bus that stops in the Junction Mall parking area. Based on my estimates of arrival and walking times, you would catch the 4:20 p.m. bus and get to Abbotsford Bus Exchange by 4:45 p.m. Walk up Bourquin Crescent to the traffic signals. You can cross South Fraser Highway and go left to the bus stop, but with any time you have to spare, you may like to look around Sevenoaks Mall and have something to eat. The City Link bus leaves the bus stop at about 6:00 p.m. for Vancouver and intermediate points.

# Mission

Today's 11½-km (7-mile) walk is full of history, with many points of interest to savour on the way. It starts at Junction Mall on the southern outskirts of Mission and passes through older areas of the city to Fraser River Heritage Park, the site of the mission settlement of the Oblates of Mary Immaculate. It skirts the cemetery, where many brothers of the order are buried, and continues up the hill to the Grotto of Our Lady of Lourdes, a shrine erected in memory of the bishop who conceived the mission. An hour-long walk through woods to the top of the 200-metre (700-foot) hill ends with a short, steep climb to the modern Westminster Abbey—home of the Seminary of Christ the King. This hill has a beautiful view over the Fraser Valley. The walk descends by a different route to the former St. Mary's Residential School and continues through the sacred Medicine Wheel grounds to Heritage Park and Norma Kenney House.

**Getting there:** If you are using transit, follow the instructions to Abbotsford given at the start of the Matsqui Trail chapter. Then catch the #11 Valley Connector Bus at Abbotsford Bus Exchange to Junction Mall in Mission, arriving at about 11:45 a.m.

If you are driving, go to Mission, follow the City Centre highway signs, head east, follow signs to Fraser River Heritage Park, and park. Washrooms may be open. Allow 15 minutes to go uphill on Mary Street outside to 5th Avenue and follow it to Stave Lake Road. Catch a #14 bus heading downhill at about 10 minutes past the hour. Ask the driver where to transfer to the #11 Valley Connector; transfer quickly, as the bus will probably be waiting and leave as soon as you board. Get off at Junction Mall. The trip takes about 10 minutes.

**Junction Mall**        0 km    0 h    F126

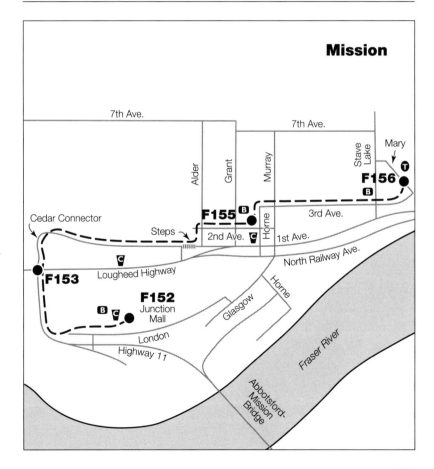

Walk west through the parking lot, continuing in the direction that the bus was heading after you got off. Follow the road within the parking area, turn briefly left at the first intersection and right to pass two fast-food restaurants. Head towards an elevated road in the distance. At the south west corner of the parking area, follow the access road to the pedestrian area at the edge of Highway 11, a strip separated from traffic by a white line. It is unnerving to walk in the same direction as the traffic, but the distance is brief and the road soon reaches Lougheed Highway.

## Lougheed Highway                    0.6 km    0 h 10m    F127

Cross and continue directly ahead on Cedar Connector. It soon bends right and heads east on a street parallel to but higher than Lougheed Highway. If you want a break, steps lead down at several points to fast-food outlets. Where the road ends, ascend the 100 steps to 1st Avenue. Go to the first intersection, cross and go left for one block to 2nd Avenue. The Wheel House on the corner is a private house fancifully decorated with a small lighthouse, wheelhouse and birdhouse to please the residents and passers-by. Turn right and follow the north side of 2nd Avenue, which has great views over the Fraser Valley. The three peaks to the south east are those of Cheam, Lady and Knight. After crossing Grand Street, you will find three heritage buildings on the left. The first is the Abbott block, where a tinsmith and plumber opened for business in 1911. A druggist named Staber built his home next door in 1927. The following year, a doctor built his residence, which is now the Katalin Rest Home. The new building at the corner of James Street is All Saints Anglican Church. Follow 2nd Avenue past Mission Museum and Mission Archives to the main bus terminal.

**Mission Bus Terminal**  2.0 km  0 h 30m  F129

If you want to take a break, you will find a coffee shop at the foot of Horne Street on the right. Go up the hill to 3rd Avenue, turn right and pass through a stretch of modern houses to Stave Lake Road. Cross carefully and continue to the end of 3rd Avenue, cross when it is clear and angle up to the gate leading into Fraser River Heritage Park.

---

## Fraser River Heritage Park

In 1974, the Oblates of Mary Immaculate sold the Mission property to the BC government. The land sat vacant for almost a decade before the government decided to use it for a high-density housing development. However, the Mission Heritage Association, led by Norma Kenney, wife of well-known bandleader Mart Kenney, persuaded the government to donate the land for a major park and heritage centre reflecting the historical significance of the area. Kenney was determined to open part of the park in time for Expo 86.

In June 1986, builders completed a replica of the original Assembly House, which the Heritage Association named Norma Kenney House. Crews have recently finished a replica of the original bell tower, and copies of other buildings from the site are in progress.

*Source: "Fraser River Heritage Park Walking Tour." Pamphlet at Norma Kenney House, Mission, BC: September 2000.*

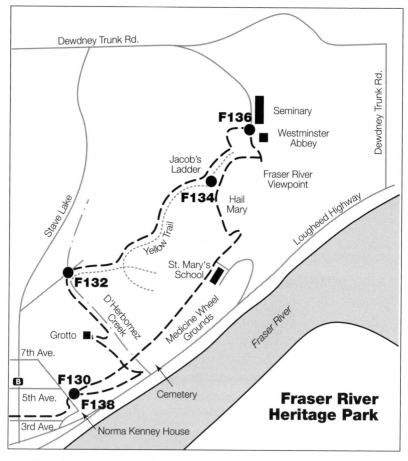

The Norma Kenney House restaurant is open in the summer for lunch and dinner, and coffee, ice cream and refreshments may be available from a window at the side; washrooms are nearby. An outside patio with picnic tables provides a view over the river, valley and town.

Walk east on the grass close to the escarpment to the cemetery gate. The cemetery contains graves of brothers and individuals associated with the mission, including that of Father Leo Fouquet, the founder of the mission, and Bishop D'Herbomez of New Westminster, who authorized it. However, the gate may be locked because vandals have desecrated many of the crosses.

**Cemetery of the Oblates of Mary Immaculate**

# The Original Mission

In 1816, a group of religious brothers founded the order of the Oblates of Mary Immaculate at Aix-en-Provence, in France, to serve the poor. In 1841, the order sent six of their 40 priests to Montréal to found a Canadian mission. In 1847, they sent five brothers to begin operations on the US west coast in the Oregon Territory. In 1858, they dispatched more brothers to establish a Western Canadian mission in Esquimalt. In 1860, Father Leo Fouquet established the New Westminster mission, subsequently headed by Bishop Louis D'Herbomez. In 1861, Fouquet continued upstream at the request of the bishop, settling by a creek entering the Fraser River. In his words: "I came up from Queensborough with 12 Indian paddlers in a war canoe, and as we rounded the bend in the Fraser, I made up my mind that I would build my mission on this beautiful hillside. I inspected it and made sure that there was a nice creek for water and a level spot for buildings and I and the Indians cooked our dinner on the beach at the mouth of the creek. I told the Indians that I was going to take this place and build a school for them, and also a church."

Father Fouquet built living quarters, a church, barn and grist mill along the river. Local farmers soon patronized the mill and picked up their mail at St. Mary's Mission. The brothers constructed French Provincial–style buildings, one to house the priests and boys of their school (1863), and the other for the Sisters of St. Ann and girls of their school (1868). A church was erected between the two buildings. When the railway arrived two decades later, the mission moved up the hill to what is now Fraser River Heritage Park. St. Mary's Mission and Residential School operated until 1961, when students moved to a new Department of Indian Affairs grade school on the eastern edge of the mission property. In 1965, the brothers cleared the site and put it on the market, finally selling it to the provincial government in 1974.

*Sources: "Fraser River Heritage Park Walking Tour." Pamphlet on the site, Mission, BC: September 2000.*

*"Oblates of Mary Immaculate Cemetery, Mission BC," by Leo Casey, O.M.I. Vancouver, BC: www3.telus.net/ruphus/her-itagepark/cemetery.htm, July 2001.*

*"Oblates of Mary Immaculate" in* **Encyclopedia of British Columbia,** *edited by Daniel Francis. Vancouver, BC: Harbour Publishing, 2000.*

Go up the set of wooden steps outside the cemetery gate, then head away from the river towards the park's open area. Across the grass, you will see a hillside with a path angling up from right to left. On the lower portion of the path, you may be able to see a yellow sign in the trees, pointing to the Grotto. Cross to the sign and follow the indicated path that leads to the right, angling uphill before it turns and rises steeply to a set of log steps. At the top, turn right on the road and left at a T-intersection to the Grotto of Our Lady of Lourdes.

On your return from the grotto, pass the T-intersection and follow the path that switchbacks to a creek below. This is the creek that attracted Father Fouquet to settle and that he named D'Herbomez Creek. Turn left and follow the track, bearing right where it passes between two concrete blocks. Continue until the trail reaches a metal gate just before a paved road. You will find a trail on the right.

# The Grotto of
# Our Lady of Lourdes

Bishop Louis D'Herbomez died on June 3, 1890. A special train from New Westminster to Mission bore his body in state. His will left instructions that a shrine be erected to honour Our Lady, similar to the Grotto at Lourdes. He asked for it to be high on a rock at St. Mary's Mission, so that the woods would be a garland for her feet; the waters of the Fraser River would bring her native sons and daughters from the hills to pray; snow-capped peaks would stand on guard; and the voices of native children laughing, playing and praying would reach her from nearby St. Mary's School.

In 1892, Bishop Durien consecrated the grotto, which featured a six-sided cupola topped with a silver dome and crowned with a white cross. It became a conspicuous landmark to all Fraser River travellers, as well as a pilgrimage site and setting for passion plays and retreats. Over time it fell into disuse, but in 1954 it reopened, only to be torn down in 1965 with the rest of St. Mary's Mission. Reconstruction began in 1996 and the outside is now complete.

*Sources: "Fraser River Heritage Park Walking Tour." Pamphlet on the site, Mission, BC: September 2000.*
*"The Grotto of Our Lady of Lourdes," Vancouver, BC: www3.telus.net/ruphus/heritagepark/grotto.htm, July 2001.*

**The Grotto of Our Lady of Lourdes**

## Yellow Trail       1.5 km    0 hr 22m    F132

These woods contain a maze of paths, so be sure to watch for the yellow markers of Yellow Trail. It crosses D'Herbomez Creek on a bridge and soon reaches a major junction, where an aluminum-marked trail bears right. However, Yellow Trail climbs left to a plateau, meanders over it and drops to a valley, which may be muddy. It then starts its climb to the top of the hill through a maple, hemlock and cedar forest that is especially attractive when the sun streams through the leaves. Reassuring yellow markers are often nailed to large cedars. Rises are punctuated by occasional elevation losses, but eventually a bend to the right around a large cedar leads to a final ascent up a steep gully, identified by a sign at the top as Jacob's Ladder. The gully passes between a rocky prominence on the right and the highest point of the mountain on the left. The trail splits near the ridge but all branches lead to the same place. The simplest way is to ignore all trails that lead off at right angles and take the left-hand trail at Y-forks.

## Top of Jacob's Ladder       2.0 km    0 hr 40 m    F134

Westminster Abbey lies a short distance to the left along the signed trail. At two points along the route, trails lead off to the left to avoid a steep ascent or descent: I usually opt to take them. The trail climbs briefly and then drops into a dip before a brief rise, where a sign indicates that dogs are not allowed past this point. You enter the monastery grounds at a soccer field. Go through the grass to reach a nearby path. A loop route takes you to the two major attractions of Westminster Abbey and Fraser River Viewpoint. Follow the path to the left to a larger track and turn right past a gate to a parking area. The building straight ahead is part of the Seminary of Christ the King; Westminster Abbey is on its right. The door on the right of the seminary leads into a reception area, where you can buy postcards and note cards or pick up pamphlets about the seminary. Washrooms are available. You can visit the abbey next door if it is open and if you are suitably dressed—shorts are not allowed. It is a magnificent and inspiring building; I look forward to the occasions when I can time my walk to find it open.

## Westminster Abbey

The Seminary of Christ the King was founded in Ladner in 1931. With the Pope's approval, the Benedictine Order took it over in 1939 and, in 1954, moved it to an 80-hectare site on the hill above the Oblate mission. The seminary is a high school, a degree-granting arts institution and a theological college where students prepare for priesthood. In addition, the order raises cows, chickens, pigs and crops. The original monks built a set of residences and celebrated prayers in the refectory. Over a 20-year period they worked with Vancouver architect Asbjorn Gathe to create an abbey near the pinnacle of their property. The modernist church has seven-metre stained glass windows in four colours representing the four seasons. A dome of coloured glass rises 18 metres above the altar, sending shafts of light into the heart of the church. It is a striking building and well worth a visit; it is open between 1:30 p.m. and 4 p.m. daily. Wear appropriate clothing—not shorts—if you want to see it.

*Sources: "The Seminary of Christ the King." Pamphlet available at Westminster Abbey, Mission, BC: July 2001.*
*"The Seminary of Christ the King, Mission, BC": www.sck.ca, July 2001.*

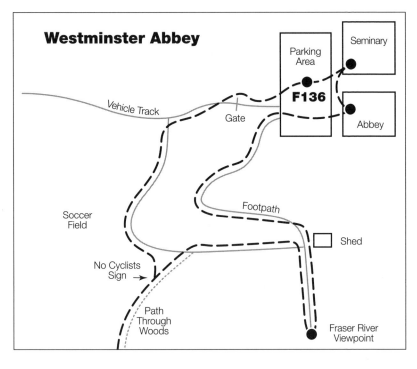

**Westminster Abbey**
0.8 km    0 hr 12 m    F135

After leaving the abbey, cross the parking area and bear left to pick up a footpath from the corner. The path winds over the hill and drops to a small shed at a trail junction. Continue straight ahead to a superb viewpoint over the Fraser River and the valley. Sumas Mountain dominates the skyline to the left, beyond the broad expanse of Fraser Valley fields. If the time is right, this is a great spot for lunch.

To return to Fraser River Heritage Park, retrace your steps to the shed and turn left to the soccer field. Find the small path through the grass and pass a sign that prohibits cyclists. Obviously it is ignored because to find your way, you could follow cycle tracks to the bottom. However, to be precise, follow the trail until you reach Jacob's Ladder. Then continue straight ahead on the lower trail, which climbs a little and then makes a steep descent. Wherever the trail forks, select the left-hand option. The prohibited cyclists call this trail the Hail Mary. At a T-junction at the bottom, turn left (trust me!) and follow the trail out to the open. Bear right to reach the grounds of the former St. Mary's Residential School. The building now serves as a native justice centre; a gift shop and a café on the other side may be open.

Continue west across the field skirting the school grounds and pick up a track that leads through a grassy area, where a notice asks you to respect the sacred Medicine Wheel grounds in memory of native ancestors. Enter the woods on the far side of the field; you will soon find the familiar territory of Fraser Valley Heritage Park. If the facilities are open, you can stop for ice cream or coffee at Norma Kenney House.

**Westminster Abbey**

## Norma Kenney House       3.1 km     0 hr 48 m     F138

**Getting home:** If using transit, walk uphill on Mary Street outside to 5th Avenue and follow it to Stave Lake Road. Catch a downhill bus at about 4:10, 4:35 or 5:00 p.m. and transfer to the #11 Valley Connector at Mission Bus Terminal. Get off at Abbotsford Bus Exchange and walk up Bourquin Crescent to the traffic signals. If you have time, you can look around Sevenoaks Mall and have something to eat; if not, cross South Fraser Highway and go left to the bus stop for the 6:00 p.m. City Link bus for Vancouver and intermediate points.

# Side Trips

# Up the Pitt River

Looking north from Pitt River Bridge, you can see a double-domed hill on the west side of the river. The higher, more pointed dome is Minnekhada Park's High Knoll. Exploring the area between the bridge and the knoll opens up views of flatlands and bird life, and the knoll itself offers a view over the whole Fraser Valley. Minnekhada Park includes a historic lodge which adds interest.

Today's 12-km (7½-mile) walk begins and ends at DeBoville Slough (Burrard Loop B70). The walk starts on a quiet road through flat Pitt River delta lands to reach a lakeside picnic site below historic Minnekhada Lodge. A fern-lined trail then winds through trees, climbing gradually to reach High Knoll lookout, a great lunch spot with a panoramic view of the Fraser Valley. The route descends to Addington Marsh Lookout, which has views over the protected Pitt wetlands. It then drops to a dike, leading back to DeBoville Slough.

**Getting there:** If using transit, take a #C38 bus from Coquitlam Station and ask the driver to let you off at DeBoville Slough.

If driving, go east on Prairie Avenue in Port Coquitlam, turn left on Cedar Drive and park at the head of DeBoville Slough, at the corner where Victoria Drive descends from the left. The round-trip will end here.

## DeBoville Slough Parking        0 km    0 hr    FP0

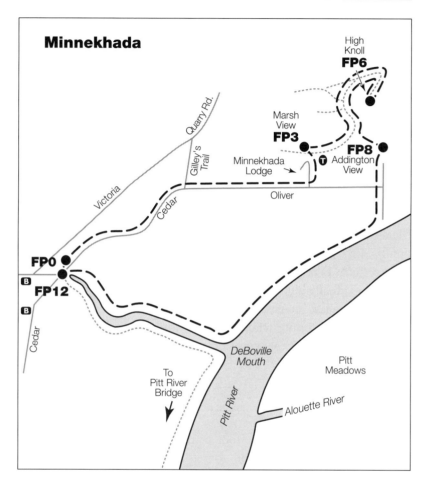

Follow the small track around the end of the inlet and head north east on Cedar Drive. On the left, Partington Creek makes its way down to the slough. Houses on the right soon give way to views over the flat marshlands. After about 20 minutes, continue straight ahead as Gilley's Trail leads off to the left. In the spring, skunk cabbages flourish in the ditches and daffodils border Berryhill Farm. Pass through the open gates across the road and continue to a yellow-barred gate. Turn left and follow the sign pointing to Minnekhada Lodge. At the top of a rise, the road makes a sharp left turn and proceeds to the lodge; do not follow it but continue straight ahead to a lake viewpoint. Picnic tables and toilets make this a good spot to take a refreshment break.

## Marsh View                    3.1 km    0 hr 45 m    FP3

After viewing the lake, take Fern Trail on the right, which is lined with swordferns. The route to High Knoll passes three trail intersections about 10 minutes apart. As the path rises to a small crest, the first intersection appears, with a sign pointing right to Addington Marsh Lookout. The return route goes there but, for now, turn left uphill. After passing a left turn to Low Knoll, you reach the second intersection. Take the right fork and continue through the trees, winding gradually higher. After passing a trail leading in from the left, you reach the last intersection. Turn right on the trail to High Knoll and make a 15-minute scramble to the top, where the Fraser Valley view more than justifies your efforts. This is a great spot for lunch.

## High Knoll                    2.5 km    0 hr 48 m    FP6

Retrace your steps to the foot of the hill and take the left-hand turn at each trail intersection to return to the Addington Marsh Lookout intersection. Go straight ahead for about 15 minutes to the lookout. A pavilion offers views across Addington Marsh, a favourite spot for birders to watch geese. The large building to the left on the other side of the river is the clubhouse of the Swan-E-Set Bay Resort and Country Club.

# Minnekhada Lodge

Harry Jenkins, a wealthy Vancouver lumber-mill owner, called his farm Minnekahda ("beside running waters") after a golf course in Minneapolis. By 1910, he practised intensive farming, using one of the first Caterpillar tractors in the area. He built his lodge on a rocky knoll, with nearby stables for draught horses and a large chicken coop. After Jenkins left in 1918 due to bad health, the property ownership changed frequently and the name spelling changed to Minnekhada.

In 1932, lumber magnate Eric Hamber bought it and the nearby uplands, renovated the farm buildings and replaced the lodge with a Tudor-style Scottish hunting lodge. Hamber entertained his friends with polo games, and his wife—Aldyen Irene, daughter of Hastings Mill owner John Hendry—hosted banquets featuring centrepieces of heather, her favourite flower. In 1936, Hamber became lieutenant governor of the province, which took him away from the property for many years. In 1958, he sold the estate to Burrard Dry Dock owner Colonel Alfred Wallace, who enjoyed duck and pheasant shooting and entertained royalty and major Vancouver businessmen. When his wife died in 1974, he remarried and sold the farm and lodge to the province for recreational purposes, although he continued to live in the lodge until 1981. The Nature Trust bought Addington Marsh in 1977 to preserve the wetlands as a home for sandhill cranes, geese and ducks.

The lodge is open from 1 p.m. to 4 p.m. from February to December on the first Sunday of each month, and often on other Sundays. Call 604-432-6352 for details.

*Source: "Minnekhada Lodge—A Dignified Past." Pamphlet at Minnekhada Lodge, Coquitlam, BC: Greater Vancouver Regional District, 2001.*

## Addington Marsh Lookout    2.5 km    0 hr 46 m    FP8

Scramble down the path to a dike road. Follow it, do not turn at the intersection with paved Oliver Drive but continue straight ahead to the end of the road and the start of the dike. A caretaker of the marsh lives in the house on the left.

Seats are strategically located along the Pitt River dike path to the mouth of DeBoville Slough. You will see Sheridan Hill on the other side of the river and a quarry on its left. Where DeBoville Slough enters Pitt River, Port Moody Boat Club lies on the opposite side of the slough. Continue west on the dike for about half an hour to the slough parking lot.

## DeBoville Slough Parking    4.3 km    1 hr 2 m    FP12

**Getting home:** Take a half-hourly southbound #C38 bus to Coquitlam Station, where you can connect to the rest of the region.

**Minnekhada Marsh from High Knoll**

# Queensborough and Burns Bog

Today's 15½-km (9½-mile) walk is the first part of a two-day walk to Boundary Bay. It explores the new Port Royal residential area facing Westminster Quay across the old rail-and-road bridge. Continuing on the riverbank across from Annacis Island and passing old fishing docks and houses and newer floating homes, it crosses Alex Fraser Bridge to the eastern edge of Burns Bog. Here a trail makes its way through a natural bog area to Cougar Creek, continuing on to end for today at Kittson Parkway.

**Getting there:** If using transit, take SkyTrain to 22nd Street Station.

If driving, take the 64th Street exit east from Annacis Highway (#91) and park near the bus stops on Kittson Parkway at the top of the hill. A #340 bus leaves the north-side bus stop at 9:06 a.m. on Saturday and reaches 22nd Street Station in 20 minutes.

## 22nd Street Station                     0 km     0 hr     FD0

From the station (F39 of the Vancouver-to-Mission route), head down to the west sidewalk of Queensborough Bridge and cross the

Fraser River. If you look over the railing towards the far side of the North Arm, you will see a large selection of accident-damaged vehicles. They belong to the Insurance Corporation of BC, which auctions them off regularly. As the bridge descends, it crosses Westminster Highway and curves west. Leave the sidewalk and take a path on the right to Westminster Highway. Do not cross; go east, crossing Wood Street. Sukh Sagar Temple on the right has served the local Sikh community for decades.

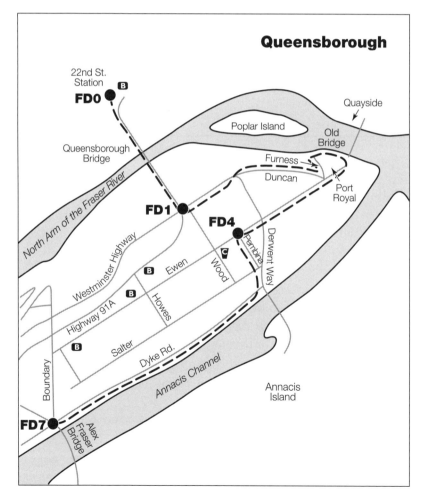

## Wood Street                    1.2 km    0 hr 17 m    FD1

Walk on the service road paralleling the highway until the highway bends right. Cross to Duncan Street when the road is clear and follow it, the trees of Poplar Island being visible beyond nearby industrial plants. Near the end of Duncan Street, you will see the Fraser Shipyard building and perhaps a ship in dock. At the next corner, turn left on Furness Street, named after the keeper of the rail-and-road bridge that once linked New Westminster and Lulu Island. The new Port Royal housing development is located here on the eastern tip of Lulu Island. Follow Queensborough Perimeter Trail around the development. Where it reaches the Fraser River, you can stop and look across to Poplar Island. A nearby sign tells the history of its rival shipyards.

---

## Star Shipyards

In the summer of 1908, two Newfoundlanders, Samuel Dawe and Edward Mercer, stood looking across to Poplar Island envisioning its potential as a shipbuilding site; they established competing shipyards. A 1910 Dawe's Shipyard contract resulted in the Anglican missionary hospital boat, *Columbia II*. During World War I, Mercer's firm built four wooden, dry-cargo steamboats of 2800 tons: *War Ewen, War Comox, War Edenshaw* and *War Kitimat*. In 1930, as business dwindled, the firms were united as Star Shipyards. When this firm closed and the site was sold in 1968, it marked the end of the longest active business in Queensborough.

*Source: "Star Shipyards." Notice board at Port Royal, New Westminster, BC: City of New Westminster, 2001.*

Continuing, you can see the Westminster Quay waterfront on the other side of the river. Soon you come to a small beach and a couple of seats on the walkway above; ahead lies the former rail-and-road bridge to New Westminster. This is a good place for a break. Loop around the rest of the Port Royal development and follow Ewen Avenue to Pembina Street. Turn left to reach the river or detour two blocks on Ewen Avenue to a café.

## Pembina Street        2.7 km    0 hr 38 m    FD4

Where Pembina Street reaches the river at Annacis Bridge, head west on the dike road. On the right, a Weyerhaeuser experimental plantation is being cut by hand to evaluate new harvesting methods. On the riverbank you pass ship-related industries and live-aboard homes; some recent ones are co-operative ventures, with services supplied from the shore. Follow the path that leads down into a small park with picnic table and benches, where you can take a break. Continuing on the dike, you pass Ryall Park on the landward side and reach Royal City Marina, a reminder that you are still in the Royal City of New Westminster. After a stretch of cottonwoods at the water's edge, the dike reaches Boundary Road at Alex Fraser Bridge, where you enter Richmond. (The South Arm trail to Massey Tunnel, FS0 to FS13, goes straight on here.)

## Boundary Road        2.7 km    0 hr 38 m    FD7

Look to the right, take the steps leading up to Alex Fraser Bridge, walk across its northern span and go down the pedestrian path to Cliveden Avenue on Annacis Island. Here you can detour briefly right across the highway bridge for a refreshment stop at a fast-food restaurant.

## Annacis Island                   1.0 km    0 hr 14 m    FD8

After the detour, if any, cross at the traffic signals onto Alex Fraser Bridge's southern span. You are on its eastern side, with a bird's-eye view of Annacis Island industries on the north side of the river; on the south side, the Burlington Northern Sante Fe Railway tracks hug the shoreline, which leads to Scott Road and Patullo Bridge. If you cross at mid-morning, you may see the Amtrak train from Seattle. Where the bridge descends into Delta, turn left and reach a red-brick road in front of the Great Pacific Forum, which has four ice rinks, a bar, a grill and upstairs washrooms.

---

# Annacis Island

First Nations peoples once used Annacis Island as a fishing site. The original written name, Annance's Island (after Métis fur trader Francis Annance), gradually corrupted to the present form. In 1953, the Duke of Westminster bought the whole island as a long-term investment to be developed by the then-Grosvenor-Laing Ltd. The industrial park leases land to automobile importers and non-polluting industries. In addition to the original Annacis Bridge to Queensborough, Alex Fraser Bridge now connects the island with the mainland.

*Source: "Annacis Island" in* **Encyclopedia of British Columbia,** *edited by Daniel Francis. Vancouver, BC: Harbour Publishing, 2000.*

---

## Great Pacific Forum              3.2 km    0 hr 45 m    FD11

Follow the red-brick path to the right around the back of the forum. At a T-intersection with another trail, turn right and pick up a bark-mulch trail to the left of a notice board. You will find a bench and a sign indicating that you are entering Delta Nature Reserve. The trail continues as a jogging and cycling track to Kittson Parkway

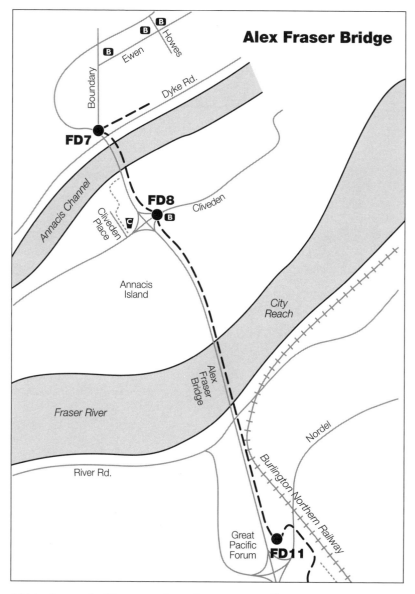

(64th Avenue). However, I prefer to turn off on a boardwalk that appears on the right in about five minutes, just beyond a transmission tower. This scenic route passes through typical peat-bog vegetation

**Tug and Barge passing Annacis Island**

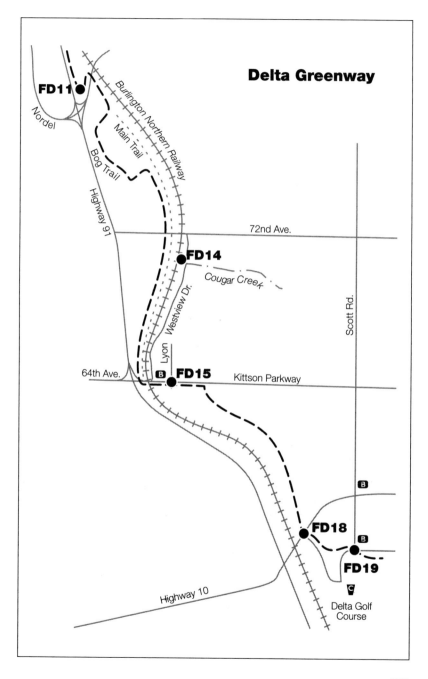

**Delta Greenway**

consisting primarily of salal, bracken, Labrador tea and hardhack. Labrador tea has dark-green leaves that appear to have a tan-coloured lining if you turn them over; hardhack has pink-flowering spikes in June and July. You will also see small pine and cedar trees.

Boardwalks take you over the wettest areas, but the trail may still be muddy in the wetter months. You soon arrive at two seats thoughtfully provided at the edge of the boardwalk. From here, the path meanders in curves, with branching trails, but stay on the main route. After about 15 minutes, you enter a cedar forest of larger trees and the path becomes firmer and drier, continuing until it rejoins the main jogging trail. Turn right and follow the path under 72nd Avenue to an open area—the site of a former Burlington Northern rail yard—with Cougar Creek Park on the other side of the railway.

## Cougar Creek Park      2.8 km    0 hr 50 m    FD14

If you choose to cross the railway to take a break in the park, note the Burlington Northern warning signs. The rail line is actively used by freight trains and by the Amtrak train that passes mid-morning on its way into Vancouver, returning in the early evening to Seattle. The crossing is well-used by local walkers who are familiar with the trains; if you are not, beware!

In June and July, the pink and white flowers of Japanese knapweed decorate the next section of the trail; on the weekend, it is well-used by cyclists. After about half an hour's walk, you pass under Kittson Parkway. Turn right, follow the trail to the road above, and follow the sidewalk of the railway bridge to reach the bus stops.

## Kittson Parkway      1.8 km    0 hr 29 m    FD15

**Getting home:** A #340 bus from the north side goes to 22nd Street Station. One from the south side goes to Scottsdale Exchange and connects to buses serving communities south of the river.

# Watershed Park to Mud Bay Park

Today's walk is the second of the walks leading to Boundary Bay; it is about 7 kilometres long. You can then continue to Serpentine Fen, making a 12½-km (8-mile) walk, or return two kilometres to 56th Avenue.

**Getting there**: If using transit, take a #340 bus from 22nd Street Station or Scottsdale Mall and get off at Lyon Road.

If driving, and finishing at Serpentine Fen, take the King George Highway and drive east on 44th Avenue to a small parking lot on the left. Walk back out to the highway. A northbound #321 bus at 9:02 a.m. on Saturday connects at Newton with a #340 22nd Street Station bus. Get off about 35 minutes later at Lyon Road.

| **Kittson Parkway** | 0 km | 0 hr | FD15 |
|---|---|---|---|

Head east on the south side of Kittson Parkway and take the trail that starts almost immediately after the last house in the street below. It starts as a narrow track through blackberry bushes and soon widens into a broad roadway through Watershed Park's cedar and maple forest. The Burlington Northern Railway is below to the right and Highway #91 is beyond that; you can hear vehicles and perhaps a train but you cannot see them. Various trails lead up the hill; ignore them and carry straight ahead. At one point, logs arranged in a circle form an auditorium around a campfire. The trail exits onto an off-ramp from Highway 10, which leads to Delta Golf Club.

## Highway 10          2.5 km     0 hr 35 m     FD18

Turn right and follow the road under Highway 10. Keep left and follow a path that hugs the base of the escarpment. Where the path meets a road coming from the right, look for a trail leading up left to the top of the escarpment. This is the trail to take, but you may want

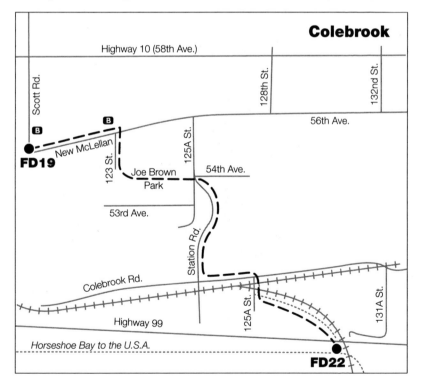

to detour briefly south to Delta Golf Club, which has a coffee shop and washrooms. Then take the trail up the hill to the foot of Scott Road at New McLellan Road.

| New McLellan Road | 1.0 km | 0 hr 16 m | FD19 |
|---|---|---|---|

Follow New McLellan Road east to 123rd Street and turn right to its end. Go across the footbridge and bend left past Panorama Stables into Joe Brown Park. The track through trees on either side leads out to 125A Street by a church and school. Follow Station Road opposite as it switchbacks downhill to the flatlands. At a T-intersection, turn left on Colebrook Road, pass Colebrook Station, and turn right onto 127A Street. Cross the railway, watching for trains, turn left and follow what maps call Railway Road but is now the access road to Surrey's Mud Bay Park. Here there is a toilet; you have joined the Horseshoe-Bay-to-the-USA route at W127.

| Mud Bay Park | 3.2 km | 0 hr 45 m | FD22 |
|---|---|---|---|

**Getting home:** If you want to carry on to Serpentine Fen, follow the Horseshoe-Bay-to-the-USA instructions. A #321 bus on King George Highway will take you to Surrey Central Station.

If you want to retrace your steps to 125A and 56th Avenue, a west-bound #322 bus at 2:31 p.m. (or 4:31 p.m.) will take you to Scottsdale Mall for transfers to Scott Road Station and elsewhere.

# Fraser South Arm

The City of Richmond is committed to a greenway along the South Arm dikes of the Fraser River from its New Westminster boundary to the Riverport complex at the eastern end of Steveston Highway. This greenway is also in the Greater Vancouver regional plan. Much of it is in place but pieces remain uncompleted. As of 2003, you can physically walk the whole trail but if you do, you will be trespassing in one or two places. This chapter describes how to walk the whole length but you will have to wait for completion before you can comfortably walk some pieces and legally walk others.

The 12½-km (8-mile) walk goes by houses and floating homes at the water's edge and passes pleasure-boat building facilities before crossing to a trail on Shelter Island. Here it reaches boat moorage and repair plants and continues on the dike to Lafarge Cement's concrete operations. The trail will pass around these to Nelson Street and then continue on the dike past new-vehicle storage and industrial plants to reach Riverport Entertainment Complex. The last two kilometres to Massey Tunnel are on road.

**Getting there:** If using transit, take a #410 bus to the western end of Ewen Avenue (the bus leaves from 22nd Street Station). Walk down Boundary Road to the dike.

If driving, you can park at Riverport (missing the last 2-km road walk) or you can try to find parking near Steveston Highway and Highway #99. From either spot, take a westbound #403 bus and change in Richmond to a #410 22nd Street Station bus. Get off at the first stop on Ewen Road. Walk down Boundary Road to the dike. A bus at 8:45 a.m. on Saturday will take just over 50 minutes and give you a good tour of Richmond in the process.

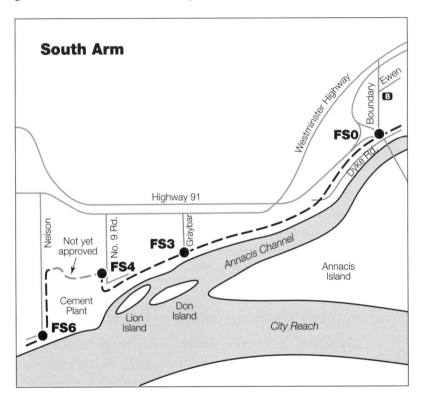

**Boundary Road**        0 km    0 hr    FS0

At the foot of Boundary Road (FD7 on the Queensborough-to-Mud-Bay-Park route), take the dike path on the right that heads south west and separates pedestrians and cyclists from the roadway.

Then continue on road, passing some condominium groups of floating homes and several pleasure-boat building and sales establishments (the trees and industrial buildings across the river are on Annacis Island). Where the road curves inland to serve new businesses in an industrial park, follow the trail as it branches off, keeping close to the river. Enter Shelter Island, a former island now virtually merged with Lulu Island, and reach Graybar Road; a restaurant is nearby.

## Graybar Road                    3.0 km    0 hr 42 m    FS3

You can continue on the dike trail for one more kilometre, passing ship maintenance, storage and repair facilities to reach No. 9 Road and the Lafarge Cement plant, whose tall towers have been visible for some time.

## No. 9 Road                      1.0 km    0 hr 14 m    FS4

No. 9 Road continues and is soon crossed by a railway line serving the plant. The greenway trail will probably leave from the land side of the railway here, following along the right side of the grassy area ahead to reach the paved road leading to Nelson Road. There it will turn left to the river's edge and branch right.

## Nelson Road                     1.5 km    0 hr 21 m    FS6

You now follow an old railway right-of-way along the riverbank. About 100m along, a small path leads through bushes to a secluded beach suitable for a lunch stop. This riverbank section ends in a pile of boulders which an angled path crosses. A sign on the other side warns that the upcoming fenced area of stored new cars is private, but a wide swath of grass is available for passage on its river side. I have met people walking their dogs here.

This stretch ends in a section of new industrial properties and service roads under construction. It is not clear where the trail will go through here. I used to be able to follow the riverbank but now I stay on the road nearest to the river and bypass any buildings on the grass verges at the river edge of their properties. After the last new building, the route emerges onto a public road that starts out close to the river. At times you must use the road, but frequently you may follow the dike. Sometimes the road reaches a small inlet, turns right to cross it and then returns to parallel the river again. After the road passes two landfill operations and a gate numbered 15000 on the right, a track leads left to rejoin the dike. The route uses this, leading through to the Riverport Sports and Entertainment complex. The dike surface is poor but will no doubt be improved when its use is encouraged. The complex has cinemas, an IMAX theatre, skating rinks, bowling lanes, a swimming pool, a wave pool, waterslides, a food court and restaurants.

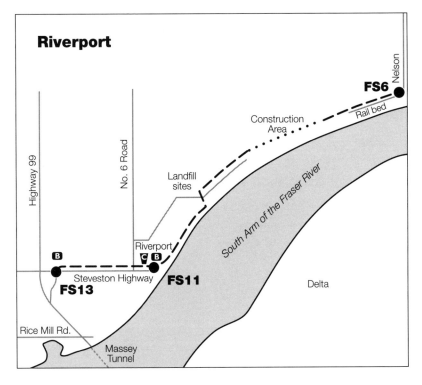

## Riverport                    5.0 km    1 hr 10 m    FS11

A two-kilometre walk west along Steveston Highway leads to Massey Tunnel (W90 on the Horseshoe-Bay-to-the-USA route).

## Massey Tunnel                2.0 km    0 hr 28 m    FS13

**Getting home:** Buses leave from the east-side bus stop at the highway exit ramp to go to Marpole, Richmond and Vancouver. Across the bridge and down at the highway edge, buses go south to Delta and White Rock.

# Walk
## Burrard

AROUND THE INLET AND
BURNABY MOUNTAIN

# Burrard Loop

Eleven walks make up a 125-km (90-mile) loop around Burrard Inlet and Vancouver's Harbour. They pass through every municipality north of the Fraser, so you can start from close to your home and walk around Burrard Loop. (From Surrey and Delta, you can start at Colony Farm, just across the Port Mann Bridge.)

Burrard Loop uses riverbank and waterfront walkways, ravine trails and dikes to explore the inner Greater Vancouver area. The route goes along the Capilano, Seymour, Coquitlam, Pitt and Fraser Rivers. Each of these is a major river and impressive when it is in flood, particularly in May. It goes beside Mackay, Mosquito, Hastings, Lynn, McCartney, Noons, Scott, Hoy, Hyde, Miller, Stoney and Still Creeks. Each of these flows through a canyon, ravine, or valley known to its nearby residents, but not many Vancouverites wander far from their homes to see them. The walks pass Beaver, Lafarge, Sasamat, Lost, Mundy, Burnaby, Deer and Trout Lakes—not forgetting the little jewel of Donovan's Pond—but few people have sat by all of them.

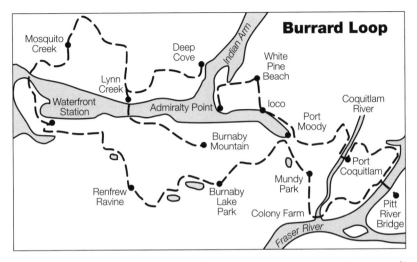

The walk starts at Canada Place, heads west over Vancouver's impressive new seawall to Stanley Park, passes over Lions Gate Bridge and reaches the North Shore. It makes its way to the lower level of the mountains above the urbanized area by going up the Lower Capilano River, crossing to MacKay Creek on the Bowser Trail, then making a jog across to Mosquito Creek and up that magnificent canyon all the way to the Baden-Powell Mosquito Bridge.

It crosses above the housing developments and comes down the hidden Hastings Creek to join Lynn Creek and follow it to its mouth by the Ironworkers Memorial Second Narrows Crossing. It continues across the Seymour River in an area where some of the first immigrants settled on Burrard Inlet and follows an old water-pipeline route through parks to Deep Cove, where it is temporarily stopped by Indian Arm. However, starting on the other side of Indian Arm, it explores the newly expanded Belcarra Regional Park, visits White Pine Beach on Sasamat Lake and follows around the northern corner of Burrard Inlet to its eastern end at Port Moody. From here, it heads further east along Hoy Creek and the wild Coquitlam River to reach Port Coquitlam. The Poco Trail along Hyde Creek reaches the Pitt River at DeBoville Slough, the most easterly point of the Loop. It now starts to wend its way back.

The walk beside the Pitt River offers a change of pace, with wide expansive views over the flat Pitt Meadows and back to the mountains in the north. The walk continues at the river's edge all the way to the mouth of the Coquitlam River and the new regional park at Colony Farm, which used to serve Riverview Hospital. The route continues up to and through Mundy Park and explores the heavily-ravined hillside above Port Moody and the southern slopes of Burnaby Mountain. It then descends, following Stoney Creek down to the Brunette River. A walk along the edge of the wetlands bordering Burnaby Lake leads to Burnaby City Hall and passes Deer Lake to reach Metrotown. It continues on the BC Parkway along the SkyTrain route to Still Creek, which it follows through Renfrew Ravine, the largest ravine in the city of Vancouver. Crossing to John Hendry Park and Trout Lake, it begins an urban and historical walk back to Canada Place. It passes Commercial Drive, with its historic associations with the Italian community. It passes the oldest school in the city of Vancouver, the oldest Italian church, and goes through the historic Strathcona area, continues on through Chinatown and offers a peek at the unique Dr. Sun Yat-Sen Park (next door to the Dr. Sun Yat-Sen Classical Chinese Garden). The route then heads through Gastown and follows the waterfront back to Canada Place and Waterfront Station.

When you have completed the Burrard Loop, you will not only have gone around Burrard Inlet but also Burnaby Mountain. However, this mountain in the middle of the loop is well worth exploring and a further three walks of 35 km (20 miles) allow you to do this. Looking out from the top, you have a bird's-eye view of the territory which you saw at closer hand in a worm's-eye view. For western outlooks, you can climb the mountain, starting at Phibbs Exchange (B24 of the Loop) and reach Simon Fraser University at the mountain top. (Or do this in reverse if you prefer downhill all the way.) For eastern views, you can descend from SFU to Port Moody Arena (B55 of the Loop). Finally, for southern views, you can sidehill around the lower slopes of the mountain, starting at Kensington in the west and ending near the Burnaby–New Westminster border in the east.

# Canada Place to Mosquito Creek

Today's 12-km (7½-mile) walk starts from Canada Place, passes along the Coal Harbour waterfront to Stanley Park and crosses the Lions Gate Bridge. It briefly follows the Capilano River, which is always interesting whatever the flow of its water. Using the little-known Bowser Trail, it crosses to Mackay Creek and follows the edge of its ravine to a plateau above. Here it crosses to Mosquito Creek and uses a trail up its impressive canyon to end the day at William Griffin Community Centre. The rest of the canyon is left for another day.

If using transit, take SkyTrain to Waterfront Station. Follow the exit signs to Canada Place and come out to the street.

If driving, go to the William Griffin Centre, just west of Westview Drive on Queens Road in North Vancouver. Leave the vehicle nearby, walk about five minutes east and catch the #246 bus south to Lonsdale Quay for a transfer to SeaBus to Waterfront Station. A bus at 8:44 a.m. on Saturday takes 30 minutes.

Coffee shops and washrooms are in the Food Fair, reached from the station.

## Canada Place                    0 km    0 hr    B0

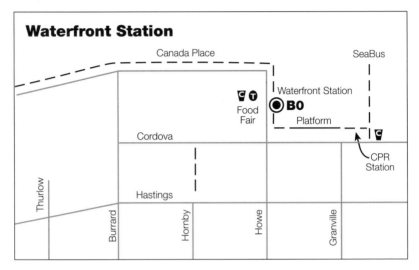

The area around Canada Place is a transportation and tourist centre. Not only does SkyTrain connect with SeaBus here, but float planes and helicopters depart for Victoria, Vancouver Island and up-coast destinations, and cruise ships head off to Alaska. Depending on the time of year, you may well see a cruise ship at the dock. You may not want to delay the start of your walk to look inside Canada Place now, but you could consider a visit at some other time or as a celebration when you finish the Burrard Loop.

Now head west downhill towards the waterfront. Canadian Pacific Railway's marshalling yards used to be here, servicing the docks on the waterfront and the various downtown industries. However, businesses and the nature of the traffic have changed, and CPR now services the docks from its rail yard in Port Coquitlam. Follow the walkway; to the north lie Grouse Mountain, with Goat Mountain and Thunderbird Ridge behind it, and the craggy Crown Mountain topping them all in the background. A forest of high-rise towers and a new community centre dominate the landward side. Soon Westin's Bayshore Inn appears on the right.

# Canada Place

Canada Place was the Canadian Pavilion at Expo 86. Vancouver needed a convention centre and an adequate terminal for the booming cruise-ship business, so the Federal Government decided to use the opportunity of Expo 86 to combine a new facility with their pavilion. Because World Fair rules require all buildings to be on a single site and the main fair was on False Creek, Canada Place was physically linked to False Creek by a dedicated SkyTrain link to Stadium Station.

The sails along the length of the pier make a strong statement of welcome to cruise ships and travellers to Vancouver. There are still exhibits from Expo 86 on display in the halls of Canada Place. There are convention rooms and exhibit space along the length of the pier, and a number of restaurants are located at the far end. An IMAX theatre from the Expo days continues to show its special large-screen productions. Visitors to the prow have a great view over the Inlet; carol ships sail past in the days before Christmas.

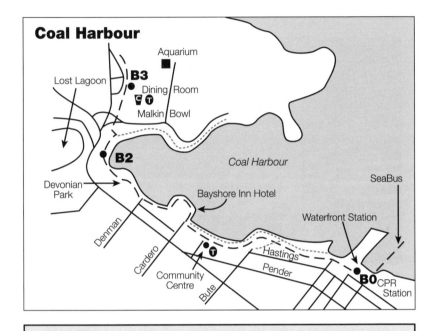

# Coal Harbour and Lost Lagoon

John Morton travelled the Douglas Trail from New Westminster to Brighton (now New Brighton Park) and then canoed down the Inlet to Coal Harbour. He evidently liked what he saw because a few months later, he joined with William Hailstone and Sam Brighouse (the "Three Greenhorns") to buy 500 acres of the West End for $555. This act is commemorated in the name Morton Street at English Bay.

Pauline Johnson also canoed regularly into Coal Harbour. One day, she arrived at low tide to find a large area of mud flats. She was so upset that she wrote a poem, titled "It is Dusk on the Lost Lagoon." The name has stayed, even though the Stanley Park Causeway has cut off the lagoon from its Coal Harbour outlet.

*Source: Vancouver: From Milltown to Metropolis, by Alan Morley. Vancouver, BC: Mitchell Press, 1974.*

Follow the walkway around the water side of the hotel and where you reach the area with no buildings between you and the water, choose the path closest to the water. Follow this around, with Devonian Park on the left, until you reach the Stanley Park seawall.

**Coal Harbour**      2.0 km    0 hr 28 m    B2

Walk briefly along the seawall towards the half-timbered Vancouver Rowing Club, but before you reach it, turn left to join the adjacent higher path, which crosses a bridge into the park. A statue of Lord Stanley welcomes you with outstretched arms, a plaque recording his dedication: "To the use and enjoyment of people of all colours, creeds and customs for all time. I name thee Stanley Park." A statue of Robert Burns lies just to the right, bearing plaques illustrating several of his poems—"Tam O'Shanter," "To the Mountain Daisy" and "The Cotter's Saturday Night."

Keep to the right, passing Lord Stanley, and immediately bear left onto a path with a children's playground to its left. Malkin Bowl, the summer home of Vancouver's famous Theatre Under the Stars, is on the right. The Rose Garden appears on the left, and a little further on the Dining Pavilion, a possible stop for refreshments and washrooms.

**Malkin Bowl**      0.8 km    0 hr 11 m    B3

Continuing on, follow the road north, passing a wishing well on the left before going through a large parking area to reach Pipeline Road. Turn right, using the sidewalk on the far side, and turn left as soon as possible to reach Beaver Lake—a broad shallow lake originally formed by beavers and beautifully flowered with water lilies when they are in season. In colder winters, you can sometimes skate on the frozen surface. Turning right, pass some benches and reach the outlet of Beaver Lake, where the path crosses a small stream running down a ravine. Look for the second of the two paths on the right at this point—this is the Ravine Trail, the first of many ravines that you will

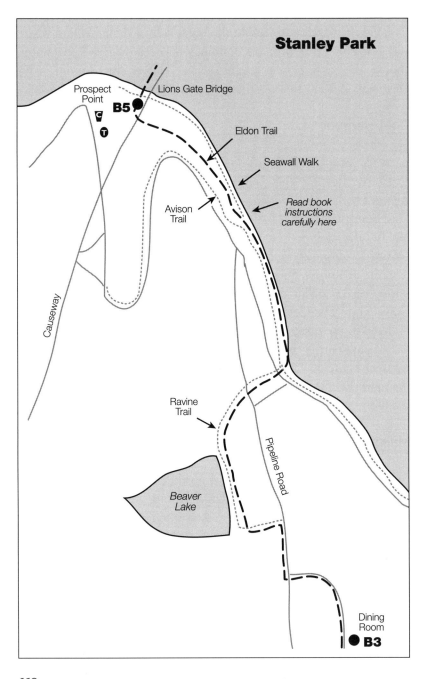

Stanley Park

Prospect Point

Lions Gate Bridge

**B5**

Eldon Trail

Seawall Walk

*Read book instructions carefully here*

Avison Trail

Causeway

Ravine Trail

Pipeline Road

*Beaver Lake*

Dining Room

**B3**

**Beaver Lake in Stanley Park**

**Stanley Park Seawall**

be following on this series of walks. On the way down, look back as you pass under the Pipeline Road bridge. You will see a large pipeline, still on the original route connecting Capilano Reservoir to Vancouver. The main water pipeline came under Pipeline Road on the North Shore, under the Inlet and then into Vancouver along Pipeline Road here.

At the bottom of the ravine, keep close to the stream and pass under the vehicle road to reach the seawall. Turn left and walk along the Burrard Inlet waterfront towards Lions Gate Bridge. The yellow piles of bulk material at Vancouver Wharves on the opposite shore consist of pellets of slated sulphur, coated to reduce the chance of the material becoming windborne. The sulphur is extracted from sour gas in Alberta as it is purified into natural gas. The wharves also store coal, potash and woodchips and load them into ships primarily destined for Japan.

As you approach Lions Gate Bridge, the bicycle path on your left merges briefly with the pedestrian path and then leaves uphill on the left. You should stay on the pedestrian path on the seawall until a set of steps with a wooden handrail leads up on the left. Follow this up to meet the bicycle path. Ignore the bicycle path which returns downhill to the waterfront level and, instead, turn briefly uphill. However, almost immediately, turn right onto the level path, which parallels the seawall walk below. This trail soon starts to rise, and switchbacks up to pass under Lions Gate Bridge and reach a junction. (A coffee shop and washrooms lie up the hill at Prospect Point.)

## Lions Gate South                   2.0 km      0 hr 28 m      B5

Bear left, take the underpass beneath the roadway and cross the bridge on its east side. The yellow sulphur piles, covered potash storage and wood-chip silos lie below you in the foreground; Stanley Park and the city of Vancouver are to the right. Marine traffic can be seen down as far as Second Narrows in the distance, with Burnaby Mountain on its right.

**Lions Gate**

Viewing balconies by the towers offer a break from the unremitting traffic noise of the major bridge sections and let you pause and take in the view. Before leaving a balcony, I check that there are no cyclists coming up before I head briskly on. On the far side of the bridge, drop off at the pedestrian underpass and go to Wardance Street. Cross the road, turn right and take the south side sidewalk onto Wardance Bridge and over the Capilano River. As soon as it reaches the far side, take the steps on the left down to a riverside trail under the bridge—the route to follow, unless you want to detour into Park Royal for a coffee or washroom break. (The Horseshoe-Bay-to-the-USA route joins here—W25.)

## Park Royal                    1.8 km    0 hr 25 m    B7

Under the Wardance Bridge, the trail continues with the Capilano River on the right. Follow the trail under Marine Drive and pass Park Royal Hotel on the left. Keep to the path, passing a sign saying

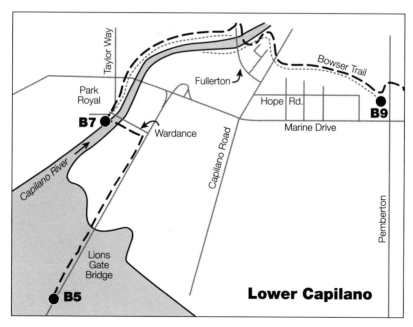

**Fullerton Bridge over Capilano River**

Capilano Care Centre and, bearing right, reach an open stretch of river with wide attractive views. People may be fishing along this stretch, either from the sides or from rocks in the middle to which they have waded. The water level can vary depending on the releases from the Cleveland Dam. Somewhere along this stretch, any of the seats would make an attractive stop for lunch (or you may prefer to wait 40 minutes for an upcoming park with picnic tables). Soon a sign appears on the left saying Capilano Pacific. This is a beautiful trail leading up to the fish hatchery and the Cleveland Dam—but not one for today. Carry straight on to Fullerton Bridge, which is visible, and turn up the steps leading to it. This bridge serves a large high-rise apartment complex on the west side, known as Woodcroft. This is located in a small, isolated piece of the municipality of North Vancouver, which happens to be west of the Capilano River. The Municipality of West Vancouver was so incensed by the construction of this complex here that they refused to provide services to it. Consequently, the developers had to build the bridge to connect themselves to North Vancouver's road system. The route now crosses this private bridge to reach the east bank of the Capilano River.

At the end of the bridge structure on the left, follow a small trail leading upstream by the river. Pass the backs of houses and where the fences come close to the trail and after the last house, take the small trail to the right into the trees. This passes a road end, but stay on the grassy trail and you will come out to busy Capilano Road, with heavy traffic in both directions. If you can find a gap in which to cross, you will find that the trail continues just south on the other side. It soon leads to a marker indicating Bowser Trail, a green and pleasant trail beneath an escarpment on its left.

The Bowser Trail lies just north of North Vancouver's Marine Drive and used to be an old streetcar line. It eventually terminates at the street end of Pemberton Avenue. You can take a break at any of several coffee shops on Marine Drive here, or a bus will take you to SeaBus at Lonsdale Quay, if you want to stop for the day.

## Pemberton Avenue 2.4 km 0 hr 41 m B9

Now take the steps which start from the north east corner of Pemberton Avenue and switchback up the escarpment to reach the continuation of Pemberton Avenue at the top. You may want to take

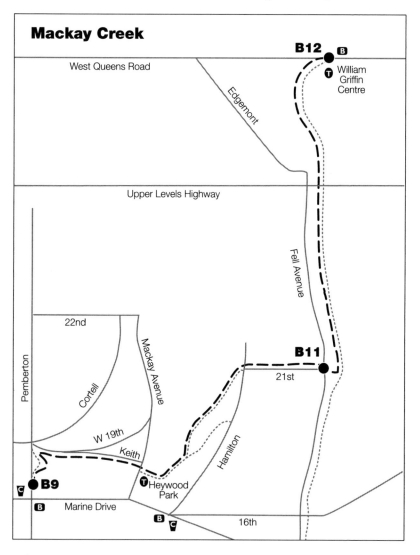

a few breaths at the top after your exertions, and admire the views over Burrard Inlet. When you continue, turn right, follow 19th Street, and bend into Keith Road when it appears on the right. The road drops gradually down and meets Mackay Avenue at the bottom, with a metal crash barrier immediately opposite. Cross Mackay Avenue when the road is clear and go down the trail at the right of the barrier, leading into Heywood Park. At the foot, the trail continues on the other side of the grass, but if you want lunch, you will find nearby picnic tables to the right. Washrooms may be open if it is municipal washroom season. If not, coffee shops and washrooms are available in the mall over the road. Buses pass outside to the SeaBus Terminal and elsewhere.

To continue, cross the grass and head north east to pick up the trail, which heads steeply up steps. Where it joins another trail, follow downhill and then uphill again as Mackay Creek appears on the left. Fairly soon up this section, if its surface is not too muddy, take the minor trail which leads down on the left towards the creek. It gradually widens into a major trail with steps leading up to the top of the ravine opposite 21st Avenue. Walking up this trail, you gain a good appreciation of the size and majesty of the ravine. However, if the minor trail looks too muddy and primitive, you can stay on the major trail, which will bring you out opposite 19th Avenue. Then walk up the grass until 21st Avenue appears. Cross the road carefully and follow 21st Street for about 400 metres until it joins Fell Avenue.

**Fell Avenue**                     1.5 km      0 hr 28 m      B11

Watch for cars where Fell Avenue bends around a corner, cross and take the trail on the immediate left down into Mosquito Creek Canyon. Here you could follow the canyon down to the right along the route of the Trans Canada Trail, and find your way to the SeaBus Terminal in about half an hour's time. However, to finish today's walk, you should head north. Soon you begin to appreciate that you have entered another major ravine with high towering walls on both sides. The west side, which you are using, has the major trail and is much used by people walking their dogs. If you don't have a dog, think about borrowing a neighbour's or you may feel ostracized on this trail. I once apologized to one of the walkers for not having a dog and was given a strong recommendation to get a Golden Labrador—they're ideal!

Soon you pass some massive columns holding up the Upper Levels Highway above. When you enter William Griffin Park and reach the paved walkways, look for the bark-mulch path on the left. It is softer on the feet and is shaded in the hot weather. Just before Queens Road blocks the way, skirt the top edge of the skateboard facility to reach the Community Centre, with washrooms, and with soft drinks available from a slot machine.

| William Griffin Centre | 1.3 km | 0 hr 22 m | B12 |
| --- | --- | --- | --- |

**Getting home:** The #232 bus heading west goes to Edgemont Village and connects to a Vancouver bus. Alternatively, you can walk five minutes east to pick up a southbound #246 bus to Lonsdale Quay to take SeaBus to connect with SkyTrain on the south shore.

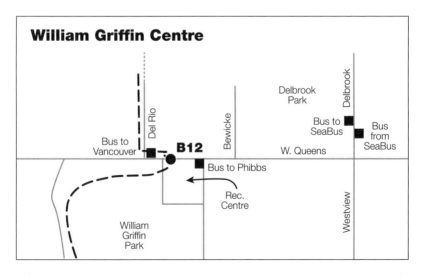

# Mosquito Creek to Lynn Creek

Today's 12-km (7½-mile) walk offers an impressive way of crossing North Vancouver. It goes up Mosquito Creek—an exciting trip—then follows a power line to Hastings Creek, which it descends on a beautiful and surprising trail to reach Lynn Creek. A trail by this wild and undammed watercourse leads down to the Second Narrows approaches. Don't expect a manicured trail—the Mosquito Creek section is definitely an adventure. The start of Hastings Creek on its way down also requires you to keep your eyes open, but it does not offer quite the same level of adventure as does Mosquito Creek.

Today, there are no restaurants en route for some time, but there is a great spot to stop and enjoy a refreshment break, so take a drink with you.

**Getting there:** If using transit, take the #232 bus to William Griffin Centre (from Vancouver, catch the #246 outside the Bay and transfer to the #232 Phibbs Exchange bus at Edgemont Village; or from SkyTrain, catch the #28 bus from Gilmore or Joyce Station and transfer at Phibbs Exchange to the #232 Grouse Mountain bus).

If driving, park at the Park-and-Ride at Phibbs Exchange at the north end of the Ironworkers Memorial Second Narrows Crossing. (From the bridge, take Exit 23A, go one block west on Main Street to the signal light, north on Mountain Highway for one short block, and east on Oxford Street to its end, and park on the left.) Take the #232 Grouse Mountain bus from Bay 10 to the William Griffin Centre; a bus at 8:47 a.m. on Saturday takes just over 20 minutes.

There are no restaurants on the early parts of the trail, but a coffee shop one block west on Main Street is available if you want a drink or snack before you catch the bus.

## William Griffin Centre  0 km  0 hr  B12

The Centre has public washrooms, the last for some time, if you want to use them. Then cross West Queens Road at the pedestrian walk, jog left and right to Del Rio Street. It says No Exit, but if you follow it to the end, you will find where it turns into a trail. This trail now follows where the stream bed used to be—the creek is underground in pipe at this point to prevent damage should it go on a rampage. Where you reach a crossing path at Evergreen Place, it is worth detouring onto the bridge to look at the facilities where the creek goes underground. Imagine big rocks being washed in here in a torrent from above and being trapped to prevent them causing catastrophic damage in the narrower canyon below.

Continue north by the creek. The valley bottom is wide and you look across the creek to the wooded areas on the east side. Occasionally, some chairs or a table may indicate that there are houses opposite, whose residents come to the creek edge in the summer to enjoy the woods and the water. In about 20 minutes, the trail passes under Montroyal Boulevard and, a minute or two later, a path comes down from Palisades Drive. This is where the adventure starts. The trail becomes rocky and then more of a scramble. If you do not fancy the uncertainty (or if the trail is, in fact, closed), you may opt to go out on Palisades Drive, turn right and follow Skyline Drive up

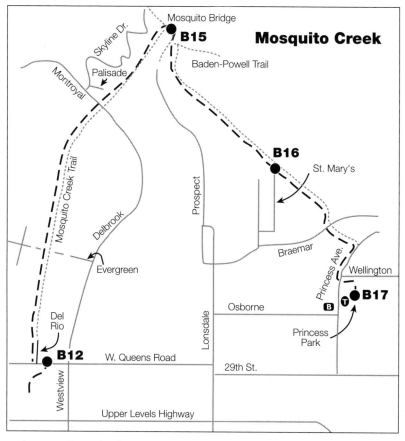

to its top. Pass the barrier on its right, and in 200 metres you reach the Baden-Powell Trail, with a sign pointing to Mosquito Creek and your destination of Mosquito Bridge. The detour takes you somewhat higher and requires about 2 kilometres of mainly road walking, compared to 750 metres of trail.

If you carry on, follow the trail to reach a point where it leaves the creek to go into the trees to switchback steeply up a bank. Stop—this is not the route (that way goes up to Skyline Drive). Although it is not obvious, you should go straight on here. If you scramble over the apparently blocking rocks, you can follow the creek up. At times, the trail is on the edge at creek level and at times on the bank above the creek but always in sight of it. I can only warn that you have to look carefully and proceed with caution over the occasional small bridging logs and scramble carefully over slippery rocks. At times you have to haul yourself steeply up; at one point someone has provided ropes to hold onto. This is not something on which you want to take a companion who is only used to easy, level walks. Eventually, it emerges to join a clear trail and reach Mosquito Bridge. This is a good place for a break—perhaps to kneel and kiss the ground. A path from the near side of the bridge leads the agile walker to the water's edge.

## Baden-Powell Centennial Trail

To mark the British Columbia Centennial in 1971, Boy Scouts and Girl Guides from the Lower Mainland undertook to establish a hiking trail on Vancouver's North Shore. They began the project in 1967, and after the main segment of the trail was routed and built, provincial, regional and municipal parks departments and various volunteer groups completed and upgraded it. The trail extends for 42 km from Horseshoe Bay to Deep Cove. It was not intended as one extensive hike, but rather as a series of short hikes. Many access points were therefore provided along its length, often accessible by bus. Much of the trail leads through areas that were logged before the North Shore municipalities were established. At that time, plank roads were used to bring logs down the mountains, and the trail follows some of these old routes.

Appropriately for the Baden-Powell trail, the section east from Mosquito Creek has been adopted by a scout troop. The Federation of Mountain Clubs operates an Adopt-A-Trail program, and many volunteer groups adopt a section of trail somewhere in the province and maintain it in co-operation with the agency which administers their particular trail.

*Source: Pamphlet of the Outdoor Recreation Council of BC*

**Mosquito Bridge on the Baden-Powell Trail**

### Mosquito Bridge · · · · · · · 2.8 km · · 1 hr 2 m · · B15

Cross the bridge and follow the signed Baden-Powell trail briefly on its route around the water towers. After passing these, drop to a junction where the Baden-Powell trail is signed left. Ignore this sign and go straight on to emerge onto a track along a transmission-line right-of-way. This starts off on the level, with wide views over the region to the right, and then rises gently to reach a high point at St. Mary's Avenue—there are gates and vehicle parking here.

### St. Mary's Avenue · · · · · · · 1.5 km · · 0 hr 22 m · · B16

Passing the gate opposite, the trail drops and becomes rocky. However, there are breaks in the rockiness from time to time, so take heart. As you near the bottom, a trail leads out right to a blacktopped pedestrian path. Ignore this, and follow the main trail for one last

165

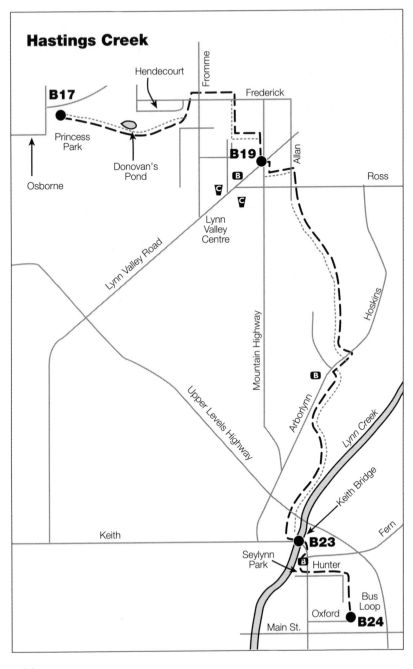

## Hastings Creek

Hendecourt

Fromme

Frederick

**B17**

Princess Park

Osborne

Donovan's Pond

**B19**

Allan

Ross

Lynn Valley Centre

Lynn Valley Road

Mountain Highway

Hoskins

Upper Levels Highway

Arborlynn

Lynn Creek

Keith Bridge

Fern

Keith

**B23**

Seylynn Park

Hunter

Bus Loop

Oxford

**B24**

Main St.

rocky switchback. You will hear and then see and cross the start of Hastings Creek. Now look carefully up into the trees on the right. In about 20 metres, you may see a tree house, just before the trail reaches a small clearing. Look here for a narrow path leading off right through the bushes. Take it and go through the trees and down to Braemar Road in greater comfort than staying with the rocky track. (If you don't find the path, don't bother. Keep on to reach Braemar Road below.) At the road, jog back to the transmission-line route, which you follow one more block to Princess Avenue. Turn right for one block to Wellington Drive and then turn left and almost immediately right to enter Princess Park.

A trail leads to a cleared area with a nearby bridge in front. Go over the grass to the bridge, but do not cross it unless you want to use the covered picnic tables on the other side. This is an excellent spot for lunch if it fits in with your schedule. I have taken advantage of these tables to have a dry lunch in the rain and have really appreciated them. (Washrooms are to the right across the grass; a bus stops on the nearby road.)

## Princess Park                   1.3 km    0 hr 21 m    B17

From the bridge, go back into the trees and bear right, following the edge of the ravine. Almost immediately, a trail comes in from the left, followed in a few metres by another minor one. About 10 metres later, the main trail branches left, but stay with the minor branch as it follows along the edge, with Hastings Creek below. These are relatively open woods, which make an attractive change from the open transmission-line route of the last hour or so. Where the trail leads out into the transmission line, turn right and make your way down the minor trail, taking the right-hand trail at any fork. You have a steep but brief descent (and I do mean steep—sit down if you have to) to reach the creek edge and then turn left into the woods again. The trail now parallels the creek all the way down. At any intersection, choose the right-hand option if it continues forwards and down (do not double back). The trail is rough but it is an attractive walk, and you may marvel that you are in such surroundings in a city of two million people. At the foot of this trail, a bridge leads to a house on the other side of Hastings Creek. Do not turn onto the bridge, but cross the road and hug the far side of the opposite fence to pass over Hastings Creek and reach a pleasant man-made lake—Donovan's Pond—named after a man who owned much of the land around here. This is another potential lunch spot or you may want to wait to use a fast-food outlet at the upcoming Lynn Valley Centre. Bear right, keeping the pond on your left initially, and pass over a footbridge when you see it on the right. On the other side, start along the path towards a street access, and then turn left onto a major trail when it appears.

You now pass through a wooded area, with houses on the right and Hastings Creek on the left. Follow this trail to its end on Hendecourt Drive. Go up the hill to the far side of Frederick Road ahead and turn right along the sidewalk opposite to reach Fromme Road. Go to the opposite corner of both roads, and take the Frederick Road sidewalk, which borders the top edge of the secondary school. Pass the school and the playing field beyond, then follow the paved path off along the far edge of the field. Where a notice says the field is reserved for users only, keep to the edge around the field and go out the exit on the far side. Bend left and then right onto a metal hand-railed bridge. Follow the path until it reaches another crossing. Turn left over a bridge to reach Mountain Highway, and then turn right and walk to the traffic signals.

## Lynn Valley Centre  2.0 km  0 hr 39 m  B19

Lynn Valley Centre is a bustle of commercial activity. It has an ample supply of coffee shops, a shopping mall with washrooms and buses if you want to end here. However, it takes a surprisingly short time to leave it and re-enter the tranquillity of Hastings Creek Ravine. Cross Mountain Highway and Lynn Valley Road and continue briefly on Mountain Highway to the midpoint of the short block. Go down the lane on the left to its end, behind some apartments and over a bridge onto a trail, which comes out on Allan Road. Go south across Ross Road and follow a path to reach the Hastings Creek trail. Keeping left, the trail drops down, with Hastings Creek on the right. This is a newly-prepared trail, with bridges, steps and boardwalks over muddy spots. The forest and steep canyon banks are on the left, and there are houses on the escarpment opposite with yards sometimes leading down to the creek edge. At the bottom, the route leads out onto Hoskins Road. It follows the road downhill for about five minutes—there are bus stops here and the downhill bus would take you to Phibbs Exchange on the hour and half hour, if you have had enough for the day.

If you prefer to finish the walk, take the trail where it appears on the left and follow it to Lynn Creek. This is a wide, fast-flowing stream with undammed headwaters. There are informal paths which follow the escarpment edge from time to time and give you a good view of the creek. However, these frequently erode and are not continuous. The main official trail is a little further back and is easier and safer to walk for longer distances. It passes a new footbridge over the creek. If

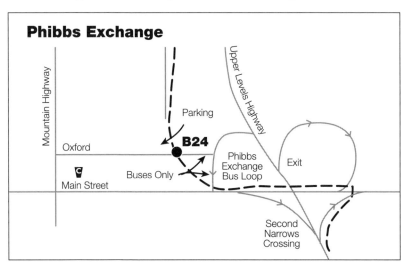

you crossed this and went upstream, you would reach the Baden-Powell Trail and then the Lynn Canyon Suspension Bridge.

Do not cross the bridge, but stay on the path which follows the river downstream and passes under the Trans-Canada Highway. Almost immediately, a second bridge appears. Detouring under this bridge would lead to picnic tables and toilets in Don Bridgman Park on the other side. However, our route continues on the main trail to the road and turns left on the footpath to reach Keith Bridge on its north side.

## Keith Bridge                    3.5 km    0 hr 49 m    B23

To stop here, you may catch a bus at about 10 or 40 minutes past the hour at the stop south of the bridge. It goes to Phibbs Exchange to connect with other buses. Or, to continue, drop down on the east side of Keith Bridge to the footpath below and follow it south into Seylynn Park. Cross the park diagonally to reach the corner of Hunter Street and Mountain Highway. Follow Hunter Street east to its end, turn south and continue to reach the park-and-ride area.

## Phibbs Exchange                 1.3 km    0 hr 18 m    B24

Next time the route carries on to Deep Cove, but a detour from here to Burnaby Mountain is also possible, starting at BM0.

**Getting home:** The #210 bus for Vancouver leaves from Bay 7 and the #28 bus to SkyTrain leaves from Bay 1.

# Lynn Creek to Indian Arm

Today's 12-km (7½-mile) walk uses lower-level walking trails in the Mount Seymour district, combined on occasion with some quieter residential streets. It passes the sites of some of the early immigrant settlements on Burrard Inlet at the mouth of the Seymour River. This area is still rural, not completely developed for housing, and the settlers are appropriately recognized by a memorial. After passing through the Windridge wooded areas, the route heads higher to follow an old gravel road, known locally as Water Line Road, to a newly constructed trail on the lower slopes of Mount Seymour around a recently developed golf course. Urban walkways continue, leading through the new Indian River development. Finally, parks connected by short stretches of road provide a route into Deep Cove from the coast and the woods at its south east corner.

**Getting there:** If using transit, take the #210 bus from Vancouver to Phibbs Exchange; or, from SkyTrain, transfer to the #28 bus at Gilmore or Joyce Station.

If driving, park at Deep Cove in the lot on Panorama Drive, which is on the left just after you turn to enter the village of Deep Cove. Washrooms lie below the parking lot and Deep Cove has several coffee shops, if you want an early refreshment. You may then catch either the #211 or the #212 bus on Banbury at Gallant. A #211 bus at 8:52 a.m. on Saturday takes just over 20 minutes to Phibbs Exchange. If you are planning to go only part-way, leave your vehicle at Phibbs Exchange, as it is easy to return there from several intermediate bus stops.

## Phibbs Exchange                               0 km     0 hr     B24

Walk north from the park-and-ride area west of the bus terminal and reach Hunter Street—the last intersecting street. Turn left and continue to Mountain Highway. Cross to Seylynn Park and head north west to the far corner of the park. Here find the trail at the side of Lynn Creek and follow it north to pass under Keith Bridge.

## Keith Bridge                           1.3 km     0 hr 18 m     B26

Continue, pass under the Trans-Canada Highway and come up to the road on the other side. The Lynn Valley Nature Trail leads north on St. David's Avenue, heading up to the Baden-Powell Trail and the Lynn Canyon Suspension Bridge—but again, another trail for another day.

Go east along Keith Road, passing the Holiday Inn and brace yourself for a brief but noisy stretch along the busy Mount Seymour Parkway to the traffic signals which you can see. At the lights, cross the Parkway and continue briefly east on the south side. When you reach the Seymour River bridge, take the opportunity to look at the river in both directions. It is surprisingly wide and still tree-lined on much of its length. The trail drops down the green bank immediately after the bridge. You may take a brisk run down the grassy slope or, if you are more cautious, go right on a shallower slope towards the water and then turn left to reach the bottom. If you don't like either of these options, continue on the sidewalk by the Parkway and turn right in due course onto the adjacent access road and come back. Here you enter Maplewood Farm Park at the edge of the river and head for the cairn.

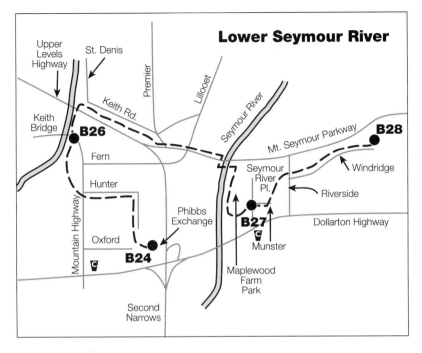

From the cairn, go towards the river to pick up the trail and head downstream. After you cross a wooden bridge, you can see Maplewood Farm behind the chain-link fencing on the left. Where the trail forks, always take the left-hand option, keeping close to the chain-link fence, until you reach a lane. Turn right to reach Seymour River Place. If you want a refreshment break, a fast-food restaurant on the Dollarton Highway just to the south opens at 10:00 a.m.

| **Seymour River Place** | 1.0 km | 0 hr 17 m | B27 |
|---|---|---|---|

From Seymour River Place, go along Munster Avenue south of the school (marked as having No Exit). After the last building on the left, turn left and enter the playground, going up steps and to the right of three large tires. Make your way across or around the football pitches to reach the path out of the diagonally opposite corner. Cross to Windridge Drive and follow it to its far end.

# Early Settlement in Burrard Inlet

In 1864, Hugh Burr, a former school teacher and early settler on Burrard Inlet, started a dairy farm just south of the present Maplewood Farm Park, at the mouth of the Seymour River on its east side. In due course, a neighbour bought the land north of him, and when the neighbour got into financial difficulties, Hugh Burr bought the land from him. Later, Hugh Burr sold his farm to C. J. Phibbs, first reeve of North Vancouver. The plaque on the commemorative cairn notes that "this monument was erected to commemorate the Diamond Jubilee [of North Vancouver] on 29 August 1951 at a place some three hundred yards south west at the milk ranch of the first reeve C. J. Phibbs."

The land on the other side of the Seymour across to the Lynn Creek was settled by John Linn in 1867. He raised cattle and horses; pigs would have been eaten by cougars. Lynn Creek is named after him.

Between 1914 and 1921, Akiyo Kogo developed the land where Maplewood Farm is now located. In 1924, he sold it to Joseph Ellis, who operated a small dairy farm and sold raw milk. When the farm ran into problems and new health regulations required pasteurization, he sold out to Fraser Valley Milk Producers and started breeding dogs. In 1970, the municipality acquired the property and operated it as a Children's Dairy Farm. It serves as a children's farm to this day.

*Source: **Echoes Across the Inlet,** by Dawn Sparks and Martha Border; edited by Damian Inwood. North Vancouver, BC: Deep Cove and Area Historical Association, 1989.*

**Jubilee Cairn in Maplewood Farm Park**

## Windridge Drive East     0.8 km     0 hr 15 m     B28

Cross the cleared area to go briefly on a major paved trail and take the first right fork, keeping a chain-link fence on your right. When the straight stretch ends, take the dirt trail leading left through the woods. These are attractive woods, with a maze of trails which offer numerous walking opportunities. You must watch carefully to find the way through. Quickly after entering, the trail dips to pass through Blueridge Creek. The state of this creek varies seasonally. Sometimes, you can just step across. At other times, you can step from the top of one stone to the next. At worst, you may have to go briefly left on the bank and jump the creek. On the other side, continue until you reach a crossing of trails. Turn left and come out at the Ron Andrews Community Centre. Now stay close to the Centre to reach the parking lot on the far side, and then take the path out to the corner of Lytton Road and the Parkway.

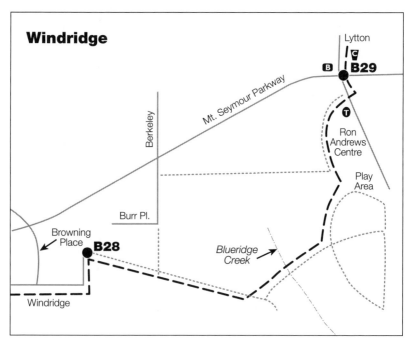

If you want, you can go into the Centre to use the washroom or get refreshments from a slot machine. Alternatively, if you wait to cross the Parkway, the gas station has a good selection of cookies, fresh muffins and drinks but with nowhere to sit down. Buses pass if you want to stop here.

## Seymour Parkway        1.8 km    0 hr 32 m    B29

Across the Parkway, Lytton Avenue leads up and ends in a trail which follows around a school, with a creek on its left side. After passing the school, do not continue to the steps you can see ahead but turn right and exit on Trillium Place. At Emerson Way, turn left until a major park appears on the right. It will be busy with the sound of children's voices on a fine weekend. Follow the tiled path into the playground area, where a chip trail leads north, following between houses. At its end, continue on a paved, lighted trail to reach Tompkins Crescent. Turn right and find a track leading uphill—this is the old Water Line Road. Just before entering trees, you reach a substation on the left.

## Tompkins Substation       1.8 km    0 hr 27 m    B31

After going through the trees, the old road reaches McCartney Creek, which can flow heavily after rain in the winter months. However, I have always found it possible to run through quickly in my boots, if I must. After the creek, there are various minor trails going through the old Blair Rifle Range down to Mount Seymour Parkway. In about 10 minutes, you reach a major junction. The old route used to run south east, following a trail called the Pipeline Trail, but a golf course now blocks its way. Instead, turn left briefly into a major trail, but quickly take the new Bailout Trail, which leads off on the right. This is not yet widely used, so follow it carefully. In just under 10 minutes more, it joins a gravelled trail. At this point, it is within three or four metres of the Bridle Trail—look uphill and you should see the trail, while uphill and to the right is a chain-link fence.

177

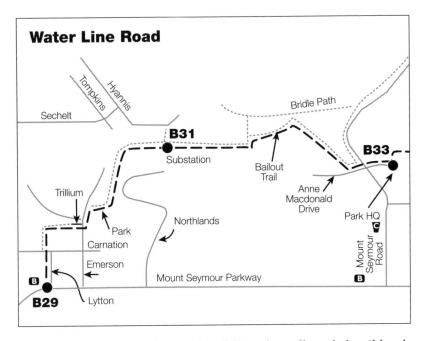

Do not take the Bridle Trail but follow the well-graded trail heading downwards, staying close to the edge of the new Northlands Golf Course as it passes through maples and hemlocks. Soon there will be further subdivision, bringing the back yards of new houses to border the trail, so enjoy the natural surroundings while you can. When the trail meets a new paved road, head down and turn left at the bottom into Anne Macdonald Drive (the entrance to the golf course is to the right). The parking lot for users of the Mount Seymour Park trails lies across the road to the left; there are toilets beyond it, just up the hill.

At the main road, a detour downhill leads to a shopping mall with restaurants, and to bus service on Mount Seymour Parkway beyond that. However, today's route crosses Mount Seymour Road and goes up the roadway opposite to Park Headquarters—known locally as the ranger station. At the first intersection, turn left up the hill and find a picnic table on the right by the building and another one when you turn right at the corner of the building. The area here is marked as Burt's Patch.

## Seymour Park HQ            1.9 km    0 hr 33 m    B33

The trail now leads off north opposite the building and almost immediately turns east, following the original pipeline alignment. Continue to follow Pipeline Trail and its successors all the way around and through the Indian River Park subdivision. The first road end passed on the right is Cascade Court. Two water towers soon appear on the left. Cross the major Indian River Crescent and, after passing a trail on the left, come to Indian River Drive. Looking to the left, you will see that a chain-link fence stops the road where it meets private property. Cross the road and almost immediately south, a paved trail leads off left and curves around in trees behind the eastern edge of the subdivision. On the right, you meet the road ends of Iron

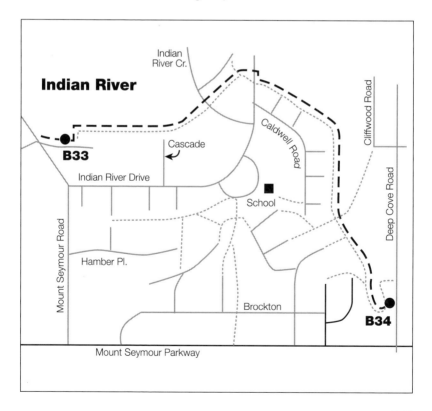

Court, Felix Court, Deane Place, Ostler Court and Theta Crescent. Then, heading downhill, you meet a crossing of trails. If you were to turn left, you would reach Cliffwood Road and would soon be in Deep Cove. However, I prefer to follow a scenic but more circuitous route, which gives a pleasant view of Deep Cove before entering its downtown.

To do this, carry straight on. Soon the paved trail yields to gravel and eventually reaches a road (Lima Road). Turn left here and head down the hill. Halfway down, ignore the trail that leads off left into a housing development and continue, reaching Deep Cove Road at the bottom.

## Deep Cove Road        1.5 km    0 hr 21 m    B34

Cross into Strathcona Road and turn left at the first road—Caledonia Avenue. You have to be watchful here to find the path. Follow the road as it curves down and enters the school grounds. You will see the words Seycove Community School on a building in front of you and the road for vehicles goes down its right-hand side. However, this is not the way for you. You must go left between two buildings and find a path which goes straight down into Myrtle Park, with a ball park and playing fields. Follow the chip path right, and where it meets a major trail at the east of the park, look for a bridge with a notice saying Noble Bridge. Go over the bridge and follow a strip of park land, passing points which used to be work stations on a fitness trail. When you emerge onto Strathcona Road, go across to Strathcona Park, which is a pleasant waterfront spot for a break and a view to a nearby island. The original population called the island Spuka-nah-ah. In 1859, Captain Richmond of *HMS Plumper* named it White Rock. Later the settler community renamed it Anderson Island after two former owners but it is now called Grey Rocks Island. Diez Vistas ridge and Belcarra lie on the other side of Indian Arm.

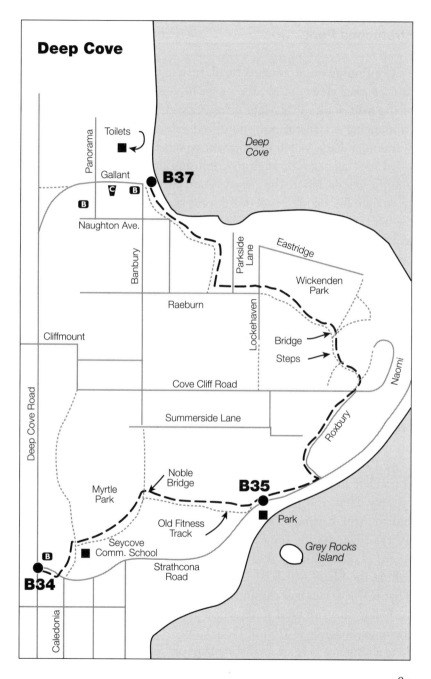

## Strathcona Park        0.8 km    0 hr 12 m    B35

Continuing on Strathcona Road, turn left up Roxbury Road with its occasional views out to sea over the houses on the right. At the end of the road, look to the right across Cove Cliff Road to see a notice announcing a trail for non-motorized vehicles. The trail leads into Wickenden Park, which has pleasant woods that you will enjoy, provided you take care through its confusing maze of trails. As you go into the woods, ignore the gravelled trail curving to the right; instead, go straight on, taking a trail down some steps. Ignore the first trail on the left (which goes back to Cove Cliff Road) and soon reach a bridge which crosses a muddy area. Go over it and continue straight ahead on a boardwalk to the T-junction with a crossing trail (ignore the trail off left immediately after the bridge). Turn left and follow the trail as it winds gradually downhill through trees, with occasional stretches of boardwalk. The tree cover is quite thick, and I have walked through here in heavy rain and kept reasonably dry.

At the end of the trail, cross Lockehaven Road to the facing Raeburn Road and go downhill, passing Parkside Lane on the right. At the foot of the hill, a sign on the right indicates you are crossing Parkside Creek, which the municipality is working to restore to its original purity. Go past a metal barred gate into the trail which comes up on the right a few metres further on. Continue through Deep Cove Park until you are almost at the water. Then take a major gravel trail left and uphill to go through the park to emerge on grass at its far end. Here you look north to the panorama of Deep Cove and Indian Arm beyond; a small picnic area lies below. Head for the water's edge, passing the canoe-rental station, where there are washrooms. Looking across Indian Arm, Belcarra is on the other side behind the island which is visible by the shore, slightly to the south. That is where you will continue on the next phase of the journey.

Follow the path until you reach steps coming down from the end of the main downtown street of Deep Cove—Gallant Avenue. The concrete abutments here are all that remains of Corfield's Dance Hall—*the* place to go on a weekend in the 1940s. You can read about the history of this location on the notice boards at the site. Today, Deep Cove offers a wide range of stores and an attractive cultural centre.

## Deep Cove             1.5 km    0 hr 26 m    B37

**Getting home:** Take a bus from Banbury at Gallant to Phibbs Exchange to connect with the #210 bus to Vancouver or the #28 bus to SkyTrain.

**Deep Cove**

# Indian Arm to Ioco

Belcarra has no weekend transit service, so today's 15-km (9-mile) walk begins inland, goes out to Belcarra and Admiralty Point, and then loops back to Ioco. It starts from the lakeshore at White Pine Beach, a popular spot on summer weekends, but you and the birds may well have it to yourself at other times. Well-built trails pass through the pleasant woods of Belcarra Regional Park to reach Belcarra. The walk continues along the coastline to Admiralty Point, with its historic marker and its panoramic view of Burrard Inlet. Retracing its tracks to Belcarra, it shortcuts to reach the gate of White Pine Beach Park and make its way to Ioco. This community is now small and quiet since activity at the Imperial Oil Company (IOCO) refinery has wound down. The general store and some of the buildings are being maintained as heritage structures.

**Getting there:** In past summers, an infrequent bus served White Pine Beach. The first bus arrived about 11 o'clock, allowing you to do the walk and finish at Ioco before 4 o'clock. However, the bus route structure changed on September 1, 2003 and only the winter timetable is available. Check with TransLink for future summer service.

If using transit, take the summer bus to White Pine Beach (or nearest available stop and walk in).

If driving, park outside Port Moody Arena and walk to the bus stop on the east side of Ioco Road. Catch the appropriate summer bus to White Pine Beach. When you end the day's walk at Ioco, catch the bus from there back to Port Moody Arena.

If you want to go at other times of the year, you can drive to White Pine Beach and do a round trip from there (White Pine, Belcarra, Admiralty Point, and back to Belcarra, White Pine). Then you could start next time at Ioco, missing only the White Pine–to–Ioco section, which is all on road until such time as the informal trails in the Ioco lands become officially available.

## White Pine Beach                    0 km    0 hr    B37

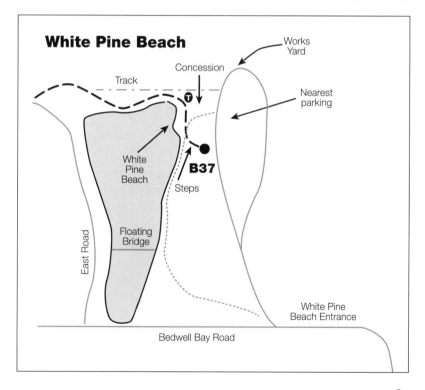

From the bus stop, go down the steps and turn right to reach the beach by Sasamat Lake. The washrooms will be open and the concession probably in the summer. After taking what time you need to appreciate the view over the lake, walk by the beach to the right and follow the lakeside walk. You may hear the sounds of children's voices reverberating across the water from Sasamat Outdoor Centre, a facility run by the Association of Neighbourhood Houses. Just before you reach the centre, the trail leaves the lakeside and climbs to the track above. Turn left, cross the centre's access road and go left on the trail on the other side as it drops down to the creek. On the other side of the creek, the trail winds back and goes up to the road by the entrance sign to Belcarra Village.

## Belcarra Village Sign       1.0 km     0 hr 17 m     B38

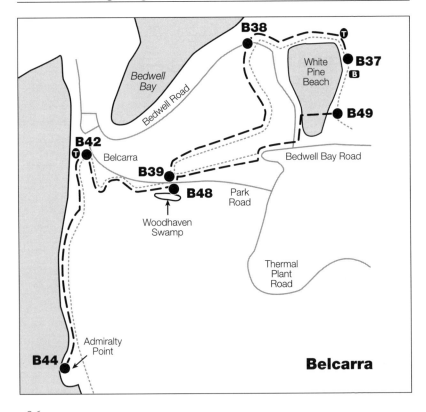

Cross the road and prepare for a little climbing. Woodhaven Trail starts by passing some houses of a subdivision and then enters a cedar and hemlock forest. After about half an hour, emerge from the forest and turn left on a track to reach the main park road. On the way down to the road, a cycle path leads out left. This will be your return route when you come back. Cross the road to the path on the other side, turn right and follow the trail to the parking lot.

## Woodhaven Swamp      1.7 km     0 hr 32 m     B39

An early road created the swamp by causing a body of water to form which could not drain out. This has resulted in snags and rotting trees, which make homes for hawks and other raptors and for woodpeckers. Frogs, amphibians and occasionally waterfowl live in the water. The normally-rare cotton grass grows in the moist hollows. A path around the lake allows the visitor to explore the swamp.

Follow Springboard Trail, which is the higher of the trails above the lake. It soon comes out onto the road, with a safe swath of blacktop to use until the path goes into the woods again. It stays in the woods for a while before again emerging briefly onto the road. After this next return into the woods, there are some tall, straight, Douglas fir trees, indicating that the climate here may be drier and the rainfall less intense, lower on the hill and closer to the coastline. The path now switchbacks down to Belcarra below. You will see the trail to Admiralty Point below you as you descend. It is worthwhile continuing to the right when you join the trail and reach Belcarra to enjoy the view.

## Belcarra      2.7 km     0 hr 38 m     B42

The covered picnic tables and washrooms make this a good place for a lunch break. The concession will likely be open if it is a summer weekend. Walk down to the pier and look across to the far shore and the community of Dollarton, which is just south of Deep Cove where the walk ended on that side.

# Belcarra

The Belcarra area's first white settler, John Hall, arrived in 1870. He lived common-law with an Indian woman, built a house, started a garden and orchard and he and his wife had two children. In 1882, John Hall shot his mother-in-law in a drunken brawl over money. Hall was defended by William Bole, who got the charge reduced from murder to manslaughter. Hall was sentenced to seven years hard labour and Bole received the house and land as payment for his fees. He used it for summer holidays and called the place Belcarra.

Belcarra comes from an Irish name meaning "fair land upon which the sun shines." Members of the Sleil Wauturh band lived here as long ago as 1000 BC. The large grassy area was once a large midden with extensive traces of habitation. Early white settlers built homesteads along the coast south of here. Their houses are gone, except for one private house just to the south. However, periwinkle and other domestic plants still indicate where there were once homes.

*Source: Echoes Across the Inlet, by Dawn Sparks and Martha Border; edited by Damian Inwood. North Vancouver, BC: Deep Cove and Area Historical Association, 1989.*

After lunch, head south on the Admiralty Point trail. At its start, the trail passes the driveway of the one remaining private house on the shoreline and then rises up the hill to go around it. When you see the house below you on the right after the top of the hill, look for its fence to appear at the trail edge. At the corner of the fence, back up the trail about 10 or 12 steps and look up into the tall Douglas fir tree ahead. Here you can see the tree house where George Dyson researched and designed his kayaks—a modernized version of the traditional kayaks used by the Aleuts to hunt the sea otters up and down the Pacific coast. He built them on the beach below. Continuing south, there are great views to sea, and soon after Maple Beach you come to the sign indicating Admiralty Point.

**The Pier at Belcarra**

# George Dyson and the Baidarka Kayak

In August 1972, the 19-year-old George Dyson was on watch, sailing down Georgia Strait. He was looking at the lights of a tug and enjoying the coming dawn, when the ship hit a huge cedar log. The captain took control, decided that the log was too valuable to leave, and took it in tow. The next evening found the boat anchored off Belcarra Park. George paddled the log ashore and secured it at the foot of a large Douglas fir.

He soon left his crew job to stay at Belcarra. He used some of the log to produce shakes which he sold to a restaurant in Deep Cove. He cut the rest of the log into boards, and as they started to accumulate, George's eye wandered up the fir tree to a possible house site with an unobstructed view. By November, he was settled almost 30 metres up in the tree, with his winter fuel of cedar trimmings stocked at the foot of the tree below. He spent three winters in this house, with a coal-oil lamp and a wood stove. The summers were spent exploring Alaskan waters to the north.

George was always fascinated by the simplicity of the Baidarka kayaks used by the Aleuts to hunt sea otters. These boats were built with a wooden framework covered with seal skins. As the son of an English astrophysicist and a Swiss mathematician, he was attracted to the use of newer materials. He built the first of many baidarkas here, using aluminum tubing, which he covered with a fibreglass-polyester skin.

*Source: **Baidarka,** by George Dyson. Edmonds, Washington: Alaska Northwest Publishing Company, 1986.*

## Admiralty Point   1.5 km  0 hr 24 m  B44

Take the side trail to a panoramic viewpoint. The mossy rocks are slippery at times, but it is worth holding on to the nearby trees to reach the bare rock and the views. You look west down the Inlet to the Second Narrows rail and road bridges, across Indian Arm to Cates Park, and south to Burnaby's Marine Foreshore Park and the slopes of Burnaby Mountain.

A metal plate fixed on an open rock reads: "Take notice that by indenture dated April 21, 1913, the areas outlined on the plan inscribed below were leased by the Government of Canada to the City of Vancouver for a term of ninety nine years computed from the 1st day of May, 1912." The plan then shows lands lying below a line to the north of Admiralty Point and extending to just beyond Burns Point to the east.

This is another good point for a longer break. But when you have enjoyed your stay, return by the same path to Belcarra. When you see Springboard Trail above you, you can short-cut to it and retrace your steps to the swamp.

## Woodhaven Swamp   4.0 km  1 hr 2 m  B48

After the swamp, cross the road and take the first trail off on the right, which is marked as the cycle trail. It leads steadily downhill through the trees and emerges onto Tum-tumay-whueton Drive—the main road to the park. Follow it briefly down to its first intersection and go left until you reach the road sign which is visible in the distance on the right. A trail from the sign leads through trees and comes to a floating bridge. Cross this to its eastern side.

## Floating Bridge East    1.5 km    0 hr 21 m    B49

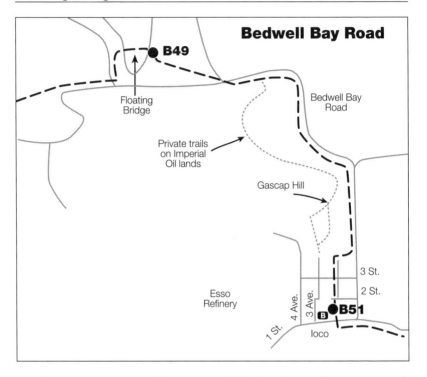

If you were to turn left, you would be back at White Pine Beach in about 15 minutes. This is the way to go if you are making a round trip from White Pine Beach. However, if you are continuing to Ioco, go up the steps to the right and follow a track that leads to the right just below the road. Continue briefly and turn off left onto an overgrown trail that leads through bushes and opens up as it leads out to the park gates.

Cross the main road carefully and follow the concrete barrier until it ends in about 200 metres. Just past here, a well-worn trail leads off on the right. No Trespassing signs used to be displayed prominently, not only at this trailhead but also where the trail emerges in Ioco. However, the sign at the Ioco end is no longer there; a sign now tells you that the property is private, there are dangers and you enter at your own risk. Cycling ramps and structures are common; the trail surface bears multiple cycle tracks and even the salmonberry bushes have been kept at bay by the level of use. Trespassing appears to be tolerated if you respect the property and assume the risk. If Ioco becomes a heritage site, perhaps the trails will become freely useable, but for the present, the legal route is the main road into Ioco. I describe the forest route for possible future legitimate use.

The trail goes through bushes and reaches a track leading west. Directly across, at the start of the track, a small trail leads down and across the pipeline route, then goes to the right and into the woods. A major trail now continues, going first towards the refinery and then bearing left and heading down, eventually reaching a creek which has to be crossed (there are provisions for diversions at high-water times). The trail continues to a T-intersection where the route turns right between bushes and reaches a hill going up—named Gascap Hill by the cyclists. At the top of the hill, the trail branches into two, but the right fork is wider and clearer. Both trails lead out to 3 Avenue, which leads downhill to a T-intersection. The right turn leads to old Ioco, the community hall and the groceteria, all boarded up but maintained. The street to the left crosses on a pedestrian bridge to reach the bus loop, with the bus stop on the right.

## Ioco                    2.2 km    0 hr 35 m    B51

**Getting home:** The #C25 bus leaves from the terminus here. You can transfer to the #97 bus at Port Moody to reach Lougheed Town Centre Station.

# Ioco to the Coquitlam River

Today's 12-km (7½-mile) walk follows the edge of Burrard Inlet through the community of Pleasantside to Noons Creek salmon hatchery and Shoreline Park. It crosses Coronation Park to reach Hoy Creek—a surprising oasis to find so near to Coquitlam Centre. Following Hoy Creek up to its salmon hatchery, it passes through the Douglas College campus, crosses Lafarge Park and meanders beside the wild Coquitlam River to reach Port Coquitlam.

**Getting there:** If using transit, take the #C25 bus to Ioco (you can transfer to it from the #97 bus from Lougheed Town Centre Station).

If driving, go to Port Coquitlam and park by the Lions Park on Lions Way, one block south of Lougheed Highway off the west side of Shaughnessy Street; washrooms are nearby in the park. After parking, come out to Shaughnessy Street and when it is safe, cross to the bus stop opposite. Take the #160 bus and transfer in Port Moody to the #C25 Ioco bus (ask the driver where). A bus at 8:49 a.m. on Saturday takes about 35 minutes.

## Ioco                    0 km    0 hr    B51

Walk from the bus to Ioco Road; start by the church and follow Ioco Road east. I enjoy the sign which is just down the first road on the right, Beach Avenue. People who walk with me know my attitude towards trespassing on private land. I never go on land where the owner genuinely wants me to stay away, but I am not deterred by ones put up for legal protection. A railway line crosses Beach Avenue and serves some houses with no other access. The sign at the railway says: Private Crossing. Use by Public Forbidden. Persons Using This Crossing Do So at Their Own Risk. In other words, it is forbidden but you can do it. I take this to mean that I may cross but cannot successfully sue them. I find this completely acceptable.

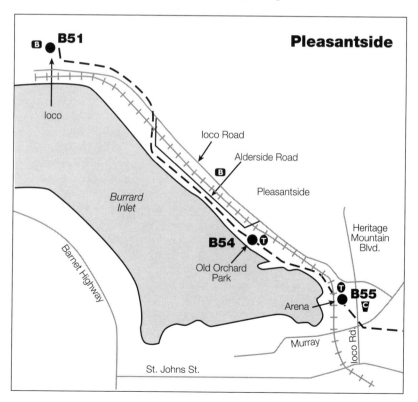

**Channel at Noons Creek Hatchery**

Continue on Ioco Road (with a wide swath on the right for much of the way) and turn right onto Alderside Road. This road has the railway on its left and waterfront houses on the right. Looking between the houses, you can see Burnaby Mountain on the other side of the Inlet. You make your way from the 1200 block to the 600 block; steps lead up to Ioco Road at 1100 and 900, if you want to stop and get a bus back.

In the 1100 block, the waterside houses use the whole of their space for house, decks and car parking, so the owners have created some attractive gardens on railway property on the other side of the street. One former owner was a retired railway worker from the Kettle Valley Railway, and he created a railway scene, with a model locomotive and tunnel; it is now deteriorating but I still enjoy his handiwork.

Enter Old Orchard Park at #644. Picnic tables are by the entrance and washrooms are by the cycle path at the upper level. The pedestrian trail starts off at beach level.

## Old Orchard Park  2.5 km  0 hr 35 m  B54

Follow the lower-level path to the end of the Inlet. Profuse skunk cabbage and bleeding hearts decorate the woodland trail in the spring. Occasional detours to the waterfront edge give you the opportunity to explore.

In about 15 minutes, the boardwalk takes a sharp right turn to a bridge to cross Noons Creek. This is the short way out. If that is your choice, take this trail, turn left at the first opportunity, and you will come out to the left of the arena. If you have more time, it is worth taking the detour left, also crossing Noons Creek and going to the hatchery. In the spring, there may be some 20,000 coho fry, waiting to be released into the creek. In October, there may be some 6,000 or so coho salmon. Continuing on the trail past the hatchery, you come out to the left side of the arena. Follow past the front of it (there are washrooms inside) and continue further to find where the cars leave the parking lot to enter Ioco Road outside. Both shopping centres across the main road have restaurants if you want a refreshment break at this point. (The trail from Burnaby Mountain ends here at BM21; it makes an interesting trip for another day.)

---

# Noons Creek Hatchery

Brian, Margaret and Gavin Waite of Maude Street, whose property backed onto Noons Creek, started the present Noons Creek Hatchery. With the help of advisers from the federal Salmonid Enhancement Program, they dug rearing ponds, installed troughs and released thousands of young coho each year. Gradually the coho started to return to their historic home. When the Waites moved out, members of the Noons Creek Housing Co-op took over the project. The City donated the present site, downstream from the Waites' hatchery. Volunteers dug new rearing ponds and a side channel from the creek, and the new Noons Creek Hatchery was born. The Centennial Senior Secondary School students and teachers who operated the nearby Mossom Creek Hatchery donated the stock; the local community donated labour, equipment, materials and money.

*Source: "Welcome to the Noons Creek Hatchery," a pamphlet of the Port Moody Ecological Society, Port Moody, BC 1999.*

---

**Port Moody Arena**      1.0 km    0 hr 20 m    B55

When you have taken any stop you may want, proceed south to the major intersection with its traffic signals. Cross to the far south eastern corner, follow up the footpath just to the south and turn right when you reach Balmoral Drive. Go past Coronation Hill School on the left and turn left to enter Coronation Park behind the school. Cross the park to its far corner and go down the steps, looking at a view of the strip of land and developments bordering Barnet Highway.

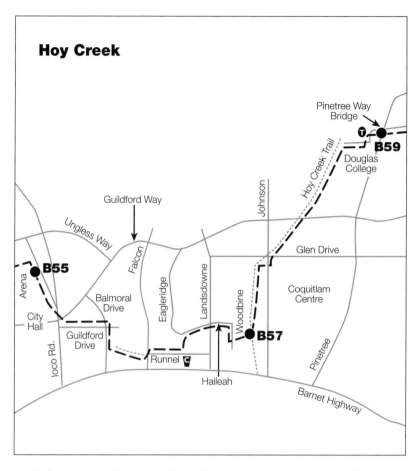

# Hoy Creek

Follow the right-hand sidewalk and continue down until you see a clock on a building in the shopping centre. You can take a refreshment break at the restaurant in here or at the McDonald's which is almost next door along the road.

Opposite McDonald's, take the path by the side of Scott Creek, which drains the Meridian Power Station area above. After a short block, turn right and go to the main road ahead, with the Mennonite Church on one corner. Continue across into Haileah Court for a block and turn right down Woodbine Street. A path leading out left between chain-link fences takes you to Hoy Creek.

## Hoy Creek                    2.3 km    0 hr 33 m    B57

Turn left and follow the creek path, being careful not to take side paths which lead off to nearby roads. Turn right where the path bends to cross a bridge signed as having a Slippery Bridge Deck and then follow it over another bridge (I have seen salmon in the creek here in October). Where the path meets a major east-west road (Glen Drive), turn right to the prominently-named Johnson Street, cross both roads and find the trail a few metres north on the east side of Johnson Street.

Follow the trail past floral gardens outside some apartments, displaying rhododendrons in bloom in April and May. Where the trail reaches the next major road (Guildford Way), it continues on the other side—you can use a pedestrian crossing just to the right. Follow this trail and stay on the east side of Hoy Creek until you reach a park building and a notice board reporting on the work of volunteers, who have adopted the creek to keep it clear and natural. You can cross a bridge to a fish hatchery to see the coho salmon. The fry are released into Hoy Creek in the early part of May at a public ceremony and mature salmon return in the fall.

After seeing the hatchery, come back to the east side of the creek and follow the trail further to the north, turning right where a trail leads off to some buildings. The Douglas College campus is on the right and the Pinetree Secondary School and Community Centre are on the left. None of these new structures was here a few years ago, when I used to find my way through these woods on muddy trails over fallen logs. At a public meeting, I once heard the recreational planner say that it took five years to get all the public, environmental and political approvals to build about a kilometre of Hoy Creek trail. I can see how that would be true. That was when I decided I did not have enough time left in my life to fight for a regional trail system. I would just publicize where the present trails are and encourage people to use them.

Follow the road, keeping close to the building on the left and go around the corner when you reach it. Pass the Community Centre (there are washrooms inside) and make your way to the staircase on the far side. Go up to the level above, follow the pathway to the bridge and pass over Pinetree Way.

## Pinetree Way Bridge                2.0 km      0 hr 28 m      B59

Look south to see Lafarge Lake, once a gravel pit and now an important attraction in Town Centre Park. On the other side, go all the way down to the parking lot, cross the parking area, and take the sidewalk going up the hill facing you. At the top, turn left along a wide red-brick path. You may hear sounds of people playing in the sports fields on the right, particularly if it is on the weekend.

As soon as you can, turn right, passing a small structure marked Coquitlam Town Recreation Centre, hug the right-hand chain-link fence and follow the path to the eastern edge of the park. Cross the road for vehicles entering the park and go on the paved path up the hill to the left.

At the top, you have to be careful to find where the trail continues. Watch for cars, cross the major road and go onto Pathan Avenue. However, bear left and head to where the road looks as if it is going to continue due north in a direct alignment with the major Pipeline Road ahead. Follow this—you will see a crash barrier, which prevents vehicles from passing to the main road; however, you will not reach this barrier. Look right after you pass a creek to see a path leading due east. Walk down this to join a road and then bear left, passing a general store, a hairdresser and a dry cleaner. Now continue on the wide swath east as it leads to the Coquitlam River. This strip of land is the right-of-way of David Avenue, which someday will be a major east-west arterial road from Westwood Plateau in the west, over the Coquitlam River to Port Coquitlam in the east. So enjoy it while you may! Street-ends enter the swath from the right, but it is more interesting to note the houses hidden in the forest of trees on the left—

# Salmon in the Rivers

I have always enjoyed the Coquitlam River, but old-timers who remember the days of plentiful salmon harvests are upset at the amount of silt from the upstream gravel pits and the near-elimination of the salmon. It is therefore heartening to see, in the stretch of trail along its banks, the extensive amount of work that is being done in salmonid enhancement, and the new channels created. A plaque on a rock in this section pays tribute to Allan E. Grist, who did much to push this work forward. I thank him too.

Vancouver uses large amounts of gravel for roads and under new housing. There are huge quantities in the ground in areas like the Westwood Plateau, but no one wants a gravel pit as a neighbour. For this reason, the big commercial gravel pits are more remote, and, in particular, a major source is up the Coquitlam River, where there are three mines. The mines have ponds to hold back silt but these may overflow on occasion at times of high water. This silt fills in the crevices in the river bed, taking away hiding places for the salmon fry. Coho salmon are particularly vulnerable, because they remain in fresh water for up to two years after hatching. In 1999, the Outdoor Recreational Council named the Coquitlam River one of the province's 10 most-threatened rivers.

You may also have noted that the Noons Creek Hatchery and the Hoy Creek Hatchery, which you passed en route, were both raising coho, in an attempt to help to preserve a species which is under threat in many British Columbia river systems.

*Source: Various **Vancouver Sun** articles.*

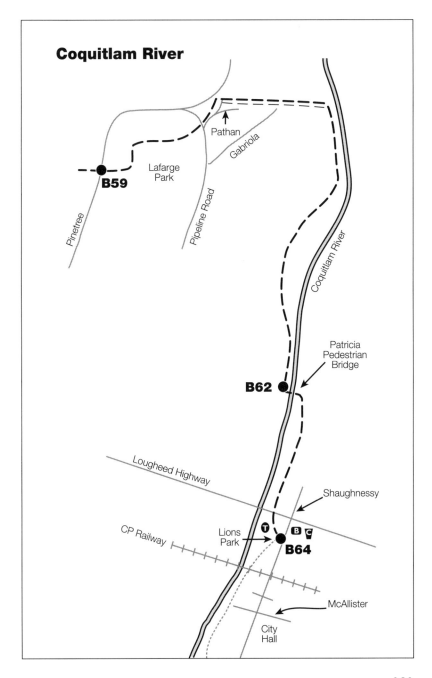

**Coquitlam River**

Pathan

Gabriola

Pinetree

Lafarge Park

Pipeline Road

**B59**

Coquitlam River

Patricia Pedestrian Bridge

**B62**

Lougheed Highway

Shaughnessy

CP Railway

Lions Park

**B64**

McAllister

City Hall

ideal for those who like their privacy, or want to play their stereos loud. When you reach the Coquitlam River, take a few moments to enjoy the flow of this wild river.

When I first walked the trail on this west side of the river, it was a muddy path, crossed by roots, and was swampy where small creeks entered. Then the salmonid enhancement started and, for a while, the trail was closed. However, the new major trail can be enjoyed by all, while the salmon are flourishing also.

As you travel south, follow the major path all the way, even where minor trails lead off. At one point, you have to turn sharp left at a chain-link fence, where the trail turns at an enhancement project. Somewhere along this stretch of river would be a great spot to have lunch. When you reach a pedestrian bridge on the left, cross the bridge to the east side. Stop at the midpoint to enjoy the sweep of the wide river.

## Patricia Bridge 3.3 km 0 hr 52 m B62

Head downstream with the river on the right and reach the Lougheed Highway. Cross under this by the river's edge and come up into Lions Park, where there may well be children enjoying themselves on a fine sunny day. Angle to the left across the grass towards the park entrance. A building with washrooms is close to the parking lot.

## Lions Park 1.3 km 0 hr 20 m B64

**Getting home:** If you cross Shaughnessy Street to the east, the #160 bus leaves from the bus stop there for Coquitlam Centre and Vancouver.

**Coquitlam River above Patricia Bridge**

# Port Coquitlam to the Pitt River

Today's 12-km (7$\frac{1}{2}$-mile) walk goes briefly up the Coquitlam River, follows the Poco Trail, going through parks and beside Hyde Creek, as it flows down into deBoville Slough. It then follows the dikes of the Pitt River, with wide sweeping views over the flat farmlands of Pitt Meadows. Northward, there are views of the various mountain ranges.

**Getting there:** If using transit, go to the intersection of Shaughnessy Street and Lougheed Highway, walk down Lions Way, one block to the south, and enter Lions Park.

If driving, follow Lougheed Highway and take the turn north at the signals at Dewdney Trunk Road, immediately east of the Pitt River Bridge. Turn almost immediately left onto a side road, drive down to the crash barrier by the Lougheed Highway and park here or nearby. The #701 bus leaves the bus stop on the other side of the barrier and goes to Port Coquitlam. Get off at Shaughnessy Street. Walk one block south to Lions Way and go one block west to enter Lions Park. A bus at 8:44 a.m. on Saturday takes less than 10 minutes.

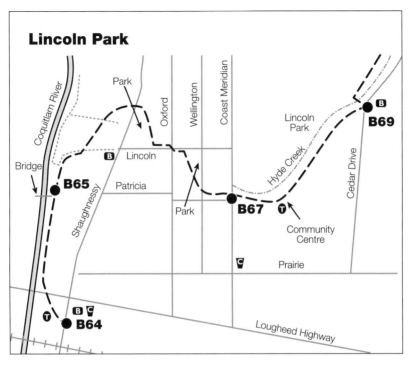

## Lincoln Park

**Lions Park**                                    0 km    0 hr    B64

The small building in the park contains washrooms if you want to use them before you start. Then walk towards the river and head north to reach the highway bridge. Go under the bridge and follow the path, with the river on the left. In about 20 minutes, you reach the Patricia pedestrian bridge.

**Patricia Bridge**                        1.3 km    0 hr 20m    B65

Continue upstream on the east side of the river until you reach a place where the main trail turns left on a wooden bridge over a creek entering the Coquitlam River. Do not turn here but go straight ahead, turning right onto a path bordered by a fence on the right. A notice board on the left describes the Oxbow Sidechannel project.

207

After reading this, continue east and take the first trail off left, leading north past a board asking you not to dump refuse. This path keeps the stream of the Sidechannel project on the left and leads out to a clearing and a joining of trails. The trail left leads to the river; the trail right leads out to a gate to Shaughnessy Street (and a bus stop back to Port Coquitlam, if you want). Our route bends toward the right initially but continues north, rather than going through the gate. Where this trail becomes gravelled and turns off right, follow it, cross Shaughnessy Street when nothing is coming, and follow the trail through the forested Coquitlam River Park. Turn right where the major trail does so, to reach a blue-topped garbage container at Lincoln Avenue. Now follow the trail east past a wooden Poco Trail sign at ground level, and continue parallel to the road until the trail comes out at the corner of Lincoln Avenue and Oxford Street. Cross both streets and follow Lincoln Avenue until the trail enters Wellington Park on the right-hand side.

Follow the trail through Wellington Park. You are at its north west corner and you want to find the south east corner on the far side. The trail curves somewhat to the left and there are several side trails leading off. Try to follow the central one, maintaining the same general curvature to the left. Soon you will reach a road edge. This may be Wellington Street or Patricia Avenue, depending on which trail you have finally followed. Make your way down to the nearest corner and check which is Wellington Street and which is Patricia Avenue. Follow Patricia Avenue east, away from the park, with a school on the right, until you reach the major Coast Meridian Road.

## Coast Meridian Road 2.5 km 0 hr 40 m B67

Cross the road and enter Lincoln Park—a protected nature area. Follow the pleasant green trail along Hyde Creek until it reaches Cedar Drive. You can see houses through the trees at times. Hyde Creek Community Centre lies in an open area on the right. Washrooms are available inside and the refreshment concession may be open. Salmonberry bushes, Himalaya weed and other vegetation line the trail to its end at a barred gate on Cedar Drive. Buses in either direction go to Port Coquitlam or Coquitlam Station.

Walk briefly north on Cedar Drive from the bus stop and go over the pedestrian bridge on the left. Follow the trail and road north to reach the corner of the main road. Cross carefully to DeBoville Slough's parking area opposite. (An interesting round trip up the Pitt River to Minnekhada starts here at FP0.)

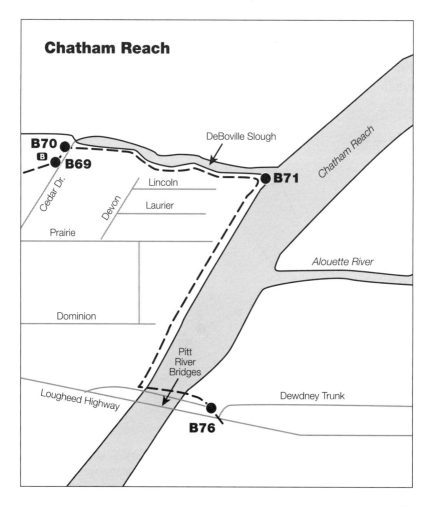

**Chatham Reach**

## DeBoville Slough Parking          2.2 km     0 hr 33 m     B70

Follow the dike path on the south side of the slough. The trail bends towards the south, passing a track that leads in from Devon Road. Walkers on the other side of the slough are going to Minnekhada Park or to Addington Marsh, prime habitat for many kinds of waterfowl. I was fortunate enough once to see a rare sandhill crane there. DeBoville Slough is one of the first areas visited by the swallows when they return, sometimes as early as February. Fireweed decorates the trail and hardhack bushes display their attractive pink spears in June or July. Two yellow barred gates just before the mouth of the slough announce the Pitt River Boat Club and its landing dock.

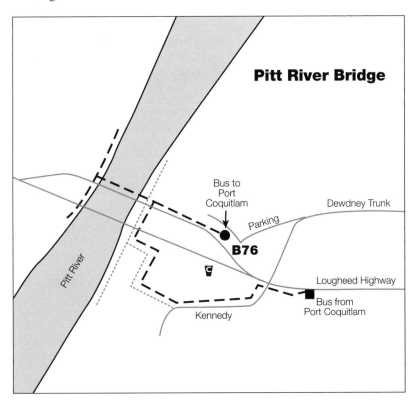

## DeBoville Slough Mouth     1.6 km    0 hr 24 m    B71

The dike now turns south down the west side of the wide Pitt River—the second-largest river in the Lower Mainland after the Fraser. You can expect to hear the honking of geese in the fall as the birds get ready to depart. A newly-constructed viewing platform near the start lets you admire Chatham Reach, as this section of the river is called. Local residents drive to the road ends which lead in from the right and walk their dogs on the dike. On the opposite side, the Alouette River comes in from Maple Ridge. Make sure you stop occasionally and look back to see the various mountain ranges there. You will first see the Pitt River Bridge and then hear its traffic as you get nearer. Cross the bridge by the pedestrian pathway, but stop halfway to look north to the mountains, with the contrasting flat marshlands in front. Continue on the path to the bus stop on the north side of Lougheed Highway, just before Dewdney Trunk Road.

## Pitt River Bridge East     4.4 km    1 hr 2 m    B76

**Getting home:** The #701 bus from the north-side bus stop goes to Coquitlam Station and makes connections to all parts of the region.

# Pitt River to Mundy Park

Today's 14-km (8½-mile) walk passes the site of an old ferry that served as a crossing of the river until just after the Pitt River Bridge of 1914 was built. After following the river south, it takes a break from the dike and climbs to the top of Mary Hill to provide a view of the whole Fraser Valley. Descending on the other side, the walk passes through the newly-created Colony Farm Park, crossing the Coquitlam River near its conjunction with the Fraser River. This area, which used to provide vegetables for Riverview Hospital, is now a bird sanctuary with great walking and biking trails. The walk concludes by climbing up to Mundy Park, offering broad views of the Fraser Valley along the way.

**Getting there:** If using transit, take the #701 Haney Place bus and get off at the first bus stop east of the Pitt River Bridge. A #158 bus at 8:25 a.m. on Saturday from Braid Station will connect at Coquitlam Station with the #701 bus.

If driving, park near the intersection of Austin Avenue and Hickey Drive. Take a #152 bus from the south side of Austin Avenue to Coquitlam Station, transfer to the #701 Haney Place bus and get off at the first stop over the Pitt River Bridge. A bus at 8:33 a.m. on Saturday takes about 40 minutes.

## Pitt River Bridge East 0 km 0 hr B76

Walk back from the bus stop and, at the traffic signals, take the road on the left which goes behind the service station visible ahead. Continue west on this road past the service station until a road marked No Through Road appears on the right. Follow this towards the dike, turn right to reach the highway embankment and then turn left to the river edge. Now go under both spans of the bridge and come up steps on the far side to the footpath on the bridge. (You now retrace the Fraser River walk from Pitt River Road, F61, for the first hour or so.)

Cross the river and turn right on the far side to follow the paved trail that leads down and under the bridge. This path leads under both spans and comes out again on the dike on the south side. The ferry to Pitt Meadows used to leave from here before the bridge was built.

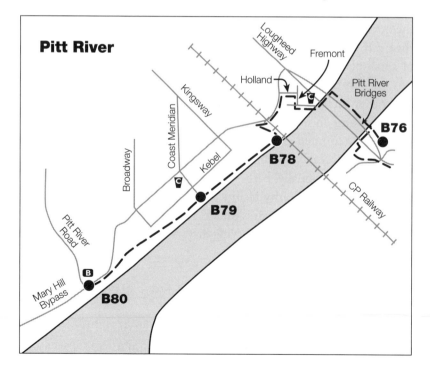

Beyond this point, a sawmill blocks further passage on the dike, and the path leaves the dike for Kingsway Avenue. Turn right at the first road, Fremont Street, and follow it almost back to the highway; an inn, pub and restaurant is on the right. Turn left along Holland Avenue and follow the path as it leads left to a sidewalk passing under the railway. When I use this, I recall the many times in the past when there was no sidewalk, and it was necessary to take your chances on the road surface, facing the oncoming trucks in a two-lane tunnel. At the far side, follow the sidewalk until the railing on the left ends. Then take the road on the left back towards the railway and pick up a trail leading through the poplar trees to the dike.

| **South Dike** | 2.1 km | 0 hr 33 m | B78 |
|---|---|---|---|

Follow the dike with its views to the long row of poplar trees lining the far side of the river; poplar is the principal tree you will see for the next hour or so. Pitt Meadows is on the opposite side, and beyond the nearby meadows is Pitt Meadows Airport. You may well see signs of small-plane activity on a fine weekend afternoon. Pitt Meadows was once in the top three airports in Canada for landings, ahead of Vancouver International Airport. This is because pilots who are training may come in many times in an afternoon, practising their landings. If they counted every bump, it would be even more! In about 20 minutes, you reach a yellow barred gate. This is Coast Meridian Road. Very occasionally, barges moor here while receiving heavy cargoes trucked from nearby facilities. There are benches to use if you have brought your own refreshments along. Also, just inland by the fuel pump area, a restaurant serving drivers of inter-city trucks is open weekdays from an early hour.

| **Coast Meridian Road** | 1.1 km | 0 hr 17 m | B79 |
|---|---|---|---|

When you are ready to resume, return to the dike. I find continuous dike walking becomes tiring on the back and legs, apart from being a little monotonous. I therefore prefer to drop down to a small dirt path that winds along the river edge below. This provides a change in pace, is out of any wind, and is in shade on a hot day. However, it can be muddy, and on a cool day you may prefer any sun there is to be had. If that is your preference, be like most people and stay on the dike. On the right are the rears of buildings of the industrial park. Where they end, the dike bends away from the river and leads out to a road with a few stores, just before the traffic signals at Pitt River Road. These include a bar, with a beer and wine store, which may be open in the late morning or afternoon. Many years ago I bought a salmon from a fishboat at a dock at the foot of Pitt River Road, but the dock is long gone. (Buses stop just up Pitt River Road; the Fraser River route joins from the south at F61).

## Pitt River Road          1.2 km    0 hr 19 m    B80

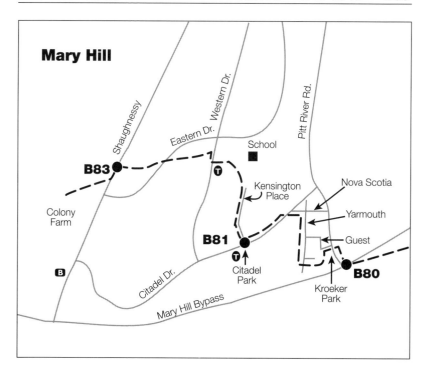

The walk now goes up to Mary Hill to see the community and to enjoy the views over the Fraser Valley and the mountains to the north. Mary Hill was originally treed but from the surrounding countryside, it now looks to some as a scar on the landscape. I used to see it in this light myself. However, a walk through the community opens one's eyes to the walks and parks that the residents enjoy, and changes one's conception of the place.

## Mary Hill

With the discovery of gold in the Fraser and the influx of 20,000 American miners, the Imperial Government became anxious that that the territories not be lost to the Americans. In 1858, the Colonial Secretary dispatched the Royal Engineers, commanded by Colonel Richard Clement Moody, with instructions to locate, survey and lay out a site for the colonial capital. Colonel Moody's first choice was Mary Hill, at the junction of the Pitt, Coquitlam and Fraser Rivers. He ordered Captain Jack Grant to cut the first tree on the site. Grant was in the very act of swinging his axe when, so much impressed with the mistake they were making, he said to the colonel, "With much submission, I will ask you not to do it. Will you yourself be pleased to take the responsibility of making the first cut?" He gave his reasons, one of which was that a lower site, being at the head of tidewater, could be reached by big ships. Another was that the lower site was easily defensible, with Mary Hill as its upstream citadel. Colonel Moody was convinced. He travelled downriver and ordered the first cut to be delivered on one of the huge cedars with which the hill was covered. He named the place Queensborough—now New Westminster.

*Source: British Columbia Year Book 1897, by R. E. Gosnell. Quoted in part in History of Our City—Port Coquitlam, by Edith Chambers. Burnaby: B. A. Thompson, 1973.*

Cross the Mary Hill Bypass over to the service station, go briefly up Pitt River Road, and turn first left along a small lane just past the service station. Turn left at its end down Guest Street into Marian Kroeker Park. Follow the small path across to the children's playground area behind the service station and backing onto the bypass. Continue past the play area, crossing a wooden bridge, and come out to a footpath leading to Yarmouth Street. Turn right and follow Yarmouth Street up the hill, turning left at the top into Nova Scotia Street. Take the set of steps that leads up past a church serving the congregations of the Mary Hill Baptist Church and the Coquitlam Chinese Baptist Church. Turn left at the top of the steps and follow Citadel Drive up for two blocks to reach Citadel Park. Take the blacktop path straight ahead and follow it as it spirals left to reach a viewpoint with seats. This is a high point on Mary Hill, named after Colonel Moody's wife, Mary Susanna. The long sloping hill that you can see in the south east is that of Iron Mountain. The large mass in the north is Burke Mountain; below, on its right-hand side at the foot, lie the humps of Minnekhada. Across the Pitt River valley to the right of Minnekhada lie the boundary hills of the Malcolm Knapp Research Forest in Maple Ridge. (The next green space a little further on has washrooms.)

| **Citadel Park** | 1.4 km | 0 hr 22 m | B81 |
|---|---|---|---|

Cross to Kensington Crescent opposite and follow it up to its end and onto the footpath leading out into the adjacent park. Take the blacktop path on the right and follow it on its way to Hazel Terembeth School. It then curves to the left and reaches a small lake, which may warn of thin ice at certain times of year. The picnic tables and toilets by the lake make this a good spot for lunch.

Now follow the path up the small rise and come down on the other side to the road. Cross the road carefully and continue north, passing under some transmission lines. (About one minute further along this road, the half-hourly #C36 bus goes down into Port Coquitlam.) Take the trail which appears very quickly on the left and follow it down to Eastern Drive. The flatlands of Colony Farm are now starting to appear. When traffic allows, cross the road and go slightly downhill to find a steeper and much less formal trail dropping down to Shaughnessy Street. Go downhill on the other side of the road to the parking turnout which you can see. (To stop here, go five minutes further on the road to reach a bus stop for a half-hourly #159 southbound bus to New Westminster, or a northbound #159 bus to Port Coquitlam.)

**Citadel Park Arbour on Mary Hill**

# Colony Farm

In 1903, the provincial government set aside 1,000 acres for a Hospital for the Mind, with an associated farm to provide activities for the patients. Land-clearing began in 1905, and construction crews finished the first permanent building, later known as West Lawn, in 1909. In 1913, the government renamed the institution Essondale after then-provincial secretary Henry Essen Young and, more recently, renamed it Riverview Mental Hospital.

The wide range of agricultural activities benefited from the farm's location on some of the best soil in the province. Cows supplied milk, some of which went directly to the hospital and the balance to a dairy which processed it into butter and cheese. A butcher shop prepared meat from the farm's cattle; pigs were sent to New Westminster for slaughter. Sheep did not arrive until 1960. Clydesdale horses ploughed fields and hauled goods. The farm grew corn for silage, hay, vegetables, apples and cherries. The farm's products won agricultural awards across Canada.

An arch over the entrance road bore the name Colony Farm. The farm had a dining room and kitchen to feed the workers, cottages for married couples and bunkhouses for single men. Hospital patients who helped on the farm earned pocket money to buy chocolate or extras.

As treatment methods for mental illness changed, the farm became less needed for therapy and the government closed it in 1985. The site became the object of much speculation. Different interest groups proposed a new Pacific National Exhibition, destination casino or golf course. In 1996 the land was transferred to the Greater Vancouver Regional District as a park.

*Source: Coquitlam, Reflections of the Past 100 Years, Coquitlam, BC: District of Coquitlam, 1990.*

**Historic Silo on Colony Farm**

## Shaughnessy Street     1.2 km     0 hr 15 m     B83

Walk down the path to the flatlands below. On the left you will see the remains of fences and an old silo that used to serve Colony Farm. Continuing on the trail for just under 10 minutes, you reach an intersection with a garbage container. If you were to turn right and follow the trail (keeping left at each fork), you would keep the Coquitlam River on your left and reach Port Coquitlam in about an hour. However, turn left today and follow the trail to a footbridge over the river.

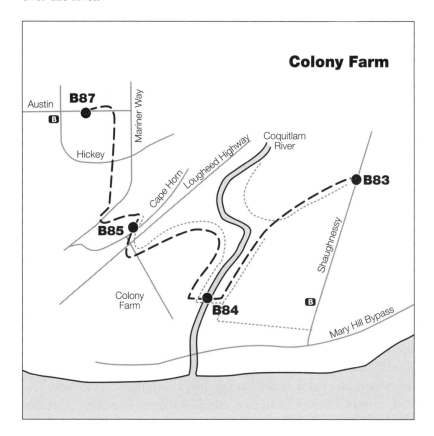

## Coquitlam Footbridge      1.2 km    0 hr 17 m    B84

Cross the river and turn right on the dike. As you get further north, you may be lucky enough to see mountains on the right. The highest is Golden Ears, with Edge Mountain on its right, then the pronounced triangle of Blanshard's Needle, followed by the long declining slope from Alouette Mountain. The dike path ends at a small parking lot at the Lougheed Highway entrance of Colony Farm Park. Cross Lougheed Highway to Cape Horn Road on the other side. The road here leads up into Riverview.

## Cape Horn      1.6 km    0 hr 23 m    B85

The route continues on an old, but now overgrown, paved road that switchbacks up the hill from Cape Horn Road, almost immediately after it starts going into Riverview from the Lougheed Highway. Follow this up—it can be slippery at the switchback corner when wet leaves cover the paved surface. The road leads out to a metal transmission tower at the top. Here you scramble up the bank to the main road at the top—Mariner Way. Vehicles have a habit of charging rapidly down around the hidden corner from above, but when you feel safe, cross here. Go briefly right and find a path coming down from the bank above.

Follow this path as it makes its way up the grassy, cleared swath. You will note that a transmission line occupies the right-hand side of the swath. The left-hand side holds a natural-gas pipeline, although this is not visible, since it is underground. Where the path forks into two, take the left-hand one and follow the gas pipeline right-of-way up the hill. Do not take all the time watching your feet; stop occasionally and enjoy the views behind. The fields of the Fraser Valley lie below and Mt. Baker in the United States dominates the skyline. The path crosses Hickey Road and continues until it meets the major Austin Road, with traffic signals to the right and a chain-link fence on the hill across the road.

Turn left, cross the road at the next intersection, and continue on the other side to reach Gate No. 9 of Mundy Park.

## Mundy Park Gate   1.9 km  0 hr 28 m  B87

**Getting home:** Two blocks west of the gate, the westbound #152 bus goes to Lougheed Town Centre Station for connections throughout the region.

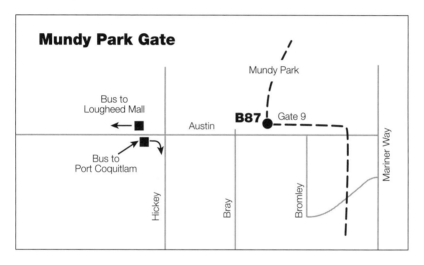

# Mundy Park to Burnaby Lake Park

Today's 13-km (8-mile) walk goes through the quiet forests of Mundy Park and down one of the many largely unexplored ravines that typify the landscape above Port Moody. I would be surprised if more than one or two per cent of the people who use busy St. Johns Street have ever seen these magnificent canyons. The walk makes its way back up the ravined hillside again to Miller Park and crosses to reach the lower slopes of Burnaby Mountain and follow Stoney Creek to reach the entrance to Burnaby Lake Park.

**Getting there:** If using transit, take the #152 bus (it passes Lougheed Town Centre Station) and get off at Austin Avenue and Hickey Drive. Walk one block east on the north side of Austin Avenue to reach Gate 9 of Mundy Park.

If driving, go to Avalon Avenue on Cariboo Road, just south of Government Road and just north of Exit 37 of the Trans-Canada Highway. Go along Avalon Avenue to Burnaby Lake Park's parking lot. Walk back along Avalon Avenue to the bus stop on the other side of Cariboo Road. Take the #101 bus to Lougheed Town Centre and transfer to the #152 bus, getting off at Austin Avenue and Hickey Drive. Walk one block east to Gate 9 of the park. A bus at 8:50 a.m. on Saturday takes 20 to 25 minutes.

## Mundy Park Gate                0 km    0 hr    B87

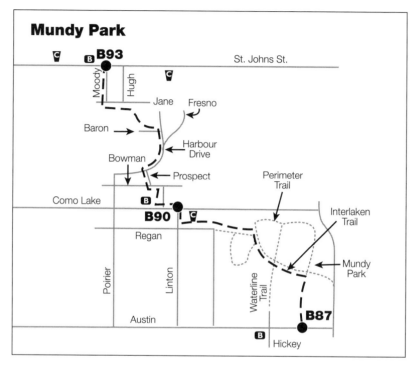

For the next half-hour, you walk through a typical West Coast cedar and hemlock forest. The walk starts on the bark-mulch Austin Trail, joins Perimeter Trail and reaches the major Interlaken Trail, which crosses the park. Turn left and follow this trail through the middle of the forest, cross Waterline Trail and Mundy Lake becomes visible on the left. You can detour down to see it or take a refreshment break, if you have brought something with you. Where Interlaken Trail meets Perimeter Trail again, turn left and where you meet School Trail, go right. Do not turn off on Nitinat Trail, neither to the left nor to the right, but continue until School Trail emerges at a school. Follow Regan Avenue west to Linton Avenue and turn right. The shopping centre on the right at the main road has some coffee shops—one being the store nearest you.

## Como Lake Avenue          2.8 km      0 hr 41 m      B90

Cross the main road, go one block east, then right onto St. Laurence Street, left onto Bowman Avenue, right onto Prospect Street and right to go down Harbour Drive. Cross to the left side of the road and continue down the hill until the little stub road of Baron Place appears on the left. It doesn't look as if it goes through, but try it and you will find a trail out of the far end on the right. The occupant of the house at the top keeps both sides of the trail neatly gardened, and you may find daffodils, hyacinths or hydrangeas out, depending on the season. The trail now leads down a ridge with views of both sides of the wild ravines where the water flows down into Burrard Inlet. It is fascinating to find such wildness near the urban centre of Port Moody.

# Port Moody

In 1859, a group of citizens named their town Port Moody, after Colonel Moody, who came to British Columbia in 1858 to develop roads into the interior of the province. One of the early settlers was John Murray, who eventually owned about half the town. His son John named many of the streets after family members; for example, John, George, William, Mary, Henry and James.

Canadian Pacific Railway selected Port Moody as its western terminus in 1879. The first passenger train to cross the continent arrived from Montreal in 1886 at the old station building located by Rocky Point Park. The locomotive of this train, after its retirement, delighted generations of children, who swarmed over it in Kitsilano Park. It is now in the Roundhouse on False Creek.

*Sources: The Canadian Encyclopedia. Edmonton: Hurtig, 1988; and "Port Moody," by J. Whitney in The Greater Vancouver Book, edited by Chuck Davis. Vancouver: Linkman*

**Historic Trans-Continental Railway Terminus, Port Moody**

227

Where the trail comes to a join, do not take the right-hand turn, but continue straight on down the somewhat steeper gullied trail ahead to reach a small park where dogs may run unleashed. Follow the trail out to reach Jane Street at the south end of Hugh Street, turn left along Jane for one block and follow down Moody Street to St. Johns Street—the major street of Port Moody. You can catch a bus if you want to stop here; you can walk one or two blocks west or east to find a coffee shop. If you would like a short detour, you can continue on Moody Street over the railway and look at the historic railway terminal below on the other side.

### St. Johns Street                     2.6 km    0 hr 49 m    B93

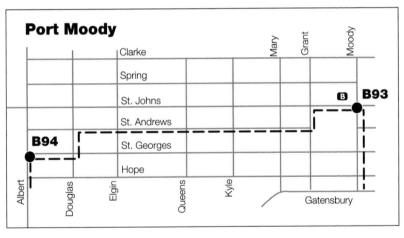

Because of the ravined nature of the hillside above Port Moody, any attempt to head west on its streets leads to roller-coaster ups and downs, these becoming larger the higher up the hillside you try to go. I find St. Johns Street too busy for enjoyable walking, so my usual route west is to follow St. Johns Street for only one block past the school, and then dodge south one block to St. Andrews Street. This continues most of the way through, but comes to an end just before Albert Street. At Douglas Street, I therefore go one more block south to St. George Street and continue to Albert Street.

## Albert Street                    1.6 km    0 hr 22 m    B94

Go south up the hill and reach a school on the right. At the end of the road, go past the gate onto the path and follow it right. Go past the back of the school towards Hillside Park, reach an opening in the chain-link fence and go up the steps on the left. These lead up to the north end of Blue Mountain Street in Coquitlam. Turn first right onto Sirmac and follow it around; then turn first right again onto Stardale to reach Oakview and find the entrance to Miller Park. Head towards the rustic arch ahead, bear left and follow the treed edge around to the bleachers by the ball ground.

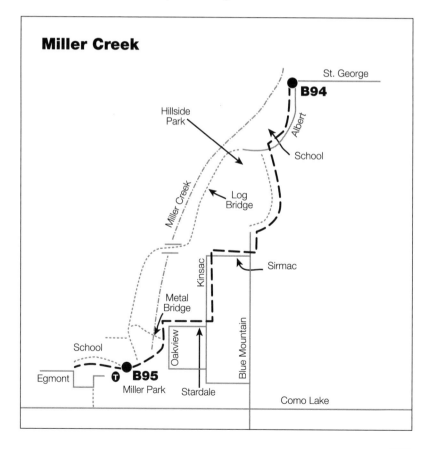

**Miller Creek**

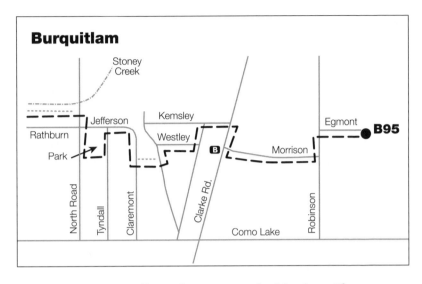

You can rest in Miller Park, sitting on the bleachers. If you want a refreshment break, you can use the half table by the ball-ground fence for a picnic table; there is a portable toilet a little further along the path towards the school.

## Miller Park                                1.0 km    0 hr 20 m    B95

Follow the path out, keeping south of the school, go into Egmont Avenue on the other side of the road, and reach Robinson Street. Jog left and then right to follow Morrison Avenue to Clarke Road. Buses go south to Lougheed Mall or north to Port Moody, if you want to stop now. To continue, cross the road at the pedestrian signal just to the north—it will probably change almost as soon as you press the button. Enter Kemsley Avenue, the street on the other side. Take the first left and, almost immediately, go right down Westley Avenue. You are now starting to drop down into the valley of Stoney Creek, with the forested slopes of Burnaby Mountain visible on the right. At the end of Westley Avenue, jog a couple of houses left, and then turn right down the footpath between numbers 643 and 645. Turn right at the bottom, and at Tyndall Street, jog left to drop down through

Tyndall Park and turn right on North Road at the bottom. A sign on the right indicates the presence of Stoney Creek, a salmon-bearing stream. Almost opposite the sign, a wide path leads west behind the houses of Rathburn Drive, with the forests of the lower slopes of Burnaby Mountain lining the far side of the creek. Soon a small weir with stepping stones appears on the right. A network of trails connects here with the top of Burnaby Mountain.

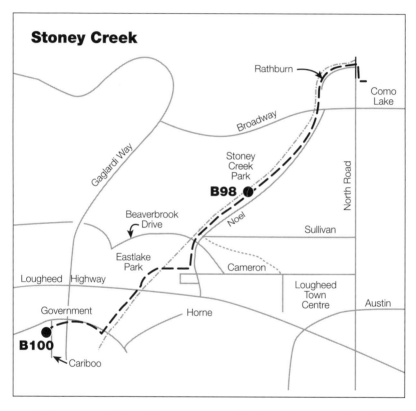

Follow the wide path on, pass under Broadway and continue, with the backs of houses on the left and Stoney Creek on the right. Soon you reach a notice board in Stoney Creek Park. The Burrard-Fraser Connection joins here (BF7). The trail on the left goes up to the nearby street.

## Stoney Creek Park 2.8 km 0 hr 40 m B98

Continue south on the wide track as it leads to Beaverbrook Drive. Turn left for one block and go right on Noel Drive to Cameron Street. Turn right and continue as the sidewalk leads off right, passing by a white post to a footpath and a bridge crossing Stoney Creek. At the foot of the hill, bend sharp left onto Burrard Fraser Greenway and follow it as it passes under Lougheed Highway and emerges onto Government Road. Turn right to the traffic signals, cross and go briefly up Cariboo Road to reach the entrance of Burnaby Lake Park on the right.

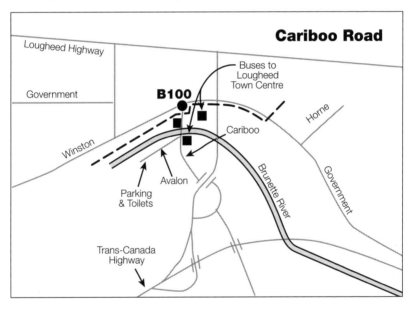

## Cariboo Road 2.3 km 0 hr 33 m B100

**Getting home:** A bus heading north on Cariboo Road at Avalon Avenue goes to Lougheed Town Centre Station. Or you can walk north to Government Road where two bus routes go to the station.

# Burnaby Lake to Renfrew Ravine

Today's 14½-km (9-mile) walk explores the shores of Burnaby Lake, with its expanse of reeds and water lilies. It continues past Burnaby City Hall, reaches Deer Lake and passes through the grounds of the former Oakalla Prison, where Pauline Johnson's Legend of Deer Lake may be read on the steps on the way up to Metrotown. The route passes through Central Park to reach the Renfrew Ravine.

If using transit, take the #101 bus (one passes Lougheed Town Centre Station on Saturday at 9:10 a.m.) to Cariboo Road.

If driving, park near 29th Avenue Station; take SkyTrain to Lougheed Town Centre Station and transfer to the #101 bus; get off at Cariboo Road. Allow 35 minutes for waiting, travelling on SkyTrain and transferring, and 5 minutes for the bus travel.

## Cariboo Road                    0 km    0 hr    B100

Enter the park from Cariboo Road and meet a picnic table almost immediately, located at the Cariboo Dam at the outlet of the lake; another one is available in about half an hour at Piper Spit. The river from the outlet of the lake is the Brunette, which drains into the Fraser River west of Fraser Mills and east of Patullo Bridge.

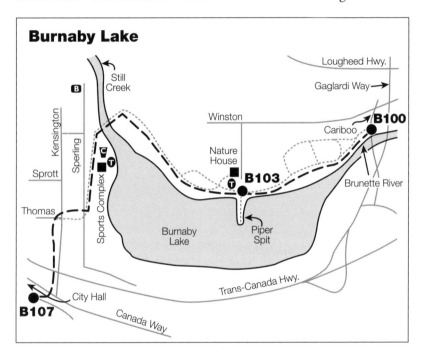

The main trail to Piper Spit is called Brunette Headwaters Trail. As you follow it along the north side of the lake, loop trails lead off to the right, but if you keep closer to the lake, you may catch the occasional glimpse of rowers or herons and you will be as far as you can get from the noise of the railway.

In about half an hour, you reach an open area; a Nature House on the right is open on summer weekends. Picnic tables and toilets lie behind the Nature House. To the left, a path leads down to Piper Spit, an impressive viewpoint. The walkway leads out onto the lake, where you can see the water lilies and yellow irises, and appreciate the size of the lake—something you cannot do from the trail.

**Wetlands of Burnaby Lake**

## Piper Spit       2.0 km     0 hr 28 m     B102

After the break, continue on Cottonwood Trail between the lake and the railway until it ends with a left turn to cross a bridge. Here you are passing over Still Creek, one of the major streams leading into Burnaby Lake. One glance will confirm that its name is correct; it is also wide and shallow. The creek rises near Central Park and you pass its much smaller headwaters later in this set of walks.

The path leads to a parking lot; follow its edge to reach the clubhouse seen ahead. This building has washrooms and the bar on the upper floor is open at 11 a.m. on weekends. If you want to stop walking here, go up the hill opposite and Sperling Station is to the right.

Continue on the path beyond the clubhouse until it ends, and turn right at the white barred gate onto Sperling Avenue. Now jog

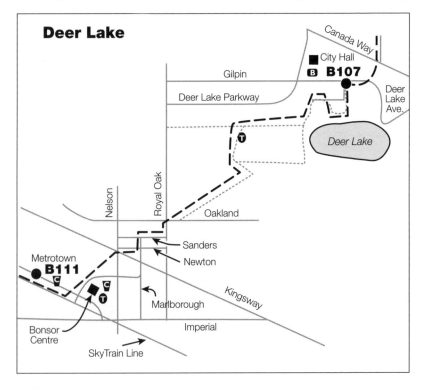

briefly left and then right to find a bark-mulch fitness loop. Go past Stop 5 Chin Up, past Stop 6 Step Up, and find a minor trail on the right at the corner before Stop 7 Push Up. This minor track leads out to Kensington Avenue, opposite Thomas Street. Cross the busy street when there is a gap in the traffic and follow the sidewalk south over the Trans-Canada Highway, carefully navigating the off ramp from the highway and continue to the traffic signal at Canada Way.

# Ceperley House

Grace Ceperley was the chatelaine of Ceperley House, with a sister who was married to a Mr. Ferguson. Mr. Ferguson had given money to help with the establishment of Stanley Park, and Ferguson Point in that park was named to recognize his benevolence. The Ceperley house was built in 1910 at a final cost equivalent to about $10 million in today's currency. As construction costs mounted, the Ceperley budget became strapped, so Mr. Ferguson gave Grace money to enable the project to be completed. His condition was that if any money ever became available from the house, it was to go to Stanley Park. When the 1922 owner of the house sold it, the proceeds went to create Ceperley Playground in Stanley Park.

In 1939, Benedictine monks from Oregon bought the house, built up the order and bought a neighbouring property which included the Seminary of Christ the King. By 1953 they had achieved the status of an abbey and in 1954 they moved to establish Westminster Abbey in Mission. The Canadian Temple of the More Abundant Life bought the property and was succeeded by other groups until the property was bought by Burnaby as a Centennial project in 1967.

*Source: "Visual Arts Burnaby." Gallery at Ceperley House, Burnaby, BC: 1999.*

At the traffic signal, cross and head right up the grass to reach Deer Lake Avenue. Follow it to the right, going up the hill, and turn left where a sign indicates Ceperley House. (If you want to end here, continue on Deer Lake Avenue and where it drops down, take the first path off on the right and walk out to the bus loop at Burnaby City Hall.)

## Burnaby City Hall    4.6 km  1 hr 6 m  B107

Follow the road, passing a chain intended to discourage drivers from taking their vehicles further down towards the lake. Ceperley House, on the immediate left, accommodates one of Burnaby's art galleries. The Shadbolt Centre of the Arts, seen across the grass to the left as you drop down to the lake, serves local performing groups.

Follow the trail to the water's edge, passing a children's playground with a yellow tower on the left. At the lake, turn right. You can see the towers of Metrotown across Deer Lake and the grassy slopes of the old Oakalla Prison; you climb through this area later today. Soon the path has to leave the lakeside because of private houses with land stretching down to the lake's edge. Where the path leads out to a road, turn left and head down to the park, which can be seen below. Follow this path around left as it makes its way to rejoin the lake. A notice tells you that the trail can be wet and soft in inclement weather; I can vouch for this, as I once found it under 50 cm of water and had to turn back. When you reach the lake, the trail turns west to reach the north west corner, where there is a crossing of trails. Choose the trail which goes straight on, and follow it for about five minutes to the first trail on the left. Turn left and make your way to the structure that you can see on the hill beyond the flats in front of you. There is a portable toilet en route, opposite an area for flying model airplanes.

When you reach the structure, go to the lookout if the weather is clear. The two peaks of the Lions are clearly identifiable to the left. Hollyburn Ridge is to their left. Then, moving right, Capilano Canyon separates the ridge from the peaks of Grouse Mountain, Crown Mountain and Mount Fromme. Then Lynn Canyon separates these from the pointed Lynn Peak, with Coliseum Peak and others behind it. The Seymour River now separates these from the ridge which contains the evident three peaks of Mount Seymour. Indian Arm provides a major separation from Eagle Ridge in the background behind Burnaby Mountain. The distinct mountain further east is that of Mount Coquitlam. Finally, the range over Deer Lake has a long sloping hill on its right which leads up left to the flat ridge of Alouette Mountain. Continuing left, the sharp peak is Blanshard's Needle; then comes Edge Mountain and the high peak is that of Golden Ears.

Follow up the path, passing through the subdivision built on the grounds of the old Oakalla Prison. Round planters display daffodils, star magnolias and other flowers, depending on the season. You pass a playground on the left. Part-way up, an old terrace of stairs has been retained and a plaque summarizes the history of Oakalla. Going up these steps are plates which gradually tell Pauline Johnson's "Legend of Deer Lake." I am not going to spoil your pleasure by telling you the story—you will enjoy reading it yourself.

**Lookout at Deer Lake Park**

At the traffic signals at the top, cross both traffic streams and follow the wide path uphill. Turn first right on Sanders, left at Marlborough and right at Newton to come out at a major intersection. Metrotown is opposite. Again cross both traffic streams and follow the footpath to the left side of The Bay. Follow the footpath around and continue west and south to reach a road in front of the SkyTrain (Bonsor Centre on the left has a coffee shop and washrooms). Cross when the road is clear and turn right on the footpath under the SkyTrain structure (the first paved section is for bicycles) and continue to Metrotown Station. If you want a refreshment break, coffee shops are across the road on this stretch.

## Metrotown                4.2 km    1 hr 1 m    B111

Continue on SkyTrain's pedestrian walkway, known as the BC Parkway. Pass Patterson Station and enter Central Park. On this walk, you skirt the park's northern edge, but look south and enjoy the forest before you. There are lakes in the park and many people enjoy walking its trails. Where the walk reaches an open area, there are

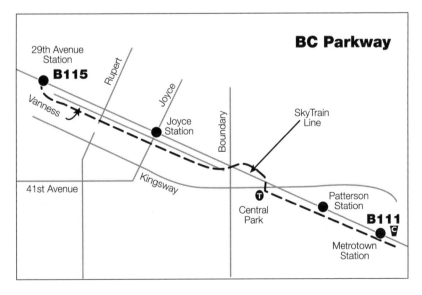

washrooms, which are usually open. From here, go north and cross the footbridge over Kingsway to the Telus office building. Spiral down the stairs to street level, turn left and left again and follow the lane at the back. Go up the ramp where it appears on the right and use the overpass to cross Boundary Road. From here, continue on the BC Parkway past Joyce Station to reach 29th Avenue Station.

**29th Avenue Station**          3.8 km     0 hr 54 m     B115

Getting home: SkyTrain provides connections throughout the region.

# Renfrew Ravine
# to Waterfront Station

Today's 12-km (7½-mile) walk follows Renfrew Ravine and Still Creek, cuts across to Beaconsfield Park by the Italian Cultural Centre, and enters John Hendry Park, with its view across Trout Lake. After crossing Broadway, it follows Commercial Drive, with its interesting mix of stores—the legacy of Italian settlement in 1957. This soon leads to an equally interesting walk through the district of Strathcona, past the oldest school in Vancouver, built in 1907, and the Italian cathedral of 1905. After the route goes through some historic parts of Chinatown and passes the gate of Dr. Sun Yat-Sen Park, it wends through the old part of Vancouver to the waterfront and back to Canada Place.

**Getting there:** If using transit, make your way to 29th Avenue Station. If driving, park near a SkyTrain station and travel to 29th Avenue Station.

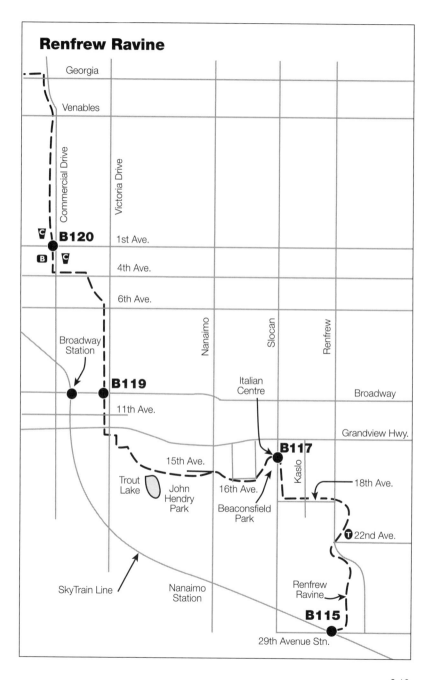

# Renfrew Ravine

Georgia

Venables

Commercial Drive

Victoria Drive

B120 · 1st Ave.

4th Ave.

6th Ave.

Nanaimo

Slocan

Renfrew

Broadway Station

B119

Italian Centre

Broadway

11th Ave.

Grandview Hwy.

15th Ave.

B117

Kaslo

18th Ave.

Trout Lake

John Hendry Park

16th Ave.

Beaconsfield Park

22nd Ave.

SkyTrain Line

Nanaimo Station

Renfrew Ravine

B115

29th Avenue Stn.

## 29th Avenue Station

0 km    0 hr    B115

Head out the north side of 29th Avenue Station, cross when the road is clear and look at the German Centre, the BC Parkway's recognition of the contribution of the German community to the life of Vancouver. Continue right and take a footpath which leads off on the left. Along its length, you can look left into Renfrew Ravine, Vancouver's largest ravine. The trails that lead down into the ravine are very wet and overgrown and it is better to stay on the top. The city has built viewing platforms and local community groups have built signs and decorative boxes. In about 10 minutes, the path comes out to the street. Follow the sidewalk down to the traffic signals and cross in both directions to the far corner. The Renfrew Community Centre has washrooms for use, if required.

Follow the path which leads down to the west side of the Community Centre and go down the steps to the edge of Still Creek in Renfrew Park. Follow the grassy trail, keeping the creek on the left all the way until it disappears into a tunnel. This is a quiet little oasis where you can see Still Creek's first appearance above ground. Then come up to Renfrew Street above, cross at the crosswalk and go briefly north to 18th Avenue. Go three blocks west, noting the Children's Hospital on the left as you go past. Turn right onto Slocan Street and take the footpath on the west side to Beaconsfield Park. If you have not visited the Italian Cultural Centre before, continue on Slocan Street, until the entrance, bearing the numbers 3075, appears on the left after the park. (If you want to miss the Centre, just cross the park to 16th Avenue on the far side.)

## Italian Cultural Centre

2.3 km    0 hr 32 m    B117

Turn left and go into the courtyard. A monument commemorates the fallen in the war—it bears the words Al Caduti per la Patria and Honoring the Fallen. The main building on the left opened in 1977. Following the walkway around, you will see a bistro straight ahead

**Still Creek in Renfrew Park**

and, in the window at its side, a highly decorated traditional Sicilian horse and cart. The Venetian gondola on the opposite side of the walkway is one of the few gondolas outside Venice and probably the only one in North America. It was built for Expo 86 and the Cultural Centre displays it here as a historic link between Vancouver's Italian community and the Immortal City of Venice. Continuing out of the building, go straight on across the outside space, walking towards and past the handicapped parking signs to pick up a trail, leading back to Beaconsfield Park. Then angle across the park to the middle of the far side to reach 16th Avenue. Go one block west on 16th Avenue and angle up right almost opposite to reach Nanaimo Street. Go to the traffic signals or find a gap in the busy traffic, cross and follow 15th Avenue down into John Hendry Park.

The house on the left as you enter the park has an overhanging trellis to hold grapes for winemaking. A number of Italian houses around here make similar use of their yards. The path continues on to pass a field house of the Little League Club and reach Trout Lake. Continue slightly right to follow the edge of the lake to reach a beach with an expansive view to the south. Trout Lake is shallow and, depending on the time of year, you may see mallards and Canada geese, or the lake may be frozen over. Now head away from the lake towards the far north west corner, picking up a bark-mulch path which leads to and along the top edge of the park. At the corner, go off to the lane and follow it to the day-care centre on the corner and come out to Victoria Drive. Walk north to the traffic signals, cross both traffic streams to the north west corner, and continue on the west side of the street. If you want to stop for the day, turn left at 11th Avenue for one block and continue to Broadway Station, two blocks to the right. If not, continue and reach the traffic signals at Broadway.

## Broadway                              1.8 km    0 hr 26 m    B119

Cross to the Tung Lin Kok Yuen Buddhist Temple opposite. Follow up to 6th Avenue, passing between historic houses on both sides of the street, and angle across McSpadden Park on the left. Head towards the day-care centre on the north side and take the northbound path out to 4th Avenue. Follow this west to reach Commercial Drive and walk along the east side of the street to the signals at 1st Avenue. You pass Olivieri's First Store with its cheeses and groceries. Other stores sell bread, meats, rabbits and produce and there are many opportunities to break for coffee. At 1st Avenue, cross both traffic streams to the north

# Italian Community at Commercial Drive

When Petronio Olivieri opened Olivieri's Ravioli Store at Commercial Drive and 3rd Avenue in 1957, there was little to suggest that Commercial Drive would eventually grow into the city's major Italian shopping area. The owner of an Italian shoe repair store a few doors south caught the attention of passers-by with puppet displays in the window. At the northern end, Nick's Spaghetti House attracted a generally non-Italian clientèle. Olivieri's intent was to make pasta for the Italian community concentrated between Main and Renfrew Streets. But he soon found out that the Italian immigrants preferred to make their own pasta at home, so as to save money to buy a house. However, they did want items such as parmesan cheese and Italian tomatoes. So Olivieri diversified and became the first Italian food store on Commercial Drive.

Little Italy boomed in the 1960s and 1970s, and then the Italian immigrants began settling in other parts of the region. Other nationalities moved in to give the area the more multicultural flavour that it now has, although the Italian influence is still evident in the names, such as Il Mercato at Commercial Drive and 1st Avenue.

*Source: Vancouver's Many Faces—Passport to the Cultures of a City, by Kevin Griffin. Vancouver: Whitecap Books, 1993.*

**Cheese Display on Commercial Drive**

west corner. A few metres north, a door leads into Il Mercato, where there are further coffee shops and washrooms. You can catch a bus on Commercial Drive if you want to stop here.

## 1st Avenue 1.1 km 0 hr 16 m B120

Walk the busy sidewalk of Commercial Drive north on the west side. Usually there will be many shoppers enjoying the wide variety of stores on both sides of the street. Half-way along the block, Grandview Park appears on the left with its Canadian Legion memorial to the soldiers who died in the two world wars. The diversity of stores begins to diminish between this park and the next signal lights at Venables Street. Cross this street and, in two blocks, reach the Raja Theatre at Georgia Street. This used to be the home of the Vancouver Little Theatre and then a home to Indian movies. Georgia Street leads west into a park, which you cross; there are washrooms here. Another short block leads to Clark Drive, which also has to be crossed (go to the signals or find a gap in traffic). On the other side, you enter an area of old historic, but well-maintained houses, starting with numbers 1224 to 1274 on the left. The playground of a school lies ahead, with a yellow wooden structure clearly visible behind. Jog briefly right and then left to enter Keefer Street and pass the school on the left. More historic Strathcona houses start to appear.

As you cross Glen Drive into the stub street ahead of you, turn back to look at the front of the school, which reads Seymour School and Public School 1907—it is the oldest still-existing school in Vancouver. Then continue to the end of the street.

## Keefer Bridge　　　　　　　1.9 km　　0 hr 27 m　　B122

Go under the totem arch and over the metal pedestrian railway bridge, taking the opportunity to look from the top at the surrounding district. The blue bulbous dome of the nearby Ukrainian Temple lies to the south west; the Raymur development to the north west was one of the last large Federal Government public-housing projects in Vancouver. Its planners intended that children in the development would make their way by roundabout streets to attend Seymour School but some children decided to try to cross the railway; after two boys were killed, the pedestrian bridge was built.

Go down the ramp on the west side and through the development to reach Keefer Street on the far side. In September 1905, the Italian community opened the Chiesa del Sacro Cuore—Catolica Romana (or Sacred Heart Church), the first Italian church in Vancouver and the second Roman Catholic Church after Holy Rosary Cathedral. In

**Seymour School, built in 1907**

the 1970s, a California artist painted a Garden of Eden scene on the wall behind the altar, showing God breathing life into Adam. The church now primarily serves a Korean congregation, rather than its Italian originators. The next building past the church on Keefer Street is a Native Catholic Centre.

Continue west on Keefer Street as it leads west into historic Chinatown. In one block, it reaches Hawks Avenue, which has been converted into a park corridor extending for three blocks to Prior Street. Going down one side and back the other makes an interesting detour.

Carrying on along Keefer Street, Maclean Park lies to the left and various old churches and schools appear in the next few blocks. Across Gore Avenue, produce stores and bustling restaurants flourish in this Chinatown shopping area. Across Main Street and half-way down the next block on the left, a Chinese market houses a variety of small stores and a food fair, where you can select dishes of rice and various toppings, all served with litres of green tea.

**Dr. Sun Yat-Sen Park**

Coming out of the market, go west to the corner, cross at the signals to the north side and then to the west and enter Dr. Sun Yat-Sen Park. This is a relaxing area for contemplation in the traditional Chinese scholars' tradition. You can make a short loop within the park and look at the balance of the soft feminine yin of the bamboo and the hard masculine yang of the rocks. Even the green water is designed to avoid the distraction of reflections.

### Dr. Sun Yat-Sen Park      1.5 km     0 hr 21 m    B124

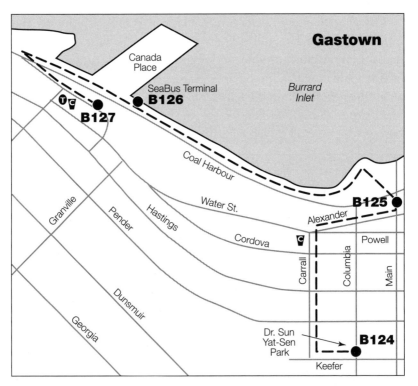

Coming out from the park, keep going right to go around the park, turn into Carrall Street and pass the entrance of Dr. Sun Yat-Sen Classical Chinese Gardens. These adjoin the park you have just visited and include buildings and rooms as well as gardens. If you decide to pay a visit some time, tour guides will explain the planning behind the gardens and the significance of the trees, plants and combinations used.

At the next street crossing, the Sam Kee Building on the near left corner is the narrowest building in the world and Ripley featured it in his Believe It Or Not!. When the city expropriated land for Pender Street, they left the owner with an uncompensated narrow strip. He was irate and determined to use the land anyhow. Also to the left, an entrance arch marking the western gate of Chinatown crosses Pender Street.

In the next block, the heritage office block of 425 Carrall Street was BC Electric Company's original home. The firm built it in 1912, used it for its headquarters and for the terminus of the interurban railway, which ran through the lobby until the late 1950s.

Crossing Hastings Street, you will see the small triangular Pigeon Park on the far side. Up to the 1920s, Canadian Pacific Railway moved traffic from the waterfront to its False Creek yards using a railway line which angled across here. You can see the gap between highrise buildings on the right; then Pigeon Park on the left and a slot back across the south side of Hastings Street. However, conflicts with vehicular traffic became too severe and the railway built a tunnel from the foot of Thurlow Street, going east generally under Dunsmuir Street. SkyTrain now uses this tunnel, deepened to carry two train lines, one above the other.

Crossing Cordova Street, you reach Water Street, a traffic circle and a statue of Gassy Jack. This is the focal point of Gastown, a historic area where old warehouses and structures have been restored as stores, restaurants, offices and homes. The triangular Hotel Europe lies on the corner between Alexander and Powell Streets.

The City plans to build a footbridge over the railway here but until they do, you should make your way round to the north side of Alexander Street and head east for two blocks, passing through the brothel area of the original city. You walk over a Working Harbour plaque inlaid in the sidewalk and reach the small Wendy Pool Park just before Main Street.

## Main Street Bridge     1.0 km     0 hr 14 m     B125

Cross to the far side of the Main Street bridge and use the sidewalk on the harbour side. You will see two Chinese lions adorning the bridge on the way over. When you can turn off right, drop down past a wharf with boats which serves the freighters that load and unload in the harbour. Entering Portside Park, follow generally along the water's edge and reach a small pier that lets you take a look up and down the working waterfront. Now make your way back to the harbour's service road, passing the parking area for buses providing local tours for cruise-ship passengers and another area for visiting cars. Carry along the edge of the road and reach the waterside terminal of the SeaBus.

## SeaBus Terminal     1.1 km     0 hr 15 m     B126

I have to tell you that I go in the door marked for heliport users and go up the escalator to the concourse of Waterfront Station. There I buy my ticket home, having temporarily passed through the area saying Fare Paid Zone only. Heliport users and a number of SeaBus users come in and out of the terminal doors at the waterfront road level. However, it is against the rules and the official way is to carry on for another 500 metres until the road comes down from the end of Burrard Street, then walk back up it to Canada Place. That is what you should do.

## Canada Place     0.9 km     0 hr 15 m     B127

**Getting home:** SkyTrain from Waterfront Station connects to all points in the region.

# Side
# Trips

UP BURNABY MOUNTAIN

DOWN TO PORT MOODY

BURRARD-FRASER CONNECTION

# Up Burnaby Mountain

This 12-km (7½-mile) walk crosses the Second Narrows, offering long views down the Inlet towards Admiralty Point, Ioco and Port Moody. A wooded path leads along the south shore of the Inlet to emerge on Hastings Street by Kensington Park and the Shellburn Oil Refinery. From here, the route makes its way up Burnaby Mountain to the top. The panoramic view over Vancouver and Burrard Inlet provides a scenic backdrop to the dramatic Ainu aboriginal Japanese totem poles. Joe's Trail leads to Simon Fraser University, offering a tour through the heart of the campus before reaching the bus exchange for the return home.

**Getting there:** If using transit, take a bus to Phibbs Exchange by the Second Narrows.

If driving, you can park at SFU at pay-parking near the bus stop and free parking further away. Or you may prefer to park for free at Phibbs Exchange at the start and catch the bus back at the end of the walk. If you choose to park at SFU, a #135 bus at 8:45 a.m. on Saturday will connect at Kootenay Loop with a #28 bus which stops at the street edge there and goes to Phibbs Exchange by 9:30 a.m.

## Phibbs Exchange  0 km  0 hr  BM0

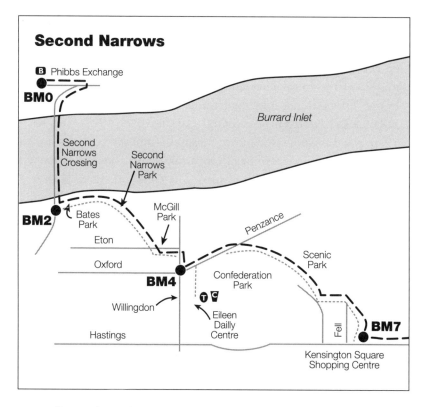

Walk east from the bus exchange (B24 of the Burrard Loop), travelling along the north side of Main Street to a signed pedestrian underpass leading south to the sidewalk of the off-ramp from the bridge. Cross over the bridge, enjoying the view eastward down the Inlet. The rail bridge below is used by Canadian National Railway to serve the North Shore. It connects with the rest of the rail system through a tunnel under Burnaby Mountain. The nearby chemical plant on the north side supplies chemicals used by the pulp mills along the coast.

At the far side of the bridge, turn off left into Fellowes Street, with Bates Park appearing on the left.

257

# Second Narrows

The Second Narrows crossing has been dogged by accidents. In 1923, the builders of a proposed new bridge removed an island known as Hwa-Hwoi-Hwoi (or Island of Evil Spirits) from the middle of the Inlet. They completed the work and opened the bridge for both rail and road traffic in November 1925. The motor vessel *Eurana* hit the central span in March 1927. Early in 1930, the *Losman* crashed into the southernmost fixed span and carried it away. In September 1930, a steel barge, *Pacific Gatherer,* became jammed under a fixed span. The rising tide lifted both it and the span, which toppled and sank. The Vancouver Harbour Commission purchased the bankrupt bridge company and reconstructed the bridge, ready for operation again in November 1934.

Increasing rail and road traffic demanded a new crossing, and construction of a new facility started in 1956. During construction, the collapse of one of the arms killed 18 men. This event is commemorated by a small cairn at the south end. A plaque on the memorial notes that the bridge, opened in 1960, is now known officially as the Ironworkers' Memorial Second Narrows Crossing.

*Sources: **A History of the City and District of North Vancouver,** by K.M. Woodward-Reynolds. Vancouver: UBC Thesis, 1943, and **The Greater Vancouver Book,** edited by Chuck Davis. Vancouver: Linkman Press, 1997.*

| **Bates Park** | 1.8 km | 0 hr 26 m | BM2 |
|---|---|---|---|

Take the trail that leads between posts, right at the start of the park. This passes along the north edge of the park and comes out onto a wide path which leads eastwards through the trees. This is the route of the Trans Canada Trail as it makes its way to and from downtown Vancouver. The route now continues through Burnaby's Second Narrows Park, with the main line of the Canadian Pacific Railway invisible below it, and occasional glimpses over the Inlet to the North Shore beyond.

The trail comes out into McGill Park, with the Chevron refinery on the left behind a chain-link fence. At first following the fence, the trail angles across to reach Eton Street, crosses it and continues on the far side. Follow the trail to Willingdon Avenue, cross when safe and continue uphill to Penzance Street.

## Willingdon Avenue               2.0 km     0 hr 28 m     BM4

Turn left very briefly to where a trail leads left into the trees. Here you have three choices for a refreshment break. You may detour south to the Eileen Dailly Fitness Centre by carefully crossing Penzance Street and following the footpath opposite through Confederation Park to the first building you reach. It has a swimming pool, washrooms, and refreshments available from vending machines.

The second choice is to go down the path through the trees. There are seats with viewpoints over the harbour, the chemical plants and ship-repair facilities. The trail returns to Penzance Street a little further east. This detour offers a good spot for a break, but it involves a drop down, crossing a swath containing a Chevron refinery pipeline right-of-way, and then a fairly steep climb back up on the return trip.

The third choice is to head to the other side of Penzance Street to the picnic tables in Confederation Park.

After your refreshment, if any, continue east along Penzance Street and take a trail when it appears on the opposite side of the street. This leads uphill and passes through a forest of tall maple trees. In the late fall and winter, the trail is relatively light with the absence of leaves. In summer, the sun streams attractively through the green foliage. Occasionally a path or road leads down from streets on the hill above. At its end, turn left and take the path over the grass by a pumping station to reach Fell Avenue. Now take the footpath on the opposite side of the street, and follow it with the Shellburn oil refinery lands on the left and the backs of houses on the right, and come out onto Hastings Street.

## Hastings Street    2.9 km    0 hr 48 m    BM7

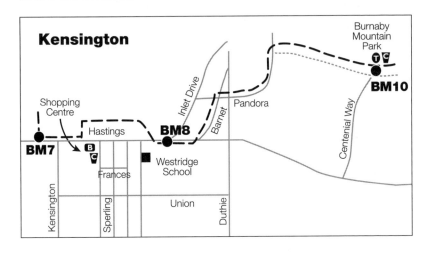

Turn left and follow down to the traffic signals. (You can catch a bus here. If you want a refreshment break, Kensington Square Shopping Centre opposite has several coffee shops.) At the Shell service station, go left and find a trail round the back of the stores; this is marked as Trans Canada Trail. Follow it round as far as you can and eventually emerge on Hastings Street further east. Continue on the sidewalk until a footbridge crosses the road. Take it and come down to the intersection of Hastings Street with Inlet Drive.

## Inlet Drive    1.0 km    0 hr 15 m    BM8

Cross the Hastings Street extension that leads up to Simon Fraser University and turn left at the first intersection—Barnet Road. After one block, head up the Pandora Street hill on the right. This climbs through a subdivision with houses on both sides and curves left along Pandora Drive at the top. At its end, head into the trail on the right and follow it up, avoiding a trail on the left which leads down, and avoiding later alternative trails on the right. When you reach the open grassy area, keep close to the fence to reach the top.

**Ainu Sculptures in Burnaby Mountain Park**

Here, 400 metres above sea level, in Burnaby Mountain Park are the famous Ainu sculptures, the Sculpture Garden, a Rose Garden and a restaurant, with public washrooms under the restaurant building. The scenic view all over the Inlet and out to sea offered from this spot is the prime reason for making the side trip. From the fence you can see Burrard Inlet and up Indian Arm. Burnaby and Vancouver lie spread out before you. On a clear day, you can see over the Gulf Islands to the high peaks of Vancouver Island.

# Kamui Mintara:
# Playground of the Gods

Naburi Toko and his son Shusei carved these wooden sculptures in 1990. The Tokos are members of the Ainu culture, Japan's first inhabitants. The spectacular setting inspired Toko to imagine it as the playground of the gods. The fifty or so totem poles tell the story of Japan's native peoples and of the gods who came down to earth to give birth to them. In the large foreground sculpture of bound poles, those with the animals on top represent the Ainu gods, while the smaller poles represent the people. On earth, the gods assume the shapes and spirits of animals, such as the bear, the owl and the orca.

The sculpture on the far left points to the west, symbolizing the 25 years of goodwill between the sister cities of Kushiro and Burnaby. These sculptures, now considered among the most successful outdoor art placements in Canada, were dedicated to the citizens of Burnaby to commemorate this friendship.

*Source: Plaques in front of the sculptures.*

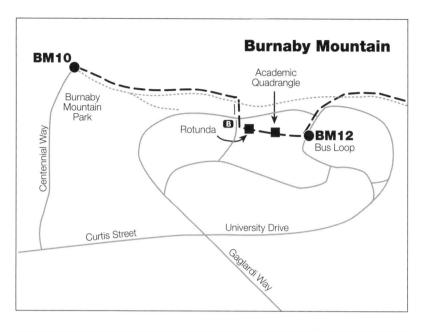

**Academic Quadrangle, Simon Fraser University**

# Simon Fraser University

Simon Fraser University was opened in 1963. It differs from traditional universities in having been built at one time and in a single style. It was designed by Arthur Erickson and Geoffrey Massey, who were little-known at the time. Arthur Erickson went on to become well-known on the world stage and was the winner of many awards. His buildings in Vancouver include the MacMillan Bloedel office tower, the provincial government offices, courthouse and art gallery, and the Museum of Anthropology at UBC. He also designed the University of Lethbridge, Roy Thomson Hall in Toronto and the Canadian Embassy in Washington, D.C.

The first chancellor of the university was Dr. Gordon Shrum, who was unusual in being both an academic and a man who made things happen in the business world. He helped UBC start up after the Second World War by floating unused huts down from Tofino on the west coast on barges—the permission arrived later. (I lived in one of these huts, known locally as "Shrum's Slums," when I first arrived in Vancouver, having been recruited by Dr. Shrum.) He later became chairman of BC Hydro for 12 years, before moving to Simon Fraser University. At age 80, he oversaw the Robson Square redevelopment project in Vancouver.

Forty years later, Simon Fraser University has 17,000 students and offers 100 programs. It is building a new residential/commercial community—UniverCity—just east of the campus. It is planning a new facility at the south west end of the campus to hold two hockey rinks, a running track and a speed-skating oval for the 2010 Winter Olympics.

## Burnaby Mountain Park 2.4 km 0 hr 44 m BM10

Follow the chain-link fence around, as it winds further up the hill and then bends left and flattens out. When the fence ends, the trail forks in two; follow the lower gravel one as it drops and then follows along the mountain side. This is known locally as Joe's Trail. In the spring or fall, there are views through the leafless trees. After about 15 minutes, a trail leads in on the right. Go up here and come out on University Drive.

Cross the road to Bus Stop 1 at the exit from the university. You may catch a bus here, if you want an early finish. Otherwise, continue and climb the steps, bearing left up to the Central Mall of the university and walk under the Rotunda. You may enjoy the brilliant reds of the trees in the fall. Pass through to the Academic Quadrangle, with its pools of reflecting water. Continuing beyond the quadrangle, you pass some smaller buildings and reach the bus loop and major parking areas.

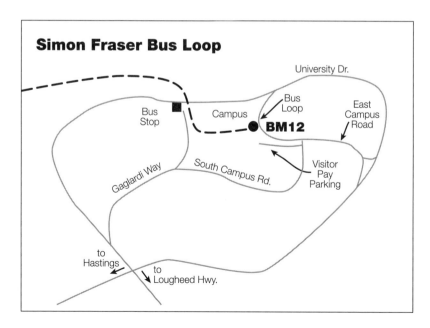

## Simon Fraser Bus Exchange    1.8 km    0 hr 26 m    BM12

**Getting home:** The #135 bus goes from Bay 1 to Vancouver (or will connect at Kootenay Loop with a #28 bus to Phibbs Exchange, if you parked there). The #145 bus goes from Bay 2 to Production City University Station.

# Down to Port Moody

Today's 9-km (5½-mile) walk follows an interesting new trail, constructed in places specifically for the Trans Canada Trail. It descends from Burnaby Mountain through forest to the edge of Burrard Inlet and follows a shoreline trail to Port Moody. It makes its way to the site of CPR's first western terminal and then continues along the shoreline to Port Moody's City Hall at the inlet's end.

**Getting there:** If using transit, go to Simon Fraser Bus Exchange.

If driving, park in the lot in front of Port Moody City Hall and the arena. Take a #97 bus from the stop on the street outside and go to Lougheed Town Centre Station. Go one station west on SkyTrain to Production Way University Station and take a #145 bus to the bus exchange at the top. Starting on the #97 bus at 9:29 a.m. on Saturday, the trip takes about 50 minutes.

**Simon Fraser Bus Exchange**     1.8 km     0 hr 26 m     BM12

Walk downhill on the road to the left to meet University Drive, which circles the University. Cross when all is clear and find a trail leading off to the left. This is known as Cardiac Hill, the reason for its name being apparent as you continue downhill to join Joe's Trail.

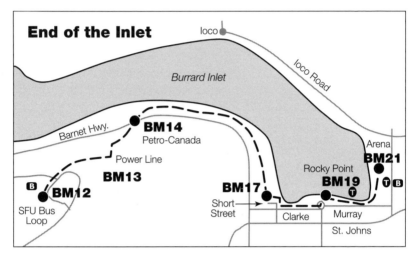

Continue right and downhill on the track. This is a pleasant walk in the winter when the leaves are off the trees and you have views out over the inlet. You pass a point where Mel's Trail joins from the right. There is a spring here and I have never seen it without water running. A few minutes later you meet BC Hydro's power-line right-of-way. Turn left and head down the hill for about 200 metres before turning right to dive down through the forest to busy Barnet Highway, beside the Petro-Canada refinery.

## Petro-Canada                    2.1 km    0 hr 31 m    BM14

Cross the road at the traffic signals and go down the road opposite, branching off right when the trail appears lower down. Follow it up and down as it makes its way between the highway and the railway bordering the inlet. You reach Reed Point Marina where the concession and toilets may be open at certain times of the year. You can enjoy a refreshment break here.

Head up the access road and find the trail on the left higher up. This makes its way along the inlet, passing the sulphur piles of Pacific Coast Terminals and reaching a paved path leading to Short Street at the western edge of Port Moody.

| **Short Street** | 3.0 km | 0 hr 55 m | BM17 |
|---|---|---|---|

Take Short Street, turn right onto Douglas Street and left onto Clarke Road, one of the main roads through old Port Moody. The strip between Clarke Road and the traffic artery of St. Johns Street houses a number of restaurants, coffee shops and stores. Continue along the street and up the hill; turn left on the bridge across the rail tracks and come down to Murray Street below by a museum at the site of CPR's original rail terminus. Go under the bridge and turn left to reach Rocky Point Park. Washrooms are just inside the park and a concession may be open for refreshments. This is a good spot for lunch.

| **Rocky Point Park** | 1.5 km | 0 hr 22 m | BM19 |
|---|---|---|---|

Go east along the paved path and pass through the forested Inlet Park. The route stays close to the water, using boardwalks over the muddy places. At the end of the inlet it crosses the rail tracks and bends north to pass some playing fields on the right. At the end of the field, turn right and follow the north edge to come out by the arena, where there are washrooms. Continue past the front of the arena and reach City Hall. There are stores, restaurants and coffee shops in Newport Village opposite (the Burrard Loop passed the arena at B55).

| **Port Moody Arena** | 2.1 km | 0 hr 30 m | BM21 |
|---|---|---|---|

**Getting home:** The #97 bus from outside the centre goes to Lougheed Town Centre Station.

# Burrard-Fraser Connection

Today's 13-km (8-mile) walk leads from Burrard Inlet at Inlet Drive (BM8) to Braid Street Station near the point where the Brunette River enters the Fraser River (F50). It sidehills around the south slopes of Burnaby Mountain, offering views over the Fraser River to the south, then reaches the Brunette River close to its outlet from Burnaby Lake. It follows the forested banks of the river, passing under the Trans-Canada Highway where not one in a hundred motorists realizes what lies below. It enters Hume Park at the New Westminster boundary and continues to Braid Street Station.

**Getting there:** If using transit, take a bus to the eastern end of Hastings Street, just before it starts up the hill to SFU. Go to Cliff Avenue, which heads south into a park, right at the signalized intersection. The trail starts on the left a few metres up Cliff Avenue.

If driving, park near Braid Street Station (probably on a side street) and take SkyTrain for three stops to Sperling Station. Catch a #134 bus to Sperling Avenue and Curtis Street. Walk about 500 metres north, take the lane opposite Frances Street, go left and right to pass Westridge School and keep left through the park to emerge at Cliff Avenue. The path leads off on the other side of Cliff Avenue. If you are at Braid Station by about 8:40 a.m. on Saturday, you should catch the 8:56 a.m. bus from Sperling Station and be at the start of the walk by 9:15 a.m.

## Cliff Avenue

0 km    0 hr    BF0

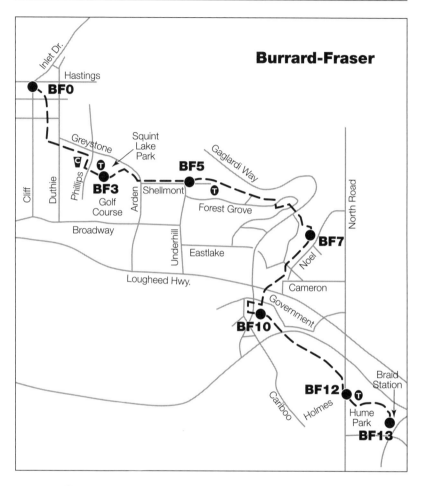

Set off on the paved trail as it wanders between houses, crosses Union Street and reaches Curtis Street. Continue straight on the facing roadway and turn left when the walkway leads off. Cross Duthie Avenue and follow the wide paved swath on the south side of Greystone Drive. When you reach a small shopping mall, turn right. The supermarket has a small coffee counter with seats if you want a break here.

At the first intersection, cross the road carefully and follow the dirt path opposite, beside a road that leads to Burnaby Mountain Golf Course. Soon trees shelter the path from the road and when a trail leads off left, take it, cross Eagle Creek on a bridge and continue straight on to reach a building with washrooms.

## Squint Lake Park       2.8 km     0 hr 39 m     BF3

Go to the left of the washrooms and take the path to the right, keeping the wooden fencing on your left. Follow this trail in a general easterly direction. It bends, always keeping Burnaby Mountain Golf Course on its right, and eventually comes out on Arden Avenue. Cross to the attractive Trans Mountain Trail, which the company has built between Shellmont Street and its property. The trail is gravelled and graded and is provided with seats for the occasional rest. At the top of the hill you leave the company land and enter the Trans Mountain Pipeline right-of-way.

## Shellmont Street East       2.4 km     0 hr 36 m     BF5

Follow the broad trail through the trees (there are washrooms down the first trail to the left and a playground and picnic table at the next one, with a school next door). The trail reaches Mountainside Village, with a small general store that sells ice creams and soft drinks. Carry straight on along a small trail which is still on the pipe right-of-way. When it descends to Forest Grove Drive, cross carefully and go down steps to reach the same road as it curves back below. Cross carefully again and head down the narrow trail at the left edge of the pipeline right-of-way. When close to Gaglardi Way below, find a dirt path going up through the bushes to a footbridge over the highway. Cross it, take the road leading down below and when it reaches a school on the left, go along the small path behind Creekside Youth Centre. Follow it to a notice board at Stoney Creek Park. You have joined the Burrard Loop (B98) as it follows Stoney Creek south.

## Stoney Creek Park          2.0 km    0 hr 30 m    BF7

Continue south on the wide track as it leads to Beaverbrook Drive. Turn left for one block and go right on Noel Drive to Cameron Street. Turn right and continue as the sidewalk leads off right, passing by a white post to a footpath and a bridge crossing Stoney Creek. At the foot of the hill, bend sharply left onto Burrard Fraser Greenway and follow it as it passes under Lougheed Highway and emerges onto Government Road. Turn right to the traffic signals, cross and go briefly up Cariboo Road and take the first road left— Cariboo Place—and pass under Gaglardi Way.

## Cariboo Place          2.4 km    0 hr 34 m    BF10

You now follow the Brunette River on its way from Burnaby Lake to the Fraser River. The high-quality trail is newly constructed and is heavily forested. It stays between the railway and the river, and sounds from the railway are the only important reason why you would not feel very rural along this stretch of the walk. It emerges onto busy North Road, where you turn right and head down towards the bridge at the foot of the hill.

At present, there is no crosswalk in place. although there may well be one by the time you read these words. Until there is, I find the safest way to cross is to follow a small path in the grass on the right which leads behind the bridge structure to the riverbank. I scramble down to the river edge, go under the bridge at the river's edge, scramble up the other side and come back to the sidewalk on the other side. Alternatively, you can wait until you find a gap in the traffic when you find it safe to cross. Or you can take my lawyer's advice and go to the signal lights ahead at the top of the hill, cross and come back.

## Hume Park                    2.0 km    0 hr 32 m    BF12

Once across, enter the signed Hume Park and follow the new trail to the left of the paved road. Pass the Lower Hume Washrooms and continue to follow the trail, whose route is marked from time to time by arrows and identified as Burrard Fraser Greenway. You are warned at one point that the trail may be closed for an hour a week where a railway enters a customer's property. If this true, I calculate that if I use this trail repeatedly at varying times, my average wait for the gate to open will be about 10 seconds! I find this risk acceptable. Follow the trail along the lip of Brunette Creek canyon and continue until it emerges at Braid Station. You have joined the Vancouver-to-Mission route (F50).

## Braid Station                1.5 km    0 hr 23 m    BF13

**Getting home:** SkyTrain will connect you with the rest of the region.

# Walk
## Horseshoe Bay
### to the USA

AND BEYOND

# Horseshoe Bay to the USA

Eleven walks from Horseshoe Bay in West Vancouver to the Peace Arch at the USA border offer a variety of views of maritime Vancouver. In 145 km (90 miles), they pass through a cross-section of Vancouver neighbourhoods. The rugged coastline of West Vancouver offers several secret parks that few Vancouverites know. The walks sample the delights of Stanley Park, partly through trees and partly along the seawall. They pass Vancouver's West End with its high-rise towers and skirt English Bay. Kitsilano surprises with its deserted rocky beach below Point Grey Road, and the hospitable sign: Welcome Stranger Rest a While. The sands of Spanish Banks below Point Grey lead to the University of British Columbia. Across Wreck Beach and through Pacific Spirit Park, they make their way to the edge of the Fraser River, with its river traffic and bird habitats. Passing along the edges of some golf courses and around another, they reach Marpole and cross to Richmond.

The terrain changes to dikes with wide views over flat farmland and out to sea, leading to historic Steveston, with its marina and the

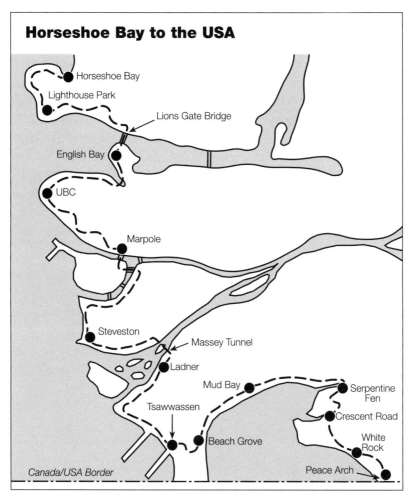

**Horseshoe Bay to the USA**

Horseshoe Bay

Lighthouse Park

Lions Gate Bridge

English Bay

UBC

Marpole

Steveston

Massey Tunnel

Ladner

Mud Bay

Serpentine Fen

Crescent Road

Tsawwassen

White Rock

Beach Grove

Canada/USA Border

Peace Arch

Gulf of Georgia Cannery museum. Continuing on dikes, they pass the interesting community of Finn Slough and reach the Massey Tunnel. On the other side, they lead through the community of Ladner with its ship building and repair facilities and reach the western tip of Delta at Brunswick Point—a remote spot left mainly to the birds. Continuing, they reach Tsawwassen and Beach Grove and make a wide sweep around Boundary Bay to reach Serpentine Fen, a protected wetland area. Pieces of the Semiahmoo and other trails lead to Centennial Park in White Rock with its waterfront and pier. A final walk leads to the USA border at the Peace Arch.

If you want to continue east beyond the Peace Arch, South Surrey and Langley contain a number of fascinating parks and historic landmarks—Campbell Valley, Langley Prairie, Derby Reach and the forest legacy of the Brown twins in Redwood Park, to mention a few. It is not easy to connect them into a set of walks because of the large farm tracts that cannot be crossed. However, you can travel 40 km (25 miles) from Peace Arch to Fort Langley in three walks of 12 to 15 km each. Or, since the middle walk contains a 6 to 7 km stretch of road which you may prefer to omit, you can see the highlights, walking 18 km the first day and 15 km the second. It's your choice.

# Horseshoe Bay to Lighthouse Park

Today's 12-km (7½-mile) walk starts along the Horseshoe Bay waterfront and passes over a rocky ridge to reach a spectacular viewpoint over Howe Sound. It continues over beaches and around the shoreline to reach Eagle Harbour. It then heads inland on a little-known trail offering marine views over the rocky coastline below and ends at Lighthouse Park.

**Getting there:** If using transit, catch the #250 Horseshoe Bay or #257 Horseshoe Bay Express bus (they stop on Georgia Street outside the Bay) and get off at the terminus in Horseshoe Bay.

If driving, go along Marine Drive and turn left into Beacon Lane at the Lighthouse Park sign. Park in Lighthouse Park and walk back to the bus stop on Marine Drive. Catch a westbound #250 bus to Horseshoe Bay from the north side of the road. A bus at 8:58 a.m. on Saturday takes you there in less than 15 minutes.

If you want coffee before you start, you will find a selection of cafés on Bay Street or just up Royal Avenue, the next avenue to the west.

## Horseshoe Bay 0 km 0 hr W0

Walk to the waterfront Horseshoe Bay Park and head west, passing washrooms in the park on the way to long-established Sewell's Marina ahead. On the right and out to sea is Bowyer Island, with Anvil Island behind it and, on the left, Bowen and Gambier Islands. On the right are Black, Harvey and Brunswick Mountains. As you walk west, the hill in front is Madrona Ridge, which you will cross. Madrona is the Spanish and American name for arbutus, the distinctive tree with a red bark which curls raggedly and then drops to the ground; it is the only native broadleaf evergreen in Canada. You will see many arbutus trees hanging at weird angles from rocky promontories like Madrona Ridge.

At the end of the waterfront, turn left up Nelson Avenue. In a few minutes, take the steps leading up by a bus stop on the right. Cross one minor road and turn right onto Wellington Avenue at the top. At its end, carry on around the corner and almost immediately go down Madrona Place. A sign at the head of the road says No Exit but this is not true; you can exit via a set of steps at the end of the road, leading steeply down to Marine Drive below. (There must be a thousand streets in Vancouver which say No Exit, but street signs are generally for drivers only and may well be false for you.)

Turn right at the bottom, pass Copper Cove Road and take the next right into Hycroft Road. This road makes a U-turn at its northern tip, going steeply up to the aptly-named Panorama Ridge. Look back as you climb and see the great views north over Howe Sound.

Take the trail leading out at the road's end, turn right at the first power pole and follow a rocky trail (slippery in wet weather). Where the trail branches, keep to the right, to the seaward side. The terrain is typical of West Vancouver; in June the ocean spray bushes decorate the drier places with showy white plumes; hardhack flaunts its pink plumes in the wetter spots; and thimbleberries abound. The thimbleberry has large single leaves and used to be known as the homesteader's toilet paper because a single leaf can be 20 cm across. The berries are

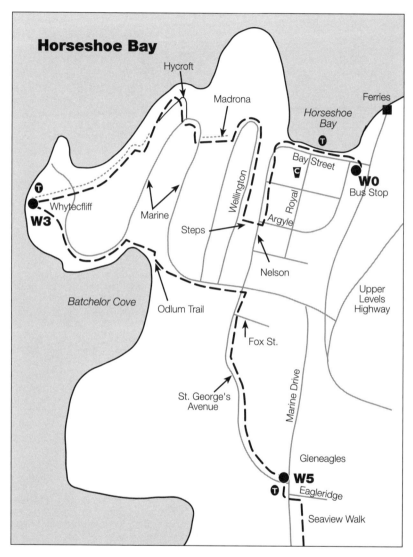

**Horseshoe Bay**

Hycroft

Madrona

Horseshoe Bay

Ferries

Bay Street

**W0**

Bus Stop

Wellington

Royal

Whytecliff

**W3**

Marine

Steps

Argyle

Nelson

Batchelor Cove

Odlum Trail

Upper Levels Highway

Fox St.

Marine Drive

St. George's Avenue

Gleneagles

**W5**

Eagleridge

Seaview Walk

flat and bright red, edible but not very tasty. You come to a small
bench, thoughtfully provided, but without any views. A little further
on, a more formal seat is dedicated to the memory of a former lover
of this ridge who asks you to "Enjoy." This seat offers views west to
Bowen Island and Howe Sound.

**The View Towards Bowen Island**

The trail now rises to a high clear knoll and immediately drops down into trees. A major trail leads down towards the left but you should take a minor trail on the right, which passes through bordering salal bushes. (The berries on these are black, pulpy and edible.) Soon the trail heads down a hill to a fire hydrant by a Douglas fir tree which carries a white-arrow trail marker. (If you should miss the minor trail, don't worry; provided you keep bearing right, you will get to this same spot in the end.)

From the marker, go down steps on a wide trail and reach Whytecliff Park's overflow parking lot. Keep to the right-hand side of the loop and cross the major road, walking onto the grass by the No Dogs sign. Here you enter a playground area, provided with covered picnic tables. Walk towards the western edge of the grass, keeping reasonably close to the chain-linked northern edge, and bear right when you reach the paved road. The washrooms on the right will probably be open, even in winter. Continue on to reach an observation platform—one of Vancouver's prime viewing spots—with the majestic cone of Mount Wrottesley in the centre to the north, the low Gulf Islands to the south west and the higher mountains of Vancouver Island behind them. This makes a good spot for a refreshment break.

**Whytecliff**                          3.0 km     0 hr 51 m     W3

Continue south through the park, with Whyte Islet (accessible at low tide) on the right side. Follow Marine Drive briefly around the point. After you have turned the corner, look across to Garrow Bay—a favourite spot for snorkellers and scuba divers because of the bright fish and the clear water. Houses are perched like aeries on the rocks and many are architectural marvels. In about five minutes, take the steps on the right, following Odlum Trail down to Batchelor Cove. In the centre of the seaward view is Passage Island, owned by twelve families, who commute as necessary to the mainland in their own boats.

# Captain George Vancouver's View

Captain George Vancouver was the first European to view this area. He passed through on June 13, 1792. Later he recorded these impressions:

"The shores of this canal, which after Sir Harry Burrard of the navy I have distinguished by the name of BURRARD'S CANAL, may be considered, on the southern side, of a moderate height, and though rocky, well covered with trees of large growth, principally of the pine tribe. On the northern side, the rugged snowy barrier, whose base we had now nearly approached, rose very abruptly, and was only protected from the wash of the sea by a very narrow border of low land. By seven o'clock we had reached the NW point of the canal, which forms also the south point of the main branch of the sound: this also, after another particular friend, I called POINT ATKINSON, situated north from point Grey, about a league distant. Here the opposite point of entrance into the sound bore by compass west, at the distance of about 3 miles; and nearly in the center between these two points, is a low rocky island producing some trees, to which the name of PASSAGE ISLAND was given. We passed in an uninterrupted channel to the east of it, with the appearance of an equally good one on the other side."

*Source: Voyage of Discovery Around the World by Captain George Vancouver (1798), as cited in Nature West Coast: A Study of Plants, Insects, Birds, Mammals and Marine Life as Seen in Lighthouse Park. (Compiled and illustrated by members of the Vancouver Natural History Society.) Edited by Kathleen Smith, Nancy Anderson, Katherine Beamish. Vancouver: Discovery Press, 1973*

Cross the cove to the far side and take the trail that goes up the steps, leading out to Marine Drive. Follow the road, turn right onto Nelson Avenue at the fire hall and continue along into St. George Avenue as it bends, with Gleneagles Golf Course on the left. At the road's end, turn left into the golf clubhouse area (offering washrooms but no coffee shop) and pass through to Marine Drive. Buses stop here.

## Gleneagles                          2.3 km    0 hr 39 m    W5

Turn right and follow the sidewalk to the first intersection. Cross when the road is clear and pick up Seaview Walk, a track which used to be the rail-bed of the British Columbia Railway. The railway was relocated to a tunnel through the hill because the residents below the tracks did not like the derailed cars rolling down into their yards. The start of the tunnel is just north of Horseshoe Bay and you will meet the end of the tunnel later on the walk.

Continue, contouring around the hill with houses perched below and above, passing occasional viewpoints out to sea and to the shore below. At Thunderbird Marina in Fishermen's Cove, a few million dollars' worth of sailboats sit idle under their blue and orange tarps. Just before the trail bends right at its end, the Trans Canada Trail leads off left and passes over the tunnel mouth where the railway reappears and resumes its use of the right-of-way.

Our trail descends steps by Nelson Creek to Cranley Drive. Follow the road out to the left, passing Daffodil Avenue and reaching Marine Drive. (You can catch a bus here if you want to stop early.) Cross carefully and take Eagle Harbour Drive to Eagle Harbour. Go past the first beach access and stay on the road for just 10 metres more, before scrambling down to a walkway. Take this walkway to the right and follow past parking reserved for Eagle Island residents to reach a wharf where boats take residents to their homes visible on Eagle Island across the narrow strip of water. You could have lunch in this area.

**Eagle Island**

**Eagle Island**                     3.3 km     0 hr 46 m     W9

Retrace your steps briefly to the end of Eagle Harbour Road—the way you came in—and turn right over a footbridge which crosses Eagle Creek and leads into Keith Road. When Parc Verdun appears on the right in a few minutes, enter and follow the footpath, generally choosing the right-hand one unless it leads out into Gallagher Place, the road that can be seen on the right. At the corner of Gallagher Place and Marine Drive, again you have an opportunity for an early stop, if you want.

Cross Marine Drive at the crosswalk and go up Westport Road, turning right very soon onto the signed Sahalee Trail. Within a minute or two, the trail appears to turn left by the railway and go up steps. However, do not go up the steps. Go (trust me!) to the right, where you will find a delightful secret trail. It is a treed oasis through which the trail scrambles up, with occasional views through the conifers and maples, particularly in winter. I am thankful that it is not stable enough to be built on, like the Westport lands which can be

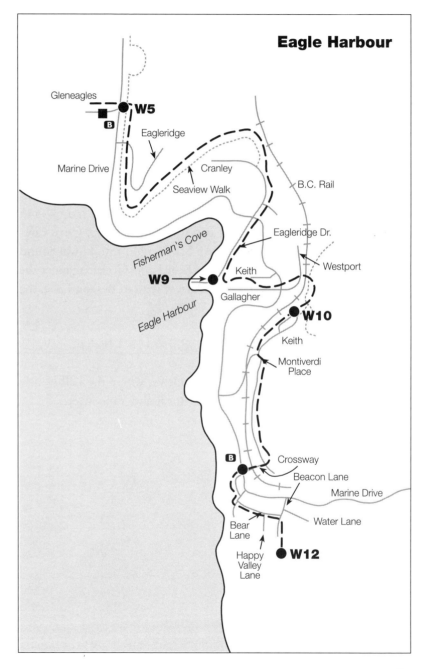

**Eagle Harbour**

Gleneagles

W5

Eagleridge

Marine Drive

Cranley

Seaview Walk

B.C. Rail

Fisherman's Cove

Eagleridge Dr.

Westport

Keith

W9

Gallagher

Eagle Harbour

W10

Keith

Montiverdi
Place

Crossway

Beacon Lane

Marine Drive

Water Lane

Bear
Lane

Happy
Valley
Lane

W12

seen through the trees, on the other side of Eagle Creek. Where the trail levels out, it goes straight to the looped end of Keith Road. Follow the lower road, passing some houses and a green strip on the right above the railway cutting below. Take the first left up Montiverdi Place (No Exit), passing some quiet townhouses and apartments. Follow the trail at its end through a small green park and rejoin a road on the far side. From here, you look south over the Inlet and west to the massive freeway structure over Nelson Canyon. Go downhill and turn right onto a paved footpath at the end of the 5100 block (you can see a barrier at its foot to make you pause at the railway). Cross the tracks—the railway is active, so watch for trains—and reach Marine Drive. Buses stop if you want to end here. Cross carefully to Crossway and, at its end, turn briefly right into Howe Sound Lane and almost immediately left into Bear Lane. Go left again at the sign to 5008 Bear Lane and take the narrow road to Beacon Lane, the access road to Lighthouse Park.

**Lighthouse Park**          3.6 km    1 hr 1 m    W12

**Getting home:** Walk up to Marine Drive, where the half-hourly eastbound #250 bus takes you to Park Royal and Vancouver.

# Lighthouse Park to Park Royal

Today's 13-km (8-mile) walk leads through the northern edge of Lighthouse Park to Caulfeild Park, passes over some little-used West Vancouver beaches, continues through McKechnie Park and some small waterside oases and concludes along the popular Dundarave-to-Ambleside-to-Park Royal seawall.

**Getting there:** If using transit, catch the #250 Horseshoe Bay bus (it stops on Georgia Street outside the Bay) and get off at Beacon Lane.

If driving, go to Park Royal and park at the south foot of Taylor Way away from the shopping centre. Walk back up to Marine Drive and catch a westbound #250 Horseshoe Bay bus on the other side of the road. Get off at Beacon Lane and walk down to Lighthouse Park. A bus at 8:37 a.m. on Saturday takes just over 30 minutes.

## Lighthouse Park — 0 km — 0 hr — W12

At the far left corner of the parking lot before the gate, find a minor trail which leads up (past a hydrant) to a loop trail at the top of a hill. Follow this trail to the right, going counter-clockwise around

289

the loop. Go past a minor trail which appears on the right within one or two minutes. In a further minute or two on the loop trail, take a minor trail which leads down on the right. (Watch carefully for it—I have missed it on occasion.) At the first intersection, go straight ahead and take the first left turn at the bottom to come out onto Water Lane. Turn right and walk down to a small triangle of green at the bottom of the hill. The interesting 1927 church of Saint Francis-in-the-Wood lies on the uphill side of this triangle. The congregation dedicated it in honour of Francis William Caulfeild (1843-1934), an early settler, who gave his name to the whole area. From the edge of the cove, you can look down at the government wharf and across to Lighthouse Park.

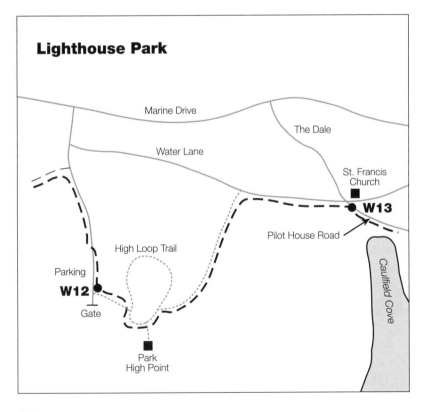

# Lighthouse Park

Lighthouse Park (like Stanley Park and Pacific Spirit Park) owes its existence to an administrative accident. When Canada accepted British Columbia as a province in 1867, the amount of logging and sawmilling increased and more and more ships started passing Point Atkinson. The Dominion Government therefore established a lighthouse here in 1875 and appointed Edward Woodward as keeper, at an annual salary of $800. In 1881, the Dominion Government acquired the area of 75 hectares immediately behind the lighthouse. In 1910, they leased it to North Vancouver and subsequently transferred the lease to West Vancouver when it incorporated in 1912. The lease has been renewed several times since. The great attractiveness of Lighthouse Park is that it is a virgin area which has never been logged.

*Source: Nature West Coast: A Study of Plants, Insects, Birds, Mammals and Marine Life as Seen in Lighthouse Park. (Compiled and illustrated by members of the Vancouver Natural History Society.) Edited by Kathleen Smith, Nancy Anderson, Katherine Beamish. Vancouver: Discovery Press, 1973*

**Caulfeild Cove**      1.2 km    0 hr 20 m    W13

Now follow along Pilot House Road, paralleling the coastline and, at the brow of the hill, enter Caulfeild Park on the right. Rough trails lead over smooth rocks above the beach. On a fine day, a patch of open rocks makes a pleasant spot for a refreshment break, looking out to the shores of Point Grey on the other side. It is humbling to realize that these granite rocks were cooling off about a hundred million years ago.

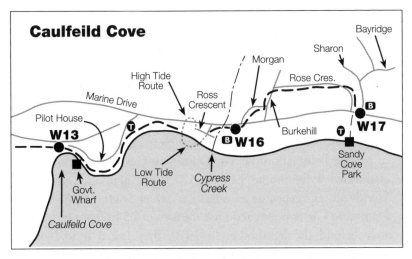

Continue, following the cliff-top trail, at one point passing some toilets, which are only open in the summer. (In winter, these and some other toilets in West Vancouver carry a sign which says Winterized. In any normal language, this would mean that you could use them in the winter. However, in bureaucratic English, it means that municipal staff have boarded up the toilets to protect them against winter weather. Heaven preserve us from any bureaucratic "all weather-ized" toilets, which would be permanently closed!) Continue along the trail, climbing up to a viewpoint with a seat, with Marine Drive passing just behind. Then drop down again past Douglas fir trees and an undergrowth including escaped domesticated plants like periwinkle and rhododendrons. Meander lower and lower until you appear to be going through private backyards. At the trail's end, you can descend to the beach by a rock scramble, provided the tide is less than 3.5 metres—and it normally is. (If the tide prevents you from dropping down, you should look left up the hill to find a trail leading out to Marine Drive. A short walk downhill past two houses brings you to some steps, which you follow down to Ross Crescent.)

Along the beach, you cross small rivulets and creeks with blue mussels. These mussels enjoy quiet streams where the water is less salty than that in the ocean. During the high tide, they open and

**Caulfeild Cove**

absorb microscopic food from the ocean. You may see geese where the creeks meet the ocean. Large driftwood logs and small pieces of bark and kelp litter the high-tide line. At the concave protective wall of a waterfront property, the walking is easier if you keep closer to the wall. On turning the corner, you will see a large arbutus tree in one of the backyards and two properties later, a white house with blue trim and a flagpole. Go through the beach-access park here, turn right and follow Ross Crescent, going left up Stearman Avenue to Marine Drive. Turn right and use Marine Drive to cross Cypress Creek, which will be roaring in the winter but may be a trickle in the summer. You have an option to catch a bus in either direction, if you want to end your walk here.

## Cypress Creek 2.5 km  0 hr 41 m  W16

Cross at the pedestrian crosswalk and go up Morgan Crescent. Cypress Park and a Montessori School lie to the right, with playing fields on the flat area below. At the road's end, head briefly uphill to reach Rose Crescent on the right, just before the railway line. A short

293

haul along Rose Crescent brings you back to Marine Drive by a bus stop, just above Sandy Cove Park. Cross to the steps opposite when it is safe and head down to the small secluded beach with a small grassy area and toilets ("winterized" in winter). This is a pleasant spot for a short break.

## Sandy Cove            1.1 km    0 hr 17 m    W17

Go back to Marine Drive, walk up Sharon Drive, cross the railway line and continue to a yellow concrete barrier block on the right at a bend in the road. Turn into the trail here and enter McKechnie Park. Go to the right and follow the path downhill. It turns left just above the railway line and is briefly level before it climbs back up. Keep going and you will see a house appear on the right as the trail bends right to come out on McKechnie Avenue. Soon McKechnie reaches an intersection with Hayes Street.

Now follow narrow one-way Hayes Street as it winds rapidly down the hillside. This in an interesting street, with houses close by on each side and views over the Inlet in front of you. When you reach Creery Avenue at the foot, follow it east—another interesting rural street. At the end, go under the railway bridge to Marine Drive. When there is a traffic gap, cross the road and, before you reach the bus stop, go

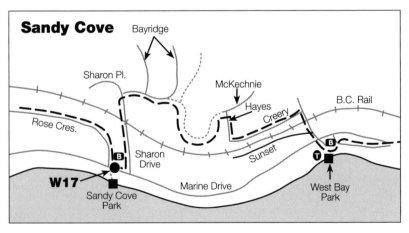

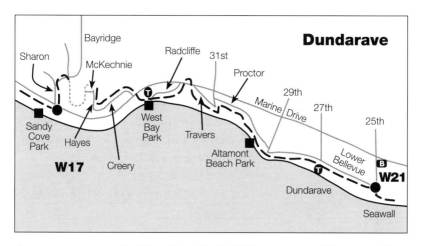

down steps to reach West Bay Park. This is a peaceful cove with a small open green area, a picnic table and a "winterized" toilet.

Now follow generally quiet streets with water views. Go up Maple Lane, turn right on Radcliffe Avenue, and then go along Marine Drive briefly to the first right at Travers Avenue. At the east end of Travers, jog left and turn right just before the railway bridge to enter Proctor Avenue and follow it east. Part-way along its length, the small treed area of Altamont Beach Park opens up on the right and narrow trails descend to the beach. You may not want to go down, but you can walk a trail briefly to make a break from the paved road. At the end of the road, use Park Lane, Bellevue Avenue and Lower Bellevue Avenue to reach Dundarave at 25th Avenue, with buses, stores and washrooms. Vancouver-bound ferries operated from the 1914 Dundarave pier for a few years. However, the waters were too exposed for safe operation and the service soon stopped. This is a good spot for lunch.

**Dundarave** 4.1 km 0 hr 59 m W21

Now follow the seawall, with views towards Stanley Park and Lions Gate Bridge and across to Kitsilano and Point Grey. This seawall walk is popular and you are certain to find lots of people on it at almost any time of day. Dogs use a separate walkway on the landward

295

side, behind a chain-link fence. I once met a couple pushing an old dog on a four-wheeled baggage trolley. He had regularly walked the wall and his owners were now helping him continue to have the pleasure of the seawall experience.

Where the seawall ends, the route follows a minor street briefly to reach the beach at Ambleside. Bus stops and at least five coffee shops lie within half a block of 15th Avenue and Marine Drive if you want a break. Public washrooms are on the left a little further on.

**Ambleside**      2.2 km    0 hr 31 m    W23

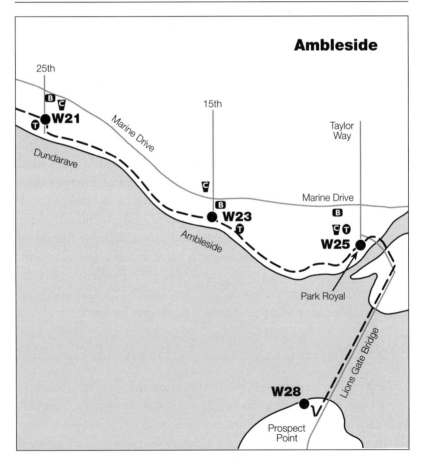

The nucleus of stores around Ambleside attests to the fact that the ferries once started their crossings to Vancouver here. A historic marker on the old ferry terminal tells you how the opening of Lions Gate Bridge in 1938 led to the routing of buses over the new bridge. Gas rationing still favoured the continuation of the ferries during World War II. The ferries survived two more years after the war, finally stopping in 1947.

Continue around the seaward edge of Ambleside Park to reach the Capilano River. Stanley Park grows progressively nearer across the inlet as you approach Lions Gate. As you pass under the railway line, the path enters the trees in the territory of the Burrard Nation. Soon you reach Park Royal, where a set of steps from the path leads up to stores, restaurants and washrooms in the shopping centre. Continue around the outside of Park Royal to reach Wardance Bridge over the Capilano River. The Burrard Nation built this bridge to connect the parts of their reserve on each side of the river. (The south side of Park Royal is located on Indian Reserve land.) You have met the Burrard Loop at B7.

**Park Royal**  2.1 km    0 hr 29 m    W25

**Getting home:** Buses from Marine Drive in front of Park Royal go to Vancouver or to SeaBus at Lonsdale Quay.

297

# Park Royal to Kitsilano

Today's 12-km (7½-mile) walk passes over Lions Gate Bridge into the forest in Stanley Park, looks out at Siwash Rock and passes Third and Second Beaches on its way to the English Bay bathhouses. It continues along the water's edge to Burrard Bridge, where it crosses to Granville Island by ferry. A walk past Vancouver's museums and planetarium leads to Kitsilano and its yacht club.

If using transit, take any West Vancouver bus (e.g., from Georgia Street outside the Bay) and get off at Park Royal.

If driving, go to Cornwall Avenue and Trafalgar Street in Vancouver and find somewhere to park on the streets. Catch a #2 or #22 bus into Vancouver, transfer to a westbound West Vancouver bus on Georgia Street and get off at Park Royal. A bus at 8:37 a.m. on Saturday takes you there in 30 minutes.

From Park Royal, walk back to the traffic signals at Taylor Way and walk south to its end.

**Park Royal**  0 km  0 hr  W25

As you head east from Taylor Way and walk over Wardance Bridge, stop in the middle to look over at the Capilano River passing below. In the fall, you may see salmon—or, unfortunately, a supermarket cart. I have seen both, although not at the same time.

At the underside of Lions Gate Bridge, select the path which uses the west side of the bridge. From balconies on the bridge, you can look at the boat traffic below. On the left, you will see the cliffs below Prospect Point where the Hudson Bay Company's ship *SS Beaver*—the first steamship on the coast—went to its fate, washing up on rocks in July 1888. On the right, you can see the high-rises of West Vancouver and beyond them Point Atkinson of Lighthouse Park. On a fine day, you may just see the peaks of the Lions on the northern skyline. When you reach Charles Marega's lion statues at the southern end of the bridge, go up the path on the right and enter Stanley Park.

# Lions Gate Bridge

The Guinness family owned large areas of the North Shore and built Lions Gate Bridge to increase the value of their lands. The increase in value more than justified the cost of building the bridge. In 1936, the Governor General in Council approved its construction and clearing of the right-of-way through Stanley Park began in 1937. On November 11, 1938, the first vehicle crossed the span, going from north to south.

Sixty years later, weather had caused significant deterioration of the road deck. In a unique engineering project, workers constructed 54 new bridge sections in advance. Traffic was stopped for 10-hour overnight periods and for some weekends. During a closure, crews cut out an old section, hauled a new one into place from a barge anchored below and fastened it with 800 bolts. They installed the last section in September 2002, skilfully completing an unusual major renovation that won praise from the engineering community.

*Sources: West Vancouver Ferry Building plaque; www.ccpe.ca/e/files/exenga_03_2.pdf, December 2003.*

# Prospect Point

Stanley Park is Vancouver's most famous landmark. The British Admiralty set it aside in 1863 as a military protection for the harbour and as a naval reserve to provide a source of timber for the construction of ships and for spars for wooden masts. In 1886, Vancouver's first year as a city, its mayor petitioned the government for control of the reserve as a park. On September 27, 1888, Mayor Oppenheimer opened it, naming it in honour of Lord Stanley, Governor General of Canada. A bridge connected the city to the island of Stanley Park. An Indian village near Prospect Point (the home of Chief Khat-sah-lanogh, now commemorated as "Kitsilano") hosted the opening ceremonies.

*Source: **Through Lions Gate**, by Anne Broadbent, (rev. ed.) Vancouver: Real Estate Board of Greater Vancouver, 1986.*

---

**Prospect Point**                    2.2 km      0 hr 33 m     W28

---

Prospect Point is the highest point in Stanley Park. It looks directly out to Lions Gate Bridge and faces west to the ocean, West Vancouver and the North Shore mountains. You can take a refreshment break and sit looking out at the ships entering and leaving the harbour. Washrooms are just past the restaurant.

Cross the road by the washrooms and take the trail where it leaves at the corner of the parking area. Keep right and you will quickly reach the Park Circular Road. Cross carefully and head down the trail opposite. Continue until you reach some steps on the right, where you will see a wooden sign: Merilees Trail. Take these steps down and follow the forested trail. Where a trail leads off to the cliff edge, follow it to reach a balcony overlooking Siwash Rock, a major Vancouver landmark. Thirty-five million years ago, boiling magma split the old rocks here. They cooled quickly, forming Siwash and other tough rocks, which are still resisting erosion today. A plaque at the overlook notes the Pauline Johnson legend which commemorates Skalsh the Unselfish, a young chief who was turned into Siwash Rock.

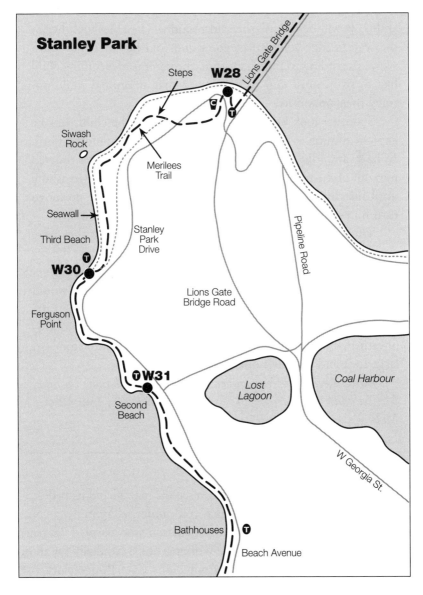

# The Legend of Siwash Rock

The girl-wife of a young chief was to give birth to their first child. "It will be today," she said proudly. The chief took her to the water's edge at Prospect Point and told her that they must swim. According to Indian custom, the parents of a coming child had to swim until they were so clean that an animal could not smell their proximity.

Soon, he took her ashore to give birth to the child. But he kept swimming as was required until the child should be born. As he swam, four giant men canoed up the Narrows and ordered him out of the way. The chief said he would not stop or go ashore until his child was born. The men said they had the power to turn him into a fish or a tree or a stone but still he refused.

The four men stopped and consulted together. As they were deliberating, a faint sound floated from the forest. It was the cry of a child. The strongest of the men then rose and told the chief that since he had defied them for the sake of his child, he would not die but would live where all eyes could see him. When the chief set foot on the land, he was transformed into stone—Siwash Rock. His wife and child were also turned into stone—a large rock and a smaller one in the woods nearby.

*Source: **Legends of Vancouver**, by E. Pauline Johnson. Toronto: McClelland & Stewart, 1924. (New ed. published by Douglas & McIntyre, Vancouver, 1997.)*

Down below the overlook, you can see the seawall and its pedestrian and cyclist users. A plaque, which you cannot see from here, commemorates James Cunningham, a stonemason who devoted 32 years of his life to building the seawall. Working single-handedly for most of the time, he built all the way from Lions Gate Bridge clockwise around to this point before having to give up. From this viewpoint, you return to the main trail and continue uphill by a swordfern-covered hillside and then drop down to the Third Beach change rooms.

## Third Beach                          1.7 km     0 hr 29 m     W29

After Ferguson Point, follow the seawall. If you are walking between November and February, you may see large numbers of goldeneyes swimming close to the shore. When the interior lakes freeze up, the goldeneyes come south to Vancouver for the winter, then return north in the spring. The male Barrow's goldeneyes have a white comma under the golden eye and white markings on a partly black back. The male common goldeneyes have a white circular patch in front of the golden eye and have much more white on their bodies.

The trail continues to Second Beach Pool, with washrooms, and refreshments if the concession is open.

## Second Beach                        1.6 km     0 hr 23 m     W31

Continue on the seawall, passing out of the park. To the south, you start to get views of the coastline to Point Grey. Pass the Sylvia Hotel, a famous landmark for Vancouverites who remember its slogan of "Dine in the Sky"; at one time, its eight storeys made it a skyscraper. Washrooms are available at the English Bay bathhouses and bus service, restaurants and stores are on the streets behind.

Continue east on the seawall, reaching an Inuit welcoming statue, Inukshuk, that originally welcomed visitors to the Northwest Territories pavilion at Expo 86. Continue to Sunset Beach with year-round washrooms; I once found the concession open on a cold Saturday in January, so you could be lucky. This is a convenient lunch stop. The uniquely shaped Planetarium across the water is a prominent Kitsilano landmark as you walk on to the Aquatic Centre. You may wonder why this eyeless box is on the waterfront, but it replaced the old Crystal Pool, which used the views and took advantage of the site.

(If you walk north, you can take steps up to Burrard Street and buses.) From the Aquatic Centre, you can take one of the small ferries to Granville Island or, to see more of the shoreline, continue further to Hornby Street, where another ferry also serves Granville Island.

## Hornby Street                    2.8 km     0 hr 40 m     W34

Both of the ferries dock at on Granville Island near the Farmers' Market where all kinds of fruit, fish, meat and breads are mouth-wateringly displayed and you have a choice of eating places. You could spend the rest of the day here and at the many stores on the island. However, if you want to keep walking, the simplest way is to keep towards the western side of the island and follow around to reach the entrance. This will take you past various maritime industries and ships' chandlers with views across the water to the west and to the south shore. The route follows the causeway out to where a pedestrian walk crosses the road.

**Granville Island Ferry**

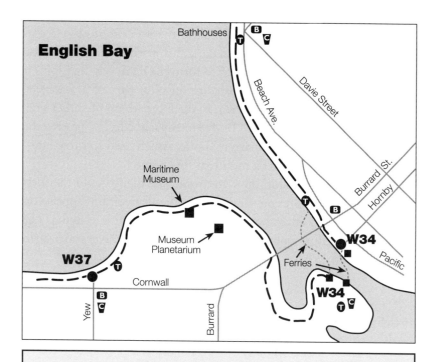

# Granville Island

Dredging operations in False Creek in the early years of the century yielded about a million cubic metres of mud, providing the base to build Granville Island in 1916. Industry occupied the whole island by 1923, with BC Equipment, Vulcan Ironworks and Wallace Shipyards as three of the early tenants. After the Second World War, industry started to pass the island by and, in 1963, Canada Mortgage and Housing Corporation took over from the National Harbours Board and the island started to take on its present character. It is now a major tourist attraction with a huge, colourful public market, two theatres, a college of art, many artist studios and a large number of restaurants and boutiques.

*Source: Island in the Creek: The Granville Island Story, by Catherine Gourley. Madeira Park, BC: Harbour Publishing, 1988.*

Turn right at the crosswalk and follow the waterfront west to pass a small marina. The crews who dredged this marina dumped the soil at the entrance to Granville Island to form the causeway that joins it to the mainland. Go along a balcony forming part of a waterside apartment complex and drop down to the footpath on the other side. Follow it and go under Burrard Bridge to Burrard Marina, passing the take-off point of the old Kitsilano Trestle, which used to carry inter-urban trains across the creek mouth at this point.

Follow the path around the waterfront. The high-rises of the West End are across the water on the right and the Planetarium appears on the left. The grassy lawns here are a favourite spot for kite-flying. The large steel sculpture commemorates Captain Vancouver's arrival in these waters in 1792.

# The Gate to the Northwest Passage

Chung Hung's 1980 hollow square sculpture stands in the grounds of the Vancouver Museum, proudly looking out to sea, commemorating the arrival in these waters of Captain George Vancouver. Its accompanying plaque reads:

"A veteran of Captain Cook's voyages of 1772–1775 and 1776–1780, Vancouver went on to become one of the most important explorers of Canada's west coast. In 1791, he was given command of an expedition to the northwest coast of North America for the purpose of establishing British sovereignty here and exploring the possibility of a northwest passage. On this voyage (1792–1794) he charted much of the coast north of the thirtieth parallel, sailing up the inside passage, circumnavigating Vancouver Island and exploring many of the geographical features in the area."

**"Gate to the Northwest Passage"**

Continue, passing between the Maritime Museum and the harbour berthing several historic boats. The A-frame part of the museum building houses the St. Roch, the first vessel to navigate the Northwest Passage in both directions and the first to circumnavigate North America. Go up the steps to the cliff-top and turn right. Stay on the trail, hugging the edge, until you come to tennis courts, Kitsilano Beach, washrooms and refreshments. Buses run along Cornwall Street, and up Yew Street opposite, a number of restaurants offer coffee, snacks or meals.

## Yew Street       2.8 km    0 hr 39 m    W37

Continue by hugging the water's edge on the wall to reach its end. You pass the outdoor Kitsilano Pool, which is popular in the summer with long-distance swimmers since it has five times the normal length of a swimming pool. You also pass the Kitsilano Yacht Club, which has races on Wednesday in the summer evenings, where small boats display their colourful spinnakers if the wind is adequate.

The last piece of the walk follows a path between the Point Grey Road houses and the sea. This walkway was once the right-of-way of the Canadian Pacific Railway, whose track came round the south side of False Creek to yards under Burrard Bridge. The right-of-way continued through Kitsilano (now housed over) and along here to the former Boundary Road (the boundary between Vancouver and Point Grey). Boundary Road is now known as Trafalgar Street. At the end of the seawall, go inland to Trafalgar Street.

## Trafalgar Street       1.0 km    0 hr 14 m    W38

**Getting home:** From Cornwall Avenue, take an eastbound #2 or #22 bus to downtown Vancouver, connecting with SkyTrain at Burrard Station.

# Kitsilano to Wreck Beach

Today's 14½-km (9-mile) walk follows Jericho and Spanish Banks beaches and continues to University of British Columbia campus. It passes the Main Mall, the library, the Chan Centre, the Museum of Anthropology, Nitobe Gardens, the Asian Centre and residences before returning down steps to a beach now popularly called Wreck Beach. A rough trail at the base of the cliffs leads to the original Wreck Beach, where steps lead up to the cliff top at Old Marine Drive.

**Getting there:** If using transit, catch a #2 or #22 bus (they stop outside Burrard Station), get off at Trafalgar Street and walk down the street to the beach path.

If driving, go to South West Marine Drive, turn off at the entrance to Old Marine Drive and park by the viewpoint. Go back to the main road, watch for the speeding traffic, then cross and follow the path left to 16th Avenue (allow 15 minutes), cross again and go up to the nearby bus stop. Catch a #41 bus, transfer to the #22 bus at Carnarvon Street across the road (ask the driver where if you are not sure). Take the bus to Trafalgar Street and walk down to the beach path. A bus at 8:40 a.m. on Saturday takes just under half an hour.

## Trafalgar Street                          0 km    0 hr    W38

The coming beach section can be walked when the tide is less than 3 metres, so check the tide tables. There is usually no problem in the summer, when daytime tide levels are relatively low, but the tide may well be too high if you chance it in the winter.

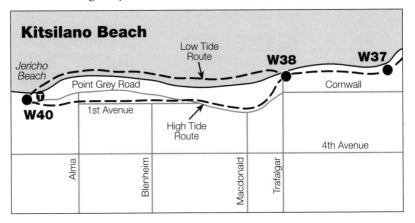

Go west along the beach, which is stony and uneven and makes an attractive change from the typical manicured sandy beach with logs. It is usually quite deserted; once at low tide, down on the rocks by the water's edge, I saw someone with a music stand playing a flute. Where else could you find a remote beach near the downtown of a major city and play your flute to the elements?

Just before reaching Jericho Park, a deck on the left bears a sign: Welcome Stranger Rest a While. It is worth resting just to enjoy all the work that has been done on this display. Take care here as the rocky beach can be quite slippery, particularly if the tide has only just gone down. After rounding the last headland, you reach a sandy beach, go under the dock pilings of Vancouver Yacht Club and pass Jericho Tennis Club and Brock House—the former home of Dean Brock of UBC and now a seniors' drop-in centre and the home of a restaurant which is popular for brunches and weddings. Come up into the park by some washrooms (closed in the winter).

(If the tide is above 3 metres, follow Point Grey Road, diverting to the quieter 1st Avenue where it joins on the south side in a few blocks. At Dunbar Street, turn right, cross Point Grey Road when there is a gap in traffic and continue onto Cameron Street. Follow it to Hastings Mill Park with its small rarely-open museum and angle across to rejoin Point Grey Road and reach Jericho Beach Park.)

**Jericho**                           2.0 km     0 hr 45 m     W40

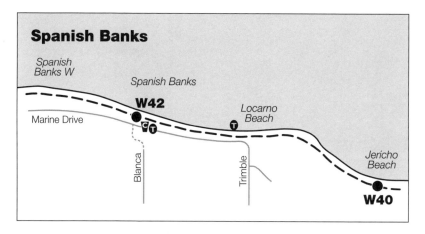

Follow the beach edge path, with the open spaces of Jericho Park on the left—the home of the Vancouver Folk Festival in July of each year. The path leads onto a large concrete apron area, which was part of a military seaplane base before the requisitioned land was returned to Vancouver as a park. It now offers impressive views of the north shore, with Vancouver's high-rise towers to the right and, on a clear day, Vancouver Island visible to the west and Texada Island to the north west. Coming off the apron, you can go round the Jericho Sailing Club on the beach or landward side and enter Locarno Park.

Continue to the Locarno Beach concession (which has washrooms and serves refreshments in the summer). Carry on along the pedestrian path to another set of concessions, where picnic tables and year-round washrooms make this a good spot for a refreshment break.

**The "Anchor" at Spanish Banks**

## Spanish Banks    2.3 km    0 hr 35 m    W42

In a further 700 metres, the route reaches the last (summer-only) concession at Spanish Banks West. Continue on the beach path, with Mount Hollyburn opposite on the North Shore and Bowen Island ahead. You will probably see freighters at anchor waiting for grain. The Canadian Wheat Board sells grain from elevators located throughout the Prairies. It has to funnel the right grade of grain down the narrow rail access through the Fraser Canyon and match it to the expected orders of ships, which have flexible arrival dates—all the time treating the farmers in all provinces equally and fairly. Ships often have to wait, particularly just after harvest and up to Christmas.

If you are walking this route on a summer evening, you will see a large number of people playing volleyball at the edge of the sand. On a Wednesday evening, you may find league games being played.

---

# Spanish Banks

Fraser River silt and erosion from Point Grey have built up the sandy "Spanish Banks," so called because Don José Maria Narvaez and his Spanish compatriots anchored here in 1791, 95 years before the founding of the City of Vancouver. In the following year, two other Spaniards, Don Dionisio Alcala-Galiano and Don Cayetano Valdez met Captain George Vancouver at this spot.

Near the end of the path on Spanish Banks the City of Vancouver erected the sculpture "Anchor" in 1986, to commemorate the city's hundredth birthday. A plaque also commemorates José Narvaez and the Spanish seamen.

Source: *Vancouver: From Milltown to Metropolis, by Alan Morley. Vancouver: Mitchell Press, 1961.*

**Beach and Trees West of Spanish Banks**

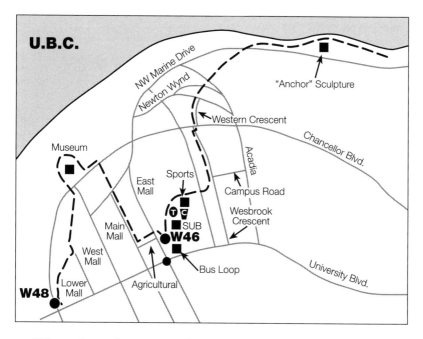

Where the path joins North West Marine Drive, use the path on the right of the road to reach a parking lot for Pacific Spirit Park. In only a minute from the end of the parking lot, wait for a gap in traffic and cross the road to a fire hydrant between the first house and the ravine. This trail leads up, going straight across any road it meets. At times, you may think you are walking through someone's yard but you are on public road allowance. The adjacent houses are interesting as are the names of the streets—for example, Newton Wynd—and the wide views of the entrance to Burrard Inlet and Howe Sound. At the top, come out to Western Crescent and follow it to Chancellor Boulevard, a main access road to the university.

Cross the boulevard and go half a block west to pass through a gap in a hedge to Wesbrook Crescent. Go along the Crescent until just past Campus Road, and cross through a gap in the hedge, and over Wesbrook Mall. Pass the Sports Building to reach the Student Union Building (SUB) with cafeterias and washrooms inside and the bus loop a few short minutes away to the south. This is a convenient lunch spot.

315

## UBC–SUB    4.1 km    1 hr 1 m    W46

In 1915, the provincial government established UBC in a campus of shacks and tents on the grounds of the present Vancouver General Hospital and relocated it to its present site after the famous "Great Trek" of 1925. The mix of ages and architectural styles that you will see as you walk through the campus demonstrate UBC's evolution over time. Cross the East Mall in front of the Student Union Building to Agricultural Road, go up to the Main Mall and turn right onto the main plaza of the campus. The new library is on the left; the old library and the Carillon Tower are visible over the gardens on the right.

Walk down the mall, keeping to the left, and reach the flagpole at its end, with Chan Centre on the right. Look over the balcony to enjoy the view for which UBC is famous; this is where UBC presidents bring the faculty they want to attract to the university. Now follow the steps down into the Rose Garden and continue down more steps to Marine Drive. Cross the road when it is safe and enter the parking lot of the Museum of Anthropology, following it left. Half-way along, a gravel path leads off right. Take this down to a path

**Museum of Anthropology at UBC**

below, go across the path and down some steps to reach the Battery. This is the site of the guns which protected Canada from the Japanese in the Second World War. Continuing on, follow the gravel path which leads behind the museum, displaying totem poles commemorating the heritage of the province's aboriginal people. Look for the bark-mulch path leading out of the western edge of the site and follow it out to Marine Drive. Cross Marine Drive at the intersection and continue on the path almost opposite, passing the Asian Centre on the left and Nitobe Gardens on the right. These gardens are reputed to be the best formal Japanese gardens outside Japan.

Past the gardens, you come out to a cobbled footpath at the side of the Lower Mall. At the end of this footpath, follow the road briefly, taking the first path on the right. Follow this path down past the residences, with an iron-railing fence on the left. When you reach Marine Drive again, continue along it until you see a sign opposite indicating the start of Trail 6 down to the beach.

## Head of Trail 6 2.5 km 0 hr 35 m W48

Go down the steps and enter a deep swordfern-covered ravine, with maples, Douglas firs, elderberries and the occasional cedar tree. Near the bottom, toilets lie to the left. Continue, and emerge to find a quite different, wild beach—home for Vancouver's clothing-optional sunbathers. To find the trail, turn left and stay at the top of the beach. Find a minor trail over downtrodden grass leading from the end of the first log you meet and going into the trees. Manoeuvre over or round one or two windfalls and reach a trail in the trees. Meander along it as it stays close to the shore and in two or three minutes come out to the sand. Follow the beach with reeds on the left until a trail leads sharply inland towards the trees. Take this and soon it leads to a well-constructed trail that carries on close to shore level for some 30 to 40 minutes until it reaches the original Wreck Beach, where a set of steps leads up beside a creek. Take the steps up to Old Marine Drive at the cliff top above.

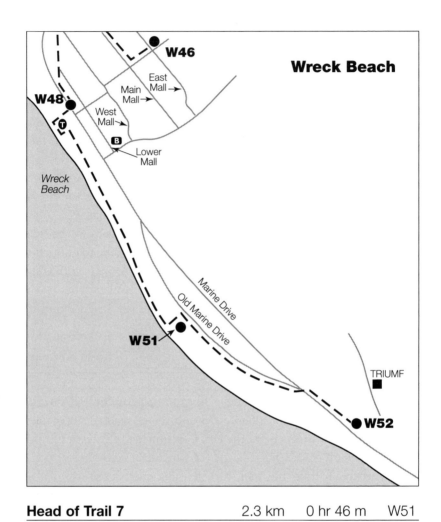

**Head of Trail 7**     2.3 km     0 hr 46 m     W51

Turn right on Old Marine Drive. UBC's Alpine Garden lies on the left behind the chain-link fence. Soon a clearing on the right lets you look south over the mouth of the Fraser River. The sea of logs below is being stored for Fraser River's sawmills, which process 60 per cent of the coastal production. If logs are stored in salt water, they risk being infested with teredos (long, worm-like creatures), which bore into them and eat most of the wood away. In fresh water, the teredos cannot live and the logs are safe. This area at the river's mouth is about the first safe storage for logs coming in from the salt water.

At South West Marine Drive, watch for fast cars, cross, go up the bank, turn right and continue for about 5 minutes to a bus stop by a trail which leads to TRIUMF, Canada's laboratory for atomic-particle research.

**Triumf Trail**                     1.5 km     0 hr 22 m     W52

**Getting home:** A half-hourly bus goes to UBC to connect to the rest of the region.

**Log Booms at the Mouth of the North Arm**

# Pacific Spirit Park to Marpole

Today's 13-km (8-mile) walk duplicates the first journey of the Vancouver-to-Mission route. Turn to the Mouth of the North Arm section, which describes how to proceed from F0 (Simon Fraser Viewpoint) to F13 (South foot of Granville). Follow the directions there and you will proceed from W52 to W65.

# Marpole and the Richmond Dikes

Today's 13-km (8-mile) walk starts through Marpole, passing a cairn commemorating the historic Great Midden. It crosses Arthur Laing Bridge, a structure which was not designed with any sympathy for the pedestrian. My wife and I have crossed the four-lane bridge alone and have led a group of 20 persons safely across, even though a painted white line was all that separated us from the oncoming vehicles. (If you prefer not to walk across the bridge, you can take the #98 bus to Airport Station at Middle Arm Bridge on the other side; or, if you leave your vehicle in Steveston, you can bus from there to Richmond Centre and transfer to the #98 bus to Airport Station.) The rest of the walk generally follows the Richmond dikes. If it is windy, button up warmly, and if it is sunny, protect yourself appropriately. Be prepared to enjoy unobstructed views out over the water.

**Getting there:** If using transit, take a bus to the corner of Granville Street and 70th Avenue and go to the south east corner of 72nd Avenue.

If driving, take Highway 99 to Steveston Highway (Exit 32) just north of the Massey Tunnel, travel west to No. 1 Road, turn left to

**Great Midden Cairn in Marpole Park**

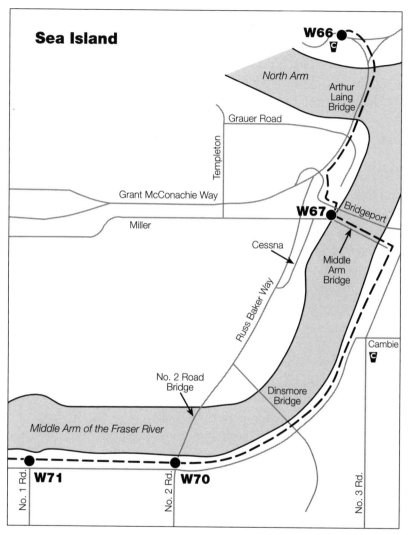

Sea Island

W66

North Arm

Arthur Laing Bridge

Grauer Road

Templeton

Grant McConachie Way

Miller

Cessna

W67 Bridgeport

Middle Arm Bridge

Russ Baker Way

Cambie

No. 2 Road Bridge

Dinsmore Bridge

Middle Arm of the Fraser River

No. 1 Rd.  W71

No. 2 Rd.  W70

No. 3 Rd.

the waterfront and park in the parking area there. Now walk back up No. 1 Road for two blocks to reach Chatham Street, and turn left to the bus stops, where buses leave for Richmond Centre. Take the first one, change at Richmond Centre to the #98 Vancouver bus and get off on Granville Street at 71st Avenue (the #401 at 8:35 a.m. on Saturday takes you there in 40 minutes). Walk back to 72nd Avenue.

## South Foot of Granville          0 km      0 hr      W65

Head east along 72nd Avenue and veer right to follow the edge of Marpole Park. Where it ends, a cairn commemorates the Great Midden. At Hudson Street, turn right to reach South West Marine Drive.

## Marpole                          0.5 km      0 hr 8m      W66

Cross to the foot of the descending ramp structure in front of you and follow it right to reach the point where it ends and vehicles from it are joining the Marine Drive traffic. Now do a U-turn onto the descending span of Arthur Laing Bridge and follow up the slope. The painted strip serves as your separation from the traffic. It takes about 20 minutes to cross the bridge, so brace yourself accordingly. As you start to rise on the bridge, the site of the old Eburne sawmill gradually appears to the right. Its owners built their sawmill here to process timber logged from what is now Pacific Spirit Park, which you explored on the previous walk. From the centre of the bridge, you have a good view of the industrial activity along the river; just before the end of the bridge, you can see the headquarters of RivTow Marine on the south bank below. Continue until the first road bridge crosses and turn left onto the footpath there. Follow it to the riverbank and turn right to pass under both the new Bridgeport Bridge and the older Middle Arm Bridge.

## Middle Arm Bridge                1.5 km      0 hr 21m      W67

Cross the Middle Arm Bridge on its right side and turn right at the far end. A few metres along the disused rail tracks, you step right onto the end of River Road. Very soon, you can climb up onto the dike and follow it all the way to Steveston. One of the first intersecting streets you meet is Cambie Road. (If you want to detour along it, you will find a coffee stop at the main road and several other restaurants nearby.)

On the dike, you reach and pass under the Dinsmore Bridge, leading across to the airport on the other side, and continue to No. 2 Road Bridge.

## No. 2 Road Bridge 2.7 km 0 hr 38 m W70

Buses stop 500 metres down No. 2 Road and again 500 metres down No.1 Road. These are your last chances to stop for some time, if you want to do so.

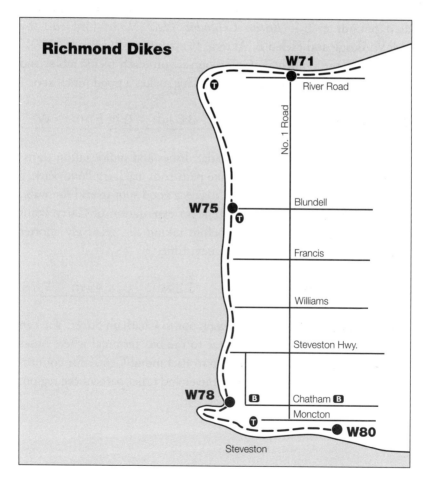

## No. 1 Road       1.6 km    0 hr 23 m    W 71

Continue along the dike, with the airport and its activities visible across the widening river. Terra Nova at the end of the road has picnic tables and toilets; the dike path turns a corner here and starts heading due south. You are now further from the housing developments and into more natural surroundings. On the right are the marshes and reeds of Sturgeon Bank—so named by Captain Vancouver "in consequence of our having purchased of the natives some excellent fish of that kind, weighing from fourteen to two hundred pounds each." (*British Columbia Place Names* (3rd ed.), by G.P.V. Akrigg and Helen B. Akrigg. Vancouver: UBC Press, 1997).

Just past the Quilchena Golf Course, you reach picnic tables and a toilet at the end of Blundell Road. This makes a good lunch spot.

## Blundell Road       3.6 km    0 hr 51 m    W75

After a straight stretch, with radar dishes and radio-station transmitter towers on the right, the dike path ends at Garry Point Park, a favourite spot for kite-fliers. This makes a good spot to end the walk, since you can conveniently combine an exploration of Garry Point with a look around Steveston before taking the relatively shorter Steveston-to-Massey-Tunnel walk next time.

## Garry Point Park       3.2 km    0 hr 45 m    W78

**Getting home:** Turn left and walk out to Chatham Street. You can catch a #410 bus here, or continue to the bus terminal where buses are more frequent. All the buses go to Richmond Centre for connections to Marpole, downtown Vancouver and other parts of the region.

# Steveston to Massey Tunnel

Today's 12-km (7½-mile) trip is a pleasant wander around the memorials on Garry Point, followed by a walk along a relatively remote section of the Fraser River. It ends at Massey Tunnel, which you cannot walk through—there is a $100 fine—and you wouldn't want to do it anyway. (I did, in fact, once see three men run through; they started at the Visitor Information Centre, got in single file, put their heads down and ran!) It is, therefore, only practical to end today on the north side of the tunnel and resume another day on the south.

**Getting there:** If using transit, catch the #410 Steveston bus from Richmond Centre and get off at Garry Point Park.

If driving from the south, go through Massey Tunnel in the right-hand lane, pull off at the Visitor Information Centre and park as far past it as possible. If driving from the north, leave Highway #99 at Exit 32, turn left at No. 5 Road at the traffic signals and left again at Rice Mill Road. Cross the tunnel mouth and park (W90). Walk down the road marked Authorized Vehicles Only to the Visitor Information Centre. From the centre, walk north to Steveston Highway and catch a #403 bus on the far side of the road, transferring at Richmond Centre to the #410 Steveston bus. A bus at 8:45 a.m. on Saturday takes about 45 minutes.

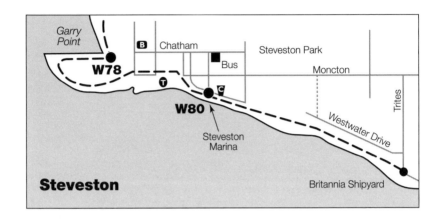

## Garry Point Park                    0 km    0 hr    W78

Follow the footpath west, passing Scotch Pond, a historic berthing spot for Steveston's gillnetter fleet. Follow the trail around to the southern point and look at the fishermen's memorial—a sculpture representing a net needle on a cairn. The bronze on the cairn is of a fisherman hauling in his net as a school of sockeye swims by. One compass rose at the base shows true north and another shows the present position of magnetic north. The openings in the surrounding walls represent the compass points north, east, south and west.

Continue east to the Kona Garden, dedicated to the first Japanese immigrant, who arrived 100 years earlier. Then follow on to the Gulf of Georgia Cannery, now a national historic site and museum. It is normally open from mid-April to early October, Thursday to Sunday. You will find washrooms in the square in front of the cannery. Staying as close to the waterfront as possible, carry on to Steveston Marina.

## Steveston Marina              2.0 km    0 hr 28 m    W80

Follow the road east from the marina and take the Imperial Landing walkway as it leads along the Fraser riverbank. The walkway passes a variety of Steveston's heritage sites, including a restored house of the Murakami family, who were interned after 50 years of residence, and Britannia Shipyard, erected in 1889 as a cannery and converted to a shipyard in 1918. After Britannia Shipyard, cross the road to a footpath and follow it along to No. 2 Road. Cross when the road is clear, follow the footpath south, passing a café on the left, and take the riverbank trail at the London's Landing sign. Cannery Channel will appear on the right, perhaps with grebes, loons and other waterfowl; historic London Farm is on the left. A signboard on the dike tells the story of the London farm and family. The farmhouse used to be a general store and post office run by Bill London until he went to California in the 1890s because of his tuberculosis. The farm was run by his brother Charles with his wife Henrietta and their five children.

**Fishing Boats at Steveston**

# Steveston

Manoah Steves left New Brunswick and arrived in British Columbia in 1877. He decided to settle in the south west corner of Lulu Island. His wife and six children came in May of the next year. Manoah's son Herbert bought land north of Chatham Street in 1880 and waterfront property in 1887. As the fishing and associated canning industry developed, workers came from the Indian villages, from European immigrants and from the Chinese community. Japanese fishermen came either seasonally or permanently from Japan. To be competitive, canneries moved as far down the Fraser River as they could, so as to be nearer the incoming fish boats. Steveston was about as far west as they could go.

By 1891, hotels lined the boardwalks and Steveston had gambling establishments, dance halls and a 900-seat opera house. The opera house, which Herbert Steves built at the south west corner of Second Avenue and Chatham Street, served as the church, meeting place, community and performance hall. By 1906, about 10,000 people lived in Steveston, but a series of poor salmon runs put Steveston into decline before 1914. Farming and fishing provided its livelihood between the wars—the interurban train (Sockeye Express) and ferries connected it with Vancouver and Victoria.

*Source: The Spirit of Steveston: A History of the Steveston Community Society, by Victoria Kendall. Richmond: Steveston Community Society, 1986.*

Between London's Landing and No. 3 Road, seats and picnic tables are spaced along the river edge. Reading the dedication plates on the seats is rather like taking a walk through a country churchyard looking at the headstones. The road surface ends at No. 3 Road by a new sports-fishing pier and year-round toilets. This makes a pleasant spot for a rest.

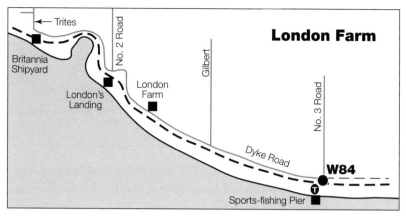

| **No. 3 Road** | 3.7 km | 0 hr 52 m | W84 |

From the pier, follow the riverbank and go around the Crown Packaging plant and back to the dike on the far side. Once as I walked here, I saw a bald eagle on a fence post, a redtail hawk on a tree, and a blue heron in the field. Continue along the dike to a road and reach the interesting little community of Finn Slough, a collection of fishing shacks and houses originally founded by Finns. It is on the water side of the dike and on Gilbert Island, reached over a footbridge. It is treasured by the residents, who have formed a Heritage Preservation Society, but is enviously eyed by developers who would like to build townhouses. From here, you can see across the wide Fraser River to Westham and the other islands in the river, with Delta in the background behind them. Next you reach a small park on the left, with parking for hikers of the Richmond trails. A few minutes later, you reach No. 5 Road and Woodward's Landing, the site of the old river ferry which was replaced by the George Massey Tunnel. It is now the site of a BC Ferries facility, as is evident from the vessels visible.

| **Woodward's Landing** | 4.0 km | 0 hr 56 m | W88 |

Turn left on No. 5 Road and right on Rice Mill Road, which crosses the Massey Tunnel portal and leads to fish plants and car-

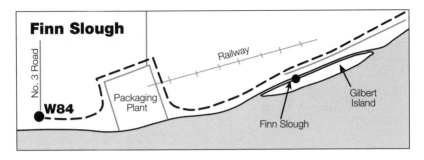

Finn Slough

No. 3 Road

W84

Packaging Plant

Railway

Finn Slough

Gilbert Island

unloading docks on the other side. The near side of the freeway leads in 800 metres to a southbound bus stop and the far side leads to the Visitor Information Centre, with washrooms (open in season) and a northbound bus stop. This is where the South Arm trail ends (FS13).

| Massey Tunnel | 2.1 km | 0 hr 29 m | W90 |
| --- | --- | --- | --- |

**Getting home:** Go to the northbound or southbound bus stop, as appropriate, and catch a bus home.

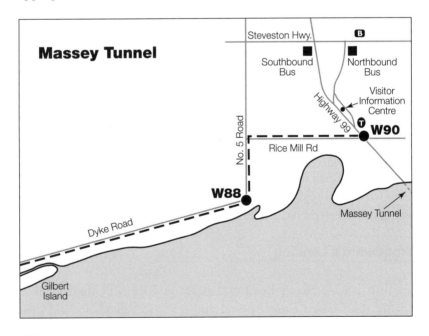

Massey Tunnel

Steveston Hwy.

Southbound Bus

Northbound Bus

Visitor Information Centre

Highway 99

No. 5 Road

W90

Rice Mill Rd

W88

Dyke Road

Massey Tunnel

Gilbert Island

# Massey Tunnel to Tsawwassen

Today's 15½-km (9½-mile) walk passes through the historic community of Ladner and makes its way by dikes and road to Wellington Point Park, which offers wide views up and down the river. It continues past the Westham Island bridge and on to one of the most remote corners of the region at Brunswick Point. It crosses the Roberts Bank access road and railway and passes through Tsawwassen Nation lands on dikes to reach the Tsawwassen Ferry highway.

**Getting there:** Take a bus to Ladner Exchange and transfer to the #606 or #608 Ladner Ring bus. Ask the driver to let you off at Admiral Boulevard at River Road.

If driving, take Highway 17 towards the Tsawwassen ferry, turn left at 52nd Street and go right on 16th Avenue to its end. Park, walk to the verge of Highway 17 and turn left to the bus stop.

The #640 leaves the Tsawwassen causeway hourly at five minutes past the hour, connecting at 20 minutes past the hour with the Ladner Ring Bus. On Saturday, the 10:05 a.m. bus is the first to connect with a Ladner Ring bus.

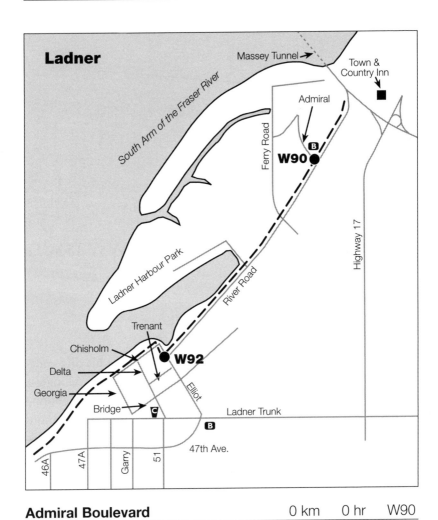

**Admiral Boulevard**                    0 km    0 hr    W90

Head west on the north side of River Road. The first major road on the right is Ferry Road, leading north to the old ferry, which crossed the Fraser River before the Massey Tunnel was built. Cross Ferry Road and go onto a dike with views over the marsh on the right. You pass a road which leads to a park on Ladner Island in the river. After a block of apartments, Elliott Street is on the left; you have now reached Ladner.

**Ladner**                              1.8 km      0 hr 25 m      W92

If you want refreshments, dodge over a block to historic Delta Street, look at the buildings and stores and find coffee shops near its end. The museum by the clock on Delta Street has historic maps and welcomes visitors. Buses pass on nearby Ladner Trunk Road.

After your break, pick up the trail on Chisholm Street back where you came in to Ladner. Go to the end of Chisholm and climb up into the dirt parking area to find a gate onto the dike. A sign on the wall says Private, but this is a plea to respect the privacy of the residences— the dike trail itself is public and is much used and enjoyed. This stretch of the walk gives you a good view of the attractions of the marshes and islands in the widening part of the river here. When you reach River

---

# Ladner

The Ladner brothers left Cornwall in England and came to Victoria in 1858. They hired some natives to canoe them to Fort Langley for the sum of $50 (equivalent to $2,500 in today's money)—entrepreneurial immigrants! The natives dropped them at Tsawwassen and from there the Ladners rowed to Fort Langley. They then tried their luck at mining and exploring for gold in the Cariboo, but had more success in running a pack-train business. In 1868, they decided to return to a piece of potential farmland they had seen from their rowboat. At that time, there were no sandbars and trees, the water was deep and large boats could go up the river. Roads did not come until later, but by 1873 there was a wharf at Ladners' Landing. Sternwheelers plying between Victoria and New Westminster would stop for passengers and freight.

*Source: **The Ladners of Ladner: By Covered Wagon to the Welfare State,** by Leon J. Ladner. Vancouver: Mitchell Press, 1972.*

---

Road again, follow it west, staying on the dike where possible. The river is on the right with the ship repair yards and boat moorages of Port Guichon. Some of the water-based facilities are chain-link fenced and you have to come off the dike and walk the grass or the road. After you leave the houses, the farm fields on the left stretch to the horizon. After the last chain-link fence forces you to the road, Wellington Point Park appears on the right. Turn into it, bear right and go across to the viewing deck. Barber Island is opposite, Westham Island is downstream to the left and another small island is to the right. There are picnic tables and toilets and this is a good spot for lunch.

**The Delta Museum in Ladner**

**Totem Poles in Ladner**

## Wellington Point Park     3.1 km     0 hr 44 m     W95

The road now bends left to follow Canoe Passage, passing Westham Bridge on the right, leading to Reifel Bird Sanctuary 5 km up the road. You can detour briefly to the water's edge to enjoy the view up and down the river.

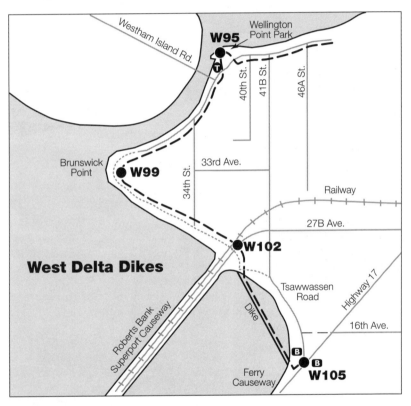

Continue along River Road. In the fall and winter, snow geese may be visible across the river. Depending on the year, between 5,000 and 25,000 of the white-feathered geese visit the Fraser River in the winter, from Wrangel Island in Alaska. After the road ends, the dike continues and brings you to Brunswick Point, the most westerly point of travel. This is an isolated spot, attractive to birders.

## Brunswick Point 3.8 km 0 hr 54 m W99

From Brunswick Point, continue south and east. You see a few houses in the fields, then reach a railway line. This is the causeway to Roberts Bank and you can see the terminal, the waiting railcars and the large black piles of coal waiting to be shipped. The coal arrives here in mile-long trains weighing 10,000 tonnes. Watching the trains arrive, you feel that we are digging up south east British Columbia and neighbouring Alberta and shipping them out to Japan.

## Roberts Bank Railway 3.3 km 0 hr 46 m W102

Looking across the railway, you can see a yellow-and-black checkerboard sign. Physically, you can just cross the tracks, but the long line of coal cars stretching to the horizon can move in either direction, presenting a real hazard. You will be safer if you go to the road crossing of the railway (about 100 metres towards the left), make sure no rail cars are near, and come back on the other side.

**Roberts Bank Port**

339

The path beyond the checkerboard sign leads to a junction, where you take the path leading right on a dike to reach a bridge over a creek outlet. The trail then continues until it reaches the Tsawwassen causeway; turn left to the traffic signal on the highway.

| **Highway 17** | 3.3 km | 0 hr 46 m | W105 |
|---|---|---|---|

**Getting home:** On the other side of Highway 17, an hourly bus (half-hourly in the summer)—at about five minutes past the hour—takes you to Ladner Exchange for connections to Vancouver or to Scott Road for SkyTrain.

# Boundary Bay

Today's 13½-km (8½-mile) walk passes through Beach Grove and then starts an exploration of Boundary Bay Regional Park. This park is protected as part of the Lower Mainland Nature Legacy. It is a great place to observe sea birds of all kinds. The walk from the dike back to the bus stop adds a further 2 km.

**Getting there:** If using transit, take a bus to Ladner Exchange and catch the #640 (or, in the summer, either the #640 or the #404) Tsawwassen Ferry bus. Ask the driver to let you off at the last stop before the causeway.

If driving, take Highway 99 and go off at Exit 20 to Highway 10—the Ladner Trunk Road. Go to the north side of the interchange and find somewhere to park. Catch an hourly #318 bus at the bus stop there to Ladner Exchange and transfer to the Tsawwassen Ferry bus. Ask the driver to let you off at the last stop before the causeway. A bus at 9:04 a.m. on Saturday takes about half an hour.

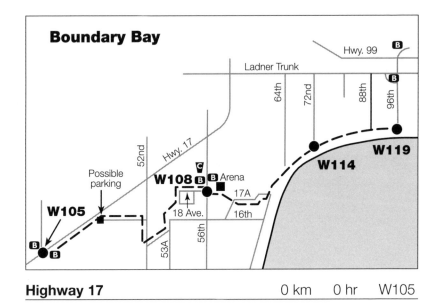

**Highway 17**        0 km    0 hr    W105

Cross to the south side of Highway 17 at the traffic signals and head briefly north on the highway edge to pick up 16th Avenue, which runs along the north edge of Tsawwassen Golf Club. The houses of a Tsawwassen development are visible on the high bluff above. Turn right up the hill of 52nd Street and, at the top, the panorama of the North Shore mountains is visible behind you (unless the day is overcast!). Turn left into Upland Drive and pass several houses to reach 53A Street. Turn left here and continue until the street ends and leads into a footpath. Follow this into Candlewyck Wynd, bear left, turn right at 18th Avenue and go down it to 56th Street opposite the arena. This is a good place to break for refreshments. (Bus service is available to Ladner Exchange and Vancouver if you want to stop your walk here.)

**South Delta Arena**        3.2 km    0 hr 45 m    W108

Cross the highway at the traffic signals and walk along the south edge of the arena. You will find a footpath out the back, going to 17A Avenue. Follow it, passing Beach Grove Park on the left, with fields visible to the north, and reach Boundary Bay. The rest of today's walk is on the dike, with the water and large areas of beach marsh on the right. These are the feeding areas for large numbers of sea birds. About a million migrating birds a year stop off here, although less than a hundred thousand will be in the bay at any one time.

As you walk along the dike, you see farm fields on the left, together with greenhouses and one or two large houses, then a BC Hydro experimental electrical area. The first street end that you reach is 64th Street—a favoured spot for snow geese in the fall. Continue and reach 72nd Street, the western boundary of Boundary Bay Airport lands.

If you want to stop at any time, you can go about 2 km up this or any street to reach Highway 10. A #318 bus will take you west to Ladner Exchange or east to the Highway 99 interchange.

## 72nd Street          5.2 km     1 hr 14 m     W114

On a fine weekend, you can see and hear plenty of airport activity as budding pilots learn to fly at Boundary Bay Airport. Anywhere on this section of dike is suitable for a lunch spot; just take your pick. As you continue, you will see fields on the left and extensive flatlands to the right, particularly when the tide is low. Pass the end of 88th Street and continue to 96th Street.

## 96th Street          5.2 km     1 hr 13 m     W119

**Getting home:** Walk 2 km up 96th Street to Highway 10. Turn left to reach the intersection with Highway 99. On the south side of the interchange, you can take the #318 bus to Scottsdale Mall or the #351 bus to White Rock. You must cross to the north side to take the #318 bus to Ladner Exchange or the #351 bus to Vancouver. If you left your vehicle on the north side, you will have to cross Highway 99 to reach it.

# Mud Bay and Serpentine Fen

Today's walk continues the exploration of Boundary Bay, passes round Mud Bay and wanders through the interesting wetlands of Serpentine Fen. You start with a 2-km walk to reach Boundary Bay from the bus and the walk itself is 15 km (9½ miles) long. Before you start on the walk, you should be aware that it crosses under Highway 99 at its Serpentine River crossing. You need the tide to be less than 3 metres, which it usually is. You have to manoeuvre over some rocks and climb up over a pipe, so go only if you feel able and agile.

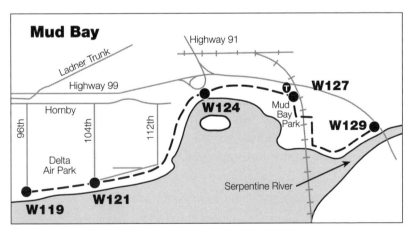

**Getting there:** If using transit, take a bus to the intersection of Highways 10 and 99—the #351 bus from Vancouver or White Rock or the #318 bus from Scottsdale Mall or Ladner Exchange. If you arrive at the bus stop on the north side of the freeway, walk over the road which crosses the freeway. Then go east to reach 96th Street and walk down it to the dike.

If driving, leave Highway 99 at Exit 10, the intersection with the King George Highway. Then park at the Park-and-Ride which is just west of the King George Highway and north of Crescent Road. Walk south at the highway edge to the traffic signals, cross the road, and go to the bus stop. Catch the #351 Vancouver bus and get off where the bus leaves the freeway at Highway 10. A bus at 8:51 a.m. on Saturday takes about 10 minutes. Walk over the freeway crossing to the south, turn left to reach 96th Street and walk down it to the dike.

**Delta Heritage Airpark**

## 96th Street                                    0 km    0 hr    W119

Follow the dike path east. The first road end you reach is that of 104th Street. This is the site of Delta Heritage Airpark, where you may find coffee and cookies if the crew room is open. The former restaurant advertised that it was open every day except Christmas, but one of the regulars told me that was untrue—it opened Christmas Day as well. However, under the new Heritage Airpark regime, there is less activity and the crew room tends to be open at the weekends only. However, you may want to go onto the site and look at the historic airplanes. Perhaps coffee will be available as a bonus.

## Delta Airpark                          1.7 km    0 hr 24 m    W121

Our route continues, sharing the dike with Irwin Road to reach 112th Street, also known as Oliver Street. The farmhouse between here and Highway 99 was the home of "Honest John" Oliver, premier of the province from 1918 until his death in 1927. Now leave the road for the dike. After you pass some trees, increasing vehicle noise indicates the approach of the intersection of Highways 91 and 99.

## Highway 91                            3.7 km    0 hr 52 m    W124

The next section of the route starts close to the noise of Highway 99, but gradually moves further away and becomes correspondingly quieter. The next major landmark is the Burlington Northern Railway line, which can be located by noting the rise in the roadway where Highway 99 goes up to cross over it. Ignore the dike which curves south before you reach this road crossing and continue straight on to reach Surrey's Mud Bay Park. This makes a good spot for lunch; it has a toilet. (The trail from Watershed Park in Delta ends here at FD22).

## Mud Bay Park  2.3 km  0 hr 35 m  W127

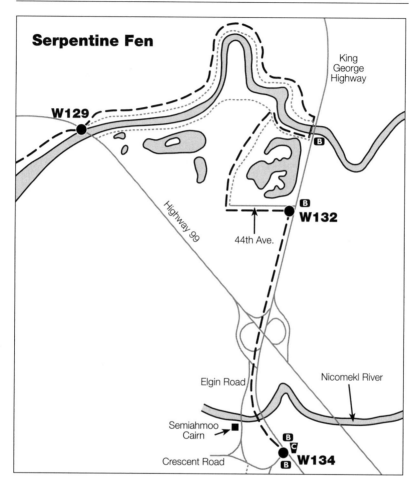

The Burlington Northern Railway is active and you should cross the tracks with care. If you head south towards the river through the gate, you will soon find a path leading over the railway to a road on the other side. The lands are private, so do as the regular park users do and keep to the road and the subsequent dike. An alternative route that avoids the road is to continue south to the riverbank, go onto the beach and, when convenient, come up to the dike on the far side.

In June, the grasses on the dike here are long and colourful and the area is aglow with tall white daisies, yellow dandelions, pink hardhack, purple thistles and red elderberries. The houses on Panorama Ridge are visible over the fields to the north. Continue along the dike until an orange gate marks the arrival of the Serpentine Bridge.

## Serpentine Bridge          2 km    0 hr 26m    W129

Pass the gate and look for a small path trodden down in the grass to take you down to the underpass route. Walk the rocks at the river's edge and go under both spans of the bridge (staying high and holding onto the concrete abutments will help you keep your balance). At the far end, climb onto a large-diameter pipe and step out onto the path at the east side.

**Passenger Train at Mud Bay**

Continue on the north side of the river to the King George Highway. The vegetation here is different, with fireweed and tall wild St. John's wort plants. The path goes around two looping curves, with several water channels visible on both sides of the path. Across the river you can see the waterfowl observation towers, and usually walkers on the riverside path.

**Serpentine Fen Lookout Tower**

When you reach King George Highway, use the highway bridge to cross the river. (Buses stop here for White Rock and Surrey Central Station.) Then detour immediately back into Serpentine Fen on the south side of the river. This in an interesting wetland, which has been preserved through the efforts of Ducks Unlimited Canada and the Sportsmen of Northern California as well as the funding of Canadian governments. A short distance along the dike, a grass trail leads left into the body of the fen. This path follows through to 44th Avenue, joining it near an observation tower by a power pole. You pass between large bodies of water and end by walking through a narrow path to the exit. Now follow 44th Avenue east to the King George Highway, passing a parking lot on the right and picnic tables.

### King George Hwy & 44th Ave.  3.7 km  0 hr 52 m  W132

From here, it is just under 2 km to the end but the route lies beside a busy noisy main road. If it is close to the hour or half hour, you might consider busing it. Alternatively, you could use the frontage roads, window-shopping as you go, coming to the highway when you must. Or you can use my method—just grit your teeth, walk the 2 km at the road edge, and give thanks when you reach the end. Riverside Golf Centre on the left may be open for refreshments.

### Crescent Road  1.8 km  0 hr 25 m  W134

**Getting home:** Cross at the traffic signals to reach the bus stop for the northbound #351 bus to Vancouver and the northbound #321 bus to Surrey Central Station.

# Semiahmoo, White Rock and the Peace Arch

Today's 11-km (7-mile) walk follows parts of the largely-disappeared Semiahmoo Trail, passes through Sunnyside Acres Urban Forest to South Surrey Athletic Park and reaches Centennial Park. A wooded trail down a gully leads to the waterfront, White Rock Pier and the historic white rock itself. A walk along the beach leads to Peace Arch Park. A further 2.3-km walk takes you back to the bus home.

**Getting there:** If using transit, take the #351 bus from Vancouver or the #321 bus from Surrey Central Station (Bay 9) and get off at Crescent Road.

If driving, follow Highway 99 to the border, exit to Peace Arch Park—signed just before Canadian Customs—and park in the parking lot. Walk back on the parking lot's west side to Beach Road. Turn left and follow the road through the First Nation reserve. Cross the footbridge over the Campbell River at its end and turn left on Marine Drive to the bus stop. Allow 40 to 45 minutes for this walk. Then, catch a community shuttle bus and transfer to the #351 or #321 bus at White Rock Centre. Get off at Crescent Road. A #C51 bus at 9:30 a.m. on Saturday takes 25 minutes.

## Crescent Road                              0 km    0 hr    W134

Start from the west side of King George Highway at Crescent Road and walk north at the highway's edge to reach the nearby Park-and-Ride lot. Go through it and turn south over the one-way bridge to reach the Semiahmoo Trail plaque at a fork in the road.

(You can sit and have coffee at Riverside Golf Centre by the bus stop at Crescent Road before you start, or stand and drink at the service station here.)

From the plaque, take the left fork to Crescent Road, go left to 144th Street and a Semiahmoo Trail marker straight ahead. Just on the right is the old one-room Elgin School. The trail passes through the grounds at the east of the building to follow through woods to reach 32nd Avenue.

---

# Semiahmoo Trail

The plaque on the historical marker states: "The Semiahmoo Trail was an ancient Indian travel-way linking tribal villages in the south to salmon grounds of the Fraser River." In 1861, the District of New Westminster upgraded the trail to become its first road—Semiahmoo Wagon Road. In 1865, the Collins Overland Telegraph Trail from San Francisco to the Stikine followed this same alignment. Only a few sections of it now remain; housing developments cover much of the rest.

*Source: Along the Way (rev. ed.), by Margaret Lang Hastings. Cloverdale, BC: D.W. Friesen and Sons, 1981.*

---

The walk continues on a paved road, also called Semiahmoo Trail. Follow this residential street until it dead-ends at 28th Avenue. Cross the avenue and follow the path curving right into the trees. Where it curves back to pass over a bridge, exit to the right and head

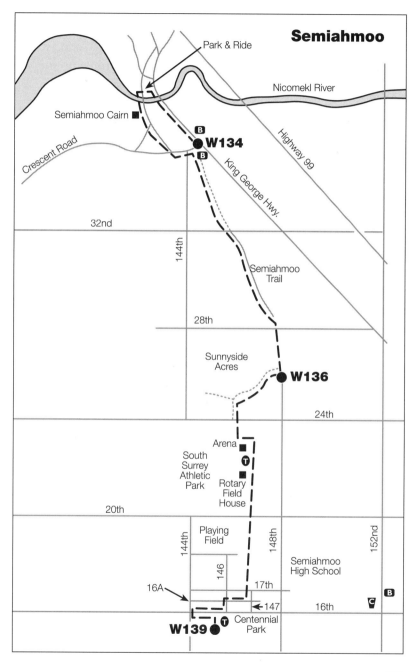

up the 148th Street hill, looking for a trail leading off right into Sunnyside Acres Urban Forest. Do not take the first one, which would lead you around the outside of the area. Continue up the hill and take the next trail in.

## Sunnyside Acres        2.2 km    0 hr 33 m    W136

The path bends slightly left and then curves in a large arc towards the right. Bleeding hearts and fringe cups line the trail, blooming in the spring. After about ten minutes, a directional sign on a triangular island in the middle of the trail indicates that 24th Avenue is to the left. Take this trail out to 24th Avenue and cross to the path into the trees to the left of South Surrey Athletic Park's entrance. Walk through the trees, emerging from dogwoods onto a path bordering the park access road. Follow the path as it curves left at its end and cross on the sidewalk to South Surrey Arena. Follow the arena around to its far side to some seats, a small pool and an arch with a broken top, commemorating the shortened lives of those killed in Canada's wars. Continue around the arena, where the grass slopes down towards the nearby Rotary Field House. Make your way there, go to its eastern side and down the steps, passing the signed public washrooms on the right. Carry on and follow the path which leads south, passing football and soccer grounds, and reach 20th Avenue.

Cross carefully to the median strip and again to the far side, entering the sports fields to the south. Walk between the football field below and the baseball field above and climb gradually to the baseball field level. At its end, follow the track down and head towards the red-and-white gate behind the school. Once there, go behind the chain-link fences of Semiahmoo High School to reach 17th Avenue; then take 147th Street, 16A Avenue and 146th Street to 16th Avenue. Cross it at the crosswalk and come back on the other side of 16th Avenue to enter Centennial Park. Just down the path, there are picnic tables and washrooms, making this a good spot for lunch. It is only a short walk east to White Rock Centre if you want to end your walk for the day.

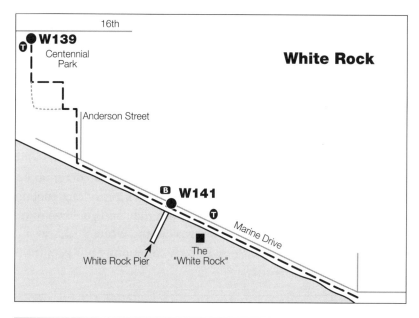

**White Rock Pier and Semiahmoo Bay**

## Centennial Park  2.9 km  0 hr 43m  W139

Continue down the path, passing a sign saying Mel Edwards Centre and follow round the fronts of the buildings to the end of the parking area near the Curling Rink and Parks Office. Take the broad main path down the hill, pass a set of old steps on the left and continue to reach a new set on the left by a seat. Go down the steps to near the bottom of the ravine and turn right at the foot. Follow this trail as it curves left into the bottom of the ravine and comes up on the other side. The ravine is a shady oasis which provides a cooling break on a warm afternoon. At the top, turn right and go down some steps to Anderson Street. Follow this street to the White Rock seawall, turning left to reach White Rock Pier. (A community bus goes from here to White Rock Centre.)

# White Rock

In the early 1900s, Semiahmoo Bay's beaches and sand dunes were famous for swimming, boating, fishing and crabbing. Recreational cottages sprouted along the shores of the bay and, in 1914, the new pier served commercial boats and provided business and recreational opportunities. A huge boulder on the beach, which was limed white by sun-bleached guano from seabirds, served as a navigation mark. The rock is still there, just east of the pier, though it is now painted white. The community slowly grew, adding a post office, schools, waterworks and a hospital. The City of White Rock separated from the Municipality of Surrey in 1957. Now the city is generally known as a residential, retirement and cultural community, with an active summer theatre company.

*Source: The Canadian Encyclopedia (2nd ed.). Edmonton: Hurtig, 1988.*

**The White Rock and Seawall Walkway**

## White Rock Pier 1.8 km 0 hr 26 m W141

Continue along the waterfront walkway, passing the large white rock from which the city takes its name. You will find washrooms at several locations along the way. Across the street from the walkway, fish-and-chip restaurants, gift shops and a variety of boutiques offer their wares. Where the adjacent Marine Drive turns directly east, you have a choice. One route follows the road through the Semiahmoo First Nation lands. Alternatively, if the tide is low, it is physically possible to walk the beach to Peace Arch Park, but be warned that this involves using the railway bridge to cross Campbell River outlet.

If you opt for the dry land route, follow Marine Drive on its south side and opposite Stayte Road, go across the footbridge over the Campbell River and follow Beach Road. You can look out to sea and across to the Semiahmoo Resort in the USA. Almost at its end the road bends and, just before the main highway, reaches the entrance to Peace Arch Park. Follow the road into the park, go past the parking lot, and walk across the grass to the Peace Arch.

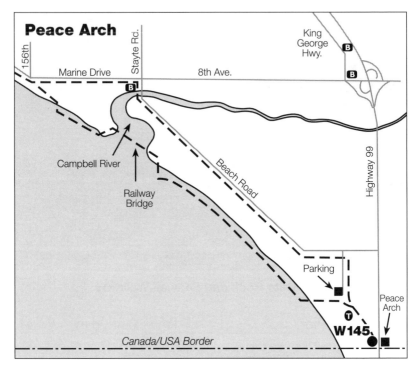

If you want to walk from White Rock using the beach, go on to the beach at the point where Marine Drive forks off east. After walking for some 15 minutes, you will reach Campbell River, which may be crossed by trespassing briefly, using the walkway at the side of the tracks over the railway bridge. The railway has posted signs which say Warning—Active Trains and you must believe them. People have been killed in arguments with these trains. Once over the bridge, turn left to scramble down to the river's edge and come back under the bridge to the beach.

Walk along the beach until you find an old concrete pipe outfall below some trees on a high bank above. The buildings of Blaine and its harbour spit are very close at this point. A climb up the trail on the left again crosses the rail tracks. A steep clamber up on the other side of the tracks leads into Peace Arch Park very near its parking lot. The park has picnic tables and washrooms. A walk across the grass leads to the Peace Arch.

You may want to cross the border, which you can do within the park, so that you can say you have reached the USA and journey's end. Enjoy the Peace Arch and its surroundings before returning home.

**Peace Arch**                    4.1 km      0 hr 58 m      W145

---

# Peace Arch

Peace Arch Park lies between the Canadian and US border stations. The Peace Arch commemorates a hundred years of peace between the two nations after the 1814 European Treaty of Ghent. Sam Hill, the famous US railroad builder, suggested the concept of a Peace Arch and used his fortune and contacts to bring the project to fruition. Construction on the arch began in 1920. At the base of the arch on the Canadian side, a tablet bears a replica of *SS Beaver*, the first steam vessel in these waters, which went aground at Prospect Point. (You visited this point earlier on these walks.) A casket embedded within the arch contains a relic of the ship. Words inscribed high up on this side of the arch read: "Brethren Dwelling Together in Unity."

On the US side, a tablet bears a replica of the *Mayflower* and a casket holds a piece of the famous sailing ship. The words on the arch are "Children of a Common Mother."

*Sources: Plaques on the Peace Arch; and **Along the Way** (rev. ed.), by Margaret Lang Hastings. Cloverdale, BC: D.W. Friesen and Sons, 1981.*

---

**Getting home**: Walk back on the parking lot's west side to Beach Road. Turn left and follow the road through the First Nation reserve. Cross the footbridge over Campbell River at its end and turn left to the bus stop. A community shuttle bus connects to regional services at White Rock Centre.

**The Peace Arch**

# Side Trips

SOUTH SURREY

BROOKSWOOD TO WALNUT GROVE

WALNUT GROVE TO FORT LANGLEY

# South Surrey

Today's 14-km (8½-mile) walk starts at the Park-and-Pool at 8th Avenue and 168th Street. You can start at the Peace Arch if you prefer (it is only 1½ km away) but the road is busy and, to me, uninteresting and the Park-and-Pool has nearby bus access. The walk starts on arterial roads for about half an hour, but then any roads are residential and quiet. It heads to Redwood Park to see the forest legacy of the Brown twins. It continues to Stokes Pit, preserved as park by the city, and passes through trails to reach Brookswood's streets and park.

**Getting there:** If using transit, a #321 bus from Surrey Central Station Bay 9 (e.g., at 8:54 a.m. and half-hourly on Saturday) will go to 8th Avenue at King George Highway, a short distance from 168th Street.

If driving, it will take two hours by bus to travel from one end to the other. Park in Brookswood Park (at 200th Street and 40th Avenue). Catch a #C60 bus on the opposite side of 200th Street and get off when the bus crosses Fraser Highway (ask the driver). Go back to the signals, cross 203rd Street and catch the #502 bus at the bus stop there. Change at Surrey Central Station to the #321 bus at Bay 9 and go to 8th Avenue at King George Highway. On Saturday, a bus at 7:44 a.m. (or hourly thereafter) will get there in about two hours.

Walk back across the bridge over the freeway to reach the Park-and-Pool.

**8th Avenue** 0 km 0 hr WS0

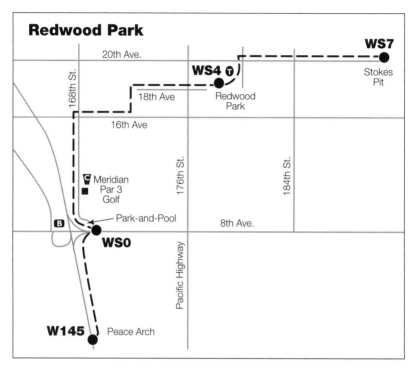

Walk north on 168th Street and within three blocks pass a par-3 golf course where you may feel the need for coffee if you have had a long journey to reach here. Then continue to 16th Avenue, cross when the road is clear and go right until you are opposite 172nd Street. Here you will see a drainage ditch on 172nd Street's right-of-way coming down on the left. Follow this public right-of-way up the hill; it looks rough, but you can choose the left or right side of the ditch, whichever is in the better condition. If necessary, you can change from one side to the other. It is going to take you less than ten minutes to reach the quiet 18th Avenue, so give it a go. (I only once found it too wet and overgrown; I had to continue to Pacific Highway (176th Street), and then go up to 18th Avenue, but this is a last resort.)

Turn right on 18th Avenue and follow it along to 176th Street. Cross carefully and follow 18th Avenue (No Exit) on the other side. At its end, a trail continues, between fences at first and after it enters Redwood Park, it makes its way along the upper edge of a meadow. Pass a barrier and carry straight on along a path under the tree cover to reach a redwood grove and tree house.

**Tree House at Redwood Park**

# The Redwoods

David and Peter Brown were born twins in 1871. Scarlet fever struck them deaf at an early age and this deafness set them apart. When they were 21, their father gave them 16 hectares (40 acres) each on the hilltop which is now Redwood Park, intending it as a fruit and nut farm. However, soon after they acquired the property, David and Peter visited California and were overwhelmed by the giant redwoods. They came back with pockets full of redwood seeds to plant on the property. Over the years they added exotic species from all over the world.

When the twins were in their thirties, their house burned down and family members assumed it was an accident. However, when a second and third house burned down, the brothers became convinced that forces were out to get them. In 1912, they built a two-storey tree house with kitchen and plant collection on the first floor and sleeping accommodation upstairs. They lined the base with barbed wire because school pranksters would vandalize the property and steal goods, taking advantage of the twins' deafness.

The redwoods grew, shutting out both the light and the neighbours, who grew antagonistic to the brothers. The twins used a shack on the ground in bad weather. One day, Peter dynamited some roots and blew them and himself skyward. He could not use the tree house again and lived in the shack until he was 86, outliving David by eight years. He had a verbal agreement that the land was to be left to the city to be preserved in its natural state, free of sports fields, and so it has.

*Source: "The Twins who Grew Giants," by John Portwood. Ottawa, BC: **Canadian Geographic,** May/June 1996.*

## Redwood Park                    3.9 km      0 hr 59 m      WS4

This is a good place for a break. Washrooms are just north of the tree house and then the route continues along the path east. Take time to read the Prayer of the Woods on the right and realize how many different roles wood plays in our lives. You can use the covered picnic tables here and drink from an interesting 2002 water fountain that serves people and dogs. The water fountain, sculpted with decorative animals, reptiles birds and insects, is called Redwood Forest Mysteries.

Continue east along the path and across the parking lot and leave the park through a gate leading onto 180th Street. Walk up the hill and turn right on 20th Avenue. This is a quiet street, with views to the south over Hazelmere Valley to BC farmlands, and to American farmlands beyond. The street becomes even quieter after crossing 184th Avenue, where it is bordered by Lombardy poplars before coming to an end at Stokes Pit.

## Stokes Pit                     3.1 km      0 hr 46 m      WS7

The City of Surrey used much of Stokes Pit to extract gravel for its road building and construction activities. They still use some parts of the site for this purpose but the excavated part is now available for the City to use for industrial and park purposes. Council has, in fact, adopted an industrial park plan so the life of the present enjoyable trails may be limited. At present, cyclists make full use of it, having created a maze of trails in the woods.

The most straightforward and enjoyable way to walk through the area is to go past 20th Avenue's end onto a track heading east. Soon you face the choice of one trail turning right and another, a little further ahead, turning left. Take the right-hand trail (there is a blue-painted band on a tree at its right) and head south. Continue south on the major trail (there will be blue-painted trees from time to time) until the trail reaches a T-junction near the southern edge of the property. Turn left and follow a perimeter trail, with fields behind a fence on the right and forest trees on the left. After the fields end, the trail

**A Pool by Little Campbell River**

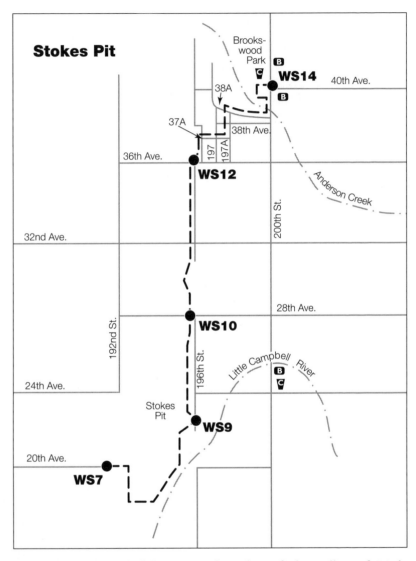

bends half-left and follows on the edge of the valley of Little Campbell River below. The wide overgrown swampy territory is typical of Campbell River and there are interesting pools if you decide to explore off to the side when you know the area better. Continue until the trail drops down into a dip towards the river and crosses a plank bridge. You are now basically on a 20th Avenue alignment and have gone from about 191st Street to close to 196th Street. You now have to go north to reach 196th Street at about a 22nd Avenue alignment.

Immediately after the bridge, turn left up the hill and keep to the top of the hogsback that separates the excavated pit on the left from the river and then road on the right. To do this, keep straight ahead if possible but go right and higher where you have to make a choice. However, don't go right if the trail drops to the river valley. (One exception is where the straight-ahead trail goes down to a creek and steeply up the other side; here it is better to take the detour down right, cross a bridge and come back up the other side.) This strategy will get you to where you can see 196th Avenue and can get out to it. You can then go out to check your bearings and confirm where you are. You should be at a seniors' trailer park.

| **Trailer Park** | 2.0 km | 0 hr 38 m | WS9 |
|---|---|---|---|

Re-enter the woods and follow the trail, keeping the pit on the left and the road on the right until you reach the top right-hand corner of the pit, where the trail bends left and follows west. At this point go out to the road. You will be close to the intersection with 28th Avenue.

| **28th Avenue** | 1.3 km | 0 hr 22 m | WS10 |
|---|---|---|---|

Watch for cars and then cross 28th Avenue, continuing up the dead-end street to its end. Immediately after you enter the trail on the left, follow the minor right-hand trail signed with two red markers. This is a short trail which leads through to a driveway continuing north on the 196th Street alignment to a paved 196th Street. Continue north, cross 32nd Avenue when the road is clear and continue on a paved but quiet road to 36th Avenue.

## 36th Avenue 1.6 km 0 hr 28 m WS12

You now meander through Langley streets to reach Brookswood Park, the numerous No Exit streets being caused by the gullies leading into Anderson Creek. Jog right and go up 196A Street, jog right on 37A Avenue and go up 197A Avenue to its end. Go right on 38A Avenue and reach 200th Street. This carries the bulk of the north-south traffic for some distance around and you don't want to stay on it for long. Go north for one block to cross Anderson Creek and turn left on 39A Avenue to its end. Turn right at a small cairn of stones and follow the footpath into the trees. To reach Brookswood Park you turn right here, but first it is worth looking at the deep impressive canyon of Anderson Creek by going straight on to its lip and then returning.

---

# Langley

Thomas Langley, a director of the Hudson Bay Company, gave his name to the 800 hectares of farmland developed by the company in Langley Prairie. In the 1840s, produce was sold to Russian forts in Alaska. Nowadays, the area has more horses than any other municipality in BC and artificial insemination and horse-breeding are big business. It is the largest mushroom-producing area in Canada, and it has more rabbit farms and sheep than anywhere else in BC. It produces vegetables, dairy and beef cattle, poultry and berries and has greenhouses and an estate winery. The City of Langley is separate from the Township of Langley; heading north, you enter the city at 44th Avenue and leave it after the shopping centre on the bypass.

*Source: "Langley" in **Encyclopedia of British Columbia**, edited by Daniel Francis. Vancouver, BC: Harbour Publishing, 2000.*

## Brookswood Park          2.0 km    0 hr 30 m    WS14

**Getting home:** Catch a #C60 bus on the opposite side of 200th Street at 44 minutes past the hour on Saturday. Get off when the bus crosses Fraser Highway (ask the driver), go back to the signals, cross 203rd Street and catch the #502 bus at the bus stop there. Transfer to SkyTrain at King George Station.

If you have to wait for the #C60, Cedarbrook Square (one block north) has stores and fast-food outlets where you can sit and get refreshment while you wait.

# Brookswood to Walnut Grove

Today's 12½-km (8-mile) walk follows a pleasantly treed creek down from Brookswood to Sendall Gardens and on to the valley of the Nicomekl River. It continues on to Michaud Crescent, which lies along the right-of-way of the railway that used to lead into Langley at this point. The route now follows six kilometres of roads through Langley and up the hill to Walnut Grove. After the first kilometre, the roads are quiet and there are views over the valley below if you turn back from time to time to enjoy them. Once in Walnut Grove, trails lead through the community to your finish point at Walnut Grove Park-and-Ride.

**Getting there:** If using transit, catch a #502 bus outside Surrey Central Station at Bay 11 (at 8:30 a.m. or hourly) and transfer at Langley Centre to the #C61 Brookswood bus, arriving at 9:25 a.m.

If driving, park at Walnut Grove Park-and-Ride. Catch a #501 Langley Centre bus and transfer to the #C63 Fernridge bus to Brookswood Park (200th Street and 40th Avenue). A bus at 9:01 a.m. on Saturday will take about 35 minutes.

## Brookswood Park      0 km    0 hr    WS14

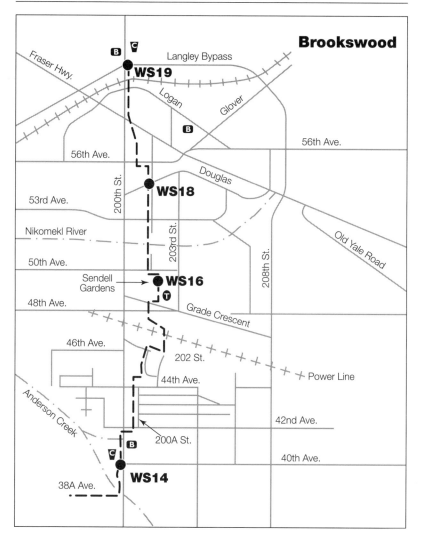

If you want, you can have coffee at one of Cedarbrook Square's fast-food outlets before you start. Then cross at the traffic signal, walk to 42nd Avenue, cross and turn right. Turn left at 200A Street and go to 44th Avenue, cross at the pedestrian crossing and go along the path

373

at the right-hand side of the school. Come out and turn left onto 201st Street, going to the right along a footpath at its end. You have now had a chance to see a Langley suburban subdivision—generally quiet and having all its wiring underground.

Turn left, go across the power-line right-of-way and follow the path left. Watch for a sign on the right saying Nature Trail and when you find it, enter an attractive, quiet, treed walkway at the side of Muckle Creek. Turn left at Simonds Elementary School and pick up the trail again on the other side of 48th Avenue. Then when the trail reaches Grade Crescent, cross at the sidewalk and jog right to pick it up again at a sign saying Sendall Gardens. This trail leads down and then left into Sendall Gardens, a beautifully planted park much in demand for wedding photographs. Picnic tables and washrooms at the centre of the gardens make this a great place for a break. The heated tropical greenhouse is another great attraction, especially in the winter.

## Sendall Gardens  2.5 km  0 hr 37 m  WS16

Walk north out of the gardens, jog left to 201A Street and go down it into the Nicomekl Valley. The Rotary Club has created an extensive set of trails along this valley but today we will only see them as we cross the river. Follow the trail off the end, go over the river, pick up 201A Street on the other side and go as far as Michaud Crescent. This used to be the right-of-way of BC Electric's railway into Langley. It is now lined with houses and townhouses, and Linwood Park's playing fields are on the left. (This is where I would end my walk, if I were coming from the Peace Arch and intended to start next time in Walnut Grove to avoid the road walking. Here I turn right up to Langley Centre and catch the #501 or #502 to Surrey Central or King George Station.)

## Michaud Crescent 1.2 km 0 hr 17 m WS18

Walk up to 56th Avenue, cross when there is a gap in traffic and go left one block to 201st Street. At the end of that street, go across the schoolyard and on to the corner of Fraser Highway and 200th Street. Now you just have to bite the bullet and go through Langley's industrial auto-oriented heartland. It is almost hilarious to note the auto dealers, auto repairers, tire stores, brake stores, muffler stores and service stations to the exclusion of almost any other enterprise. Going along 200th Street, you cross Industrial Avenue, Logan Avenue, the railway and Langley Bypass before you reach a mall on the right. Luckily there is a selection of fast-food outlets there, so you can get a strong black coffee and calm down.

## Langley Bypass 1.5 km 0 hr 24 m WS19

Go to the far north east corner of the parking area and follow around into the next mall's parking, hugging the right-hand side that adjoins a creek. Follow this up and emerge onto 64th Avenue. Go right, cross when it is safe to do so and follow 201st Street to 66th Avenue, go right and turn up 203rd Street. You are now through the heavily urbanized centre. New subdivisions are springing up rapidly on this hillside and you may be able to take in some Open Houses as you pass through. You make your way up the hill, jogging left whenever a cross-street intervenes to go from 203rd Street to 202B to 202A. When you end at 80th Avenue by a new church, turn right to 208th Street and go left to cross the Trans-Canada Highway.

## Trans-Canada Highway 6.5 km 1 hr 35 m WS26

As you come down after the bridge's midpoint, take the first left and go west along Bakerview Trail, paralleling the highway with houses below on the right, and Golden Ears and other mountains on the

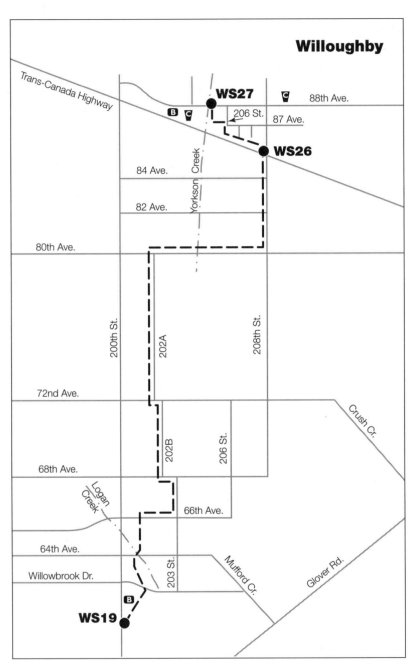

skyline beyond them. Follow the trail to its join with the signed Yorkson Creek Trail. Skirt around a playground and pass between houses on the right and Yorkson Creek on the left to reach 88th Avenue.

**Yorkson Creek**    1.0 km    0 hr 15 m    WS27

Getting home: Walk about five minutes left along 88th Avenue to Walnut Grove Park-and-Ride. Catch the half-hourly #501 bus to Surrey Central Station.

# Walnut Grove to Fort Langley

Today's 14½-km (9-mile) walk explores Walnut Grove's trails before following a relatively quiet paved road for 3 km to the Houston estate, now part of Derby Reach Regional Park. It continues on well-maintained trails through woods to reach the site of the original fort at Derby. From here, the Fort-to-Fort Trail follows the south side of the Fraser River to reach the town of Fort Langley.

**Getting there:** If using transit, take a #501 bus from Surrey Central Station Bay 1 to Walnut Grove Park-and-Ride.

If driving, park in Fort Langley, making sure to avoid the 2-hour limit zones (or park at the fort, if you plan a subsequent visit). Walk south on Glover Road to 96th Avenue and take a #C62 Walnut Grove bus to its terminus. A bus at 23 minutes past the hour takes about 20 minutes.

At Walnut Grove, there are several fast-food outlets if you want refreshment before you start. Then cross 88th Avenue when the road is clear and walk five minutes east to a bridge crossing a creek.

## Yorkson Creek | 0 km    0 hr    WS27

Take the informal trail on the east side of Yorkson Creek and follow it north briefly through tall trees, then veer right and reach a paved path following the edge of the ravine. After making a sharp right turn, take the first turn left onto a bridge over Yorkson Creek. Turn right at its end and come to 208th Street. Go left to the traffic signals, cross at the crosswalk and pick up the signed Walnut Grove Trail on the far side. This trail generally follows a Trans Mountain oil pipeline right-of-way through the community, offering you the chance to see the houses and community services while keeping away from traffic.

Pass through a townhouse development and jog briefly left then right when you meet West Munday Creek Trail. Cross the bridge over West Munday Creek and continue generally straight on, passing through the grounds of Walnut Grove Secondary School. At Walnut Grove Drive, cross at the crosswalk and follow the trail as it angles at a gentle uphill through the community. You can find coffee shops in the shopping mall areas to the right if you want a break.

At 88th Avenue, go left to the traffic signals, cross both roads and pick up Walnut Grove Trail again just to the south on 212th Street. Follow it and turn left onto the signed East Munday Creek Trail in the open low-lying Forest Hills Park. Follow into the trees and emerge onto 88th Avenue again.

## East Munday Creek | 2.6 km    0 hr 37m    WS29

Cross 88th Avenue to 214th Street and find the signed East Munday Creek on the right. Follow it, crossing the creek on a bridge and continue to 216th Street. Turn left for about a block to reach the signed trail and go back into the treed area along the creek ravine top. When the paved trail ends, ignore the informal rough trail that continues. Jog right and then left into Topham Park and follow around the edge of the grassed area to the exit on the far side at 215th Street.

Follow this street and two rights-of-way bearing East Munday Creek signs. Then decline to follow a trail that continues and crosses the creek on a long bridge. Instead, turn right onto 94A Avenue and left onto 215A Street. Follow this to its end and turn right on 95A Avenue to reach 216th Street. Turn left and go up to busy 96th Avenue. You have now negotiated Walnut Grove.

**96th Avenue**  2.1 km  0 hr 30m  WS31

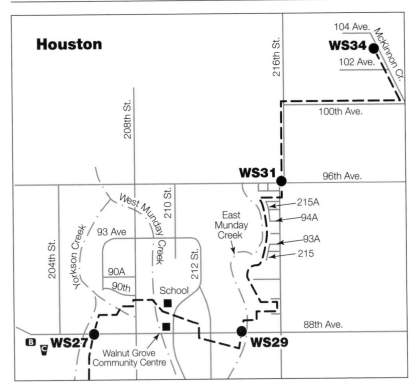

Jog right and then left up 216th Street. Continue to 100th Avenue and turn right. In this area you pass houses on large acreages, some used as pastures and others as large residential yards. Continue along 100th Avenue for the equivalent of eight blocks (about 25 minutes), passing houses on the dry ground and dropping down once or twice into dips housing shallow creek beds. Turn left at the road's end into McKinnon Crescent and find Derby Reach Regional Park's Houston Trailhead on the right in just under 10 minutes.

| **Houston** | 3.0 km | 0 hr 43 m | WS34 |
| --- | --- | --- | --- |

Turn left in the parking lot and follow the trail into the woods. This is an attractive trail at any time of year. In the summer, the tall cedar, hemlock and maple trees provide a cool welcome shade. In the winter, the well-surfaced trail provides walking that is dry, mud-free and relatively light because of the leafless maples. The trail winds up and down and after about 20 minutes you reach a grassy opening where the trail forks. Take the left-hand trail and follow it along, with trees on the right and a swampy area leading to cranberry fields on the left. Just before you reach a yellow gate, turn right into the heritage area of the park. Here there are picnic tables, toilets and notice boards describing some early history of the area. This is a good spot for a break.

# Houston

Houston Trail in Derby Reach Park is named after James Houston, one of the original settlers. He began farming in 1858 near the site of the present fort. He cleared some land and established a dairy with 12 head of cattle, which he had driven single-handedly from Oregon. He also grew and shipped potatoes, carrots, peas and cranberries, starting a farming trend that has endured for over a century. He married Mary Cutcheon, a native woman from Nanaimo, and had a son named Alexander. When Mary died, he started a second farm at Derby in 1890, which his son inherited.

*Source: "James Houston." Notice board in Derby Reach Park, Fort Langley, BC: Greater Vancouver Regional District, 2001.*

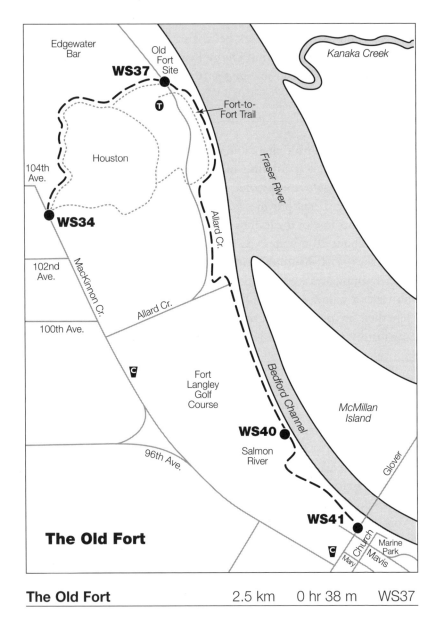

**The Old Fort**

| The Old Fort | 2.5 km | 0 hr 38 m | WS37 |

Cross the road and take the opportunity to look at the cairn on the left which marks the site of the original Fort Langley. There are

.lso notices here describing what is known of the original fort. Then turn right and follow upstream with the river on the left. Notices warn you to keep back from the undercut edge. However, a deck on the left offers a wide river view, looking across to Kanaka Creek Park, with a log sorting area to its left and Port Haney further downstream. Continuing, notice boards describe the history of the Katzie and Kwantlen members of the Sto:Lo Nation who lived in this area. When the trail reaches Allard Crescent, turn left and walk on the trail, protected from the vehicle traffic by a wooden barrier. Follow the Fort-to-Fort signs and find the trail when it leaves the road edge, passes a toilet and enters the woods. Follow the path down through trees; you may see trilliums here in the spring. The trail leads to a dike, with the river on the left and Fort Langley Golf Course on the right, screened behind the fence and upper dike. The trail continues, well provided with seats dedicated to the memory of various individuals and providing opportunities to enjoy the river views. The trail continues and reaches a pumping station where the Salmon River enters the Fraser River.

**Salmon River**       2.7 km     0 hr 38 m     WS40

Cross to the track on the far side and re-enter the woods where signed. The trail briefly follows the riverbank and re-emerges to the track, where a riverside trail may ultimately lead into Fort Langley. However, for the present the trail detours around what was Interfor's Macdonald Cedar mill, passing between the mill site and Canadian National Railway's mainline to reach Fort Langley Station. (This is F91 of the Vancouver-to-Mission route.)

**Fort Langley Station**       1.4 km     0 hr 20 m     WS41

**Getting home:** Walk up Glover Road to 96th Avenue. A #C62 bus at 23 minutes past the hour will take you to Walnut Grove to connect with the #501 bus to Surrey Central Station.

# About the Author

Charles Clapham is a retired mathematician who hikes and walks for a hobby. He and his wife Doris have hiked in Canada, the United States, Mexico, Switzerland, France, Britain, Australia, New Zealand and Japan. In the summer, they like to hike the high country of British Columbia, but in the fall and winter months, they explore the urban trails of Greater Vancouver. One year they may poke round West Vancouver and another year, explore the flat lands of Richmond and Delta. In the spring, while the snow is still on the high country, they like to explore the hills around Victoria and meander through the Gulf Islands.